T0327671

Trade-Based Money Laundering

Wiley & SAS Business Series

The Wiley & SAS Business Series presents books that help senior-level managers with their critical management decisions.

Titles in the Wiley & SAS Business Series include:

Agile by Design: An Implementation Guide to Analytic Lifecycle Management by Rachel Alt-Simmons

Analytics in a Big Data World: The Essential Guide to Data Science and its Applications by Bart Baesens

Bank Fraud: Using Technology to Combat Losses by Revathi Subramanian

Big Data Analytics: Turning Big Data into Big Money by Frank Ohlhorst

Big Data, Big Innovation: Enabling Competitive Differentiation through Business Analytics by Evan Stubbs

Business Analytics for Customer Intelligence by Gert Laursen

Business Intelligence Applied: Implementing an Effective Information and Communications Technology Infrastructure by Michael Gendron

Business Intelligence and the Cloud: Strategic Implementation Guide by Michael S. Gendron

Business Transformation: A Roadmap for Maximizing Organizational Insights by Aiman Zeid

Connecting Organizational Silos: Taking Knowledge Flow Management to the Next Level with Social Media by Frank Leistner

Data-Driven Healthcare: How Analytics and BI Are Transforming the Industry by Laura Madsen

Delivering Business Analytics: Practical Guidelines for Best Practice by Evan Stubbs

Demand-Driven Forecasting: A Structured Approach to Forecasting, Second Edition by Charles Chase

Demand-Driven Inventory Optimization and Replenishment: Creating a More Efficient Supply Chain by Robert A. Davis

Developing Human Capital: Using Analytics to Plan and Optimize Your Learning and Development Investments by Gene Pease, Barbara Beresford, and Lew Walker

The Executive's Guide to Enterprise Social Media Strategy: How Social Networks Are Radically Transforming Your Business by David Thomas and Mike Barlow

Economic and Business Forecasting: Analyzing and Interpreting Econometric Results by John Silvia, Azhar Iqbal, Kaylyn Swankoski, Sarah Watt, and Sam Bullard

Financial Institution Advantage & The Optimization of Information Processing by Sean C. Keenan

Financial Risk Management: Applications in Market, Credit, Asset and Liability Management and Firmwide Risk by Jimmy Skoglund and Wei Chen

For more information on any of the above titles, please visit www.wiley.com.

Trade-Based Money Laundering

*The Next Frontier
in International Money Laundering
Enforcement*

John A. Cassara

WILEY

Published by John Wiley & Sons, Inc., Hoboken, New Jersey.
Published simultaneously in Canada.

The manuscript of this book was submitted to the CIA's Pre-publication Review Board. This does not constitute an official release of CIA information. All statements of fact, opinion, or analysis expressed are those of the author and do not reflect the official positions or views of the Central Intelligence Agency (CIA) or any other U.S. Government agency. Nothing in the contents should be construed as asserting or implying U.S. Government authentication of information or CIA endorsement of the author's views. This material has been reviewed solely for classification.

For general information on our other products and services or for technical support, please contact our Customer Care Department within the United States at (800) 762–2974, outside the United States at (317) 572–3993 or fax (317) 572–4002.

Wiley publishes in a variety of print and electronic formats and by print-on-demand. Some material included with standard print versions of this book may not be included in e-books or in print-on-demand. If this book refers to media such as a CD or DVD that is not included in the version you purchased, you may download this material at http://booksupport.wiley.com. For more information about Wiley products, visit www.wiley.com.

Library of Congress Cataloging-in-Publication Data

Names: Cassara, John A., 1953- author.
Title: Trade-based money laundering : the next frontier in international
    money laundering enforcement / John A. Cassara.
Description: Hoboken, New Jersey : John Wiley & Sons, [2016] | Series: Wiley
    & SAS business series | Includes bibliographical references and index.
Identifiers: LCCN 2015031791 | ISBN 9781119078951 (cloth) | ISBN
    9781119125372 (epdf) | ISBN 9781119125396 (epub)
Subjects: LCSH: Money laundering. | Commercial crimes.
Classification: LCC HV6768 .C398 2016 | DDC 364.16/8–dc23 LC record available at
http://lccn.loc.gov/2015031791

Cover Design: Wiley
Cover Image: © Yi Lu / Viewstock / Corbis

Printed in the United States of America

10 9 8 7 6 5 4 3 2 1

Contents

CONTENTS

Foreword

My introduction to the name John Cassara 13 years ago created an early and instantly classic memory in my emerging career as a counter–illicit financing policy official at the U.S. Department of the Treasury. I was traveling through the Middle East on a Treasury mission to facilitate implementation of anti–money laundering (AML) systems and to explain and inform our evolving strategy to counter the financing of terrorism (CFT). Working with allies and other financial centers, the United States had recently fused many elements of the CFT strategy with global AML standards and was pressing for worldwide implementation as a collective security priority following the terrorist attacks of 9/11. After joining the Treasury mission only months before, I was both honored and a bit anxious participating in these pivotal discussions with experienced senior policymakers and AML/CFT practitioners from such a crucial region. On the margins of these discussions, and on more than one occasion, I was asked an unusual question: "Are you John Cassara?"

The clear respect, bordering on awe, with which the question was asked made the answer as disappointing as it was awkward. I returned to Washington with some frustration and abundant curiosity—who is John Cassara?

Upon my return, I quickly learned that being confused with John Cassara was a tremendous compliment. John's legendary status in the global financial investigative community at that time was mirrored by his reputation among peers across the U.S. federal government. In John's storied if not unique career in public service, he served a combined 26 years as a clandestine case officer with the Central Intelligence Agency and as a Treasury special agent with both the U.S. Secret Service and U.S. Customs.

In the 13 years since the trip that introduced me to the name John Cassara, I have had the privilege of working directly with John on multiple cases and issues. John's insights and advice, including after his retirement from government service, helped shape my perspective as I assisted Treasury leadership in creating a new strategic policy office focusing on all aspects of the counter–illicit financing mission. John's thinking informed our efforts to strengthen and expand the global commitment to combat illicit finance, including in partnership with the interagency community, the Financial Action Task Force and the global AML/CFT community, and the private sector. I have continued to rely on John's experience, talents, and insights since joining the private sector in 2013.

Throughout our relationship, John has demonstrated consistent leadership in pushing for urgent reforms required to strengthen the counter–illicit financing mission. And yet, John has never alienated those of us who might take a different view on particularly complex challenges or dimensions of this evolving mission.

I am immensely proud to call John a friend and deeply honored that he asked me to write the foreword for *Trade-Based Money Laundering: The Next Frontier in International Money Laundering Enforcement*, his fourth book.

John's latest writing comes at a crucial time in the evolution of AML/CFT regimes and the expanding role of financial and economic power as instruments of national and collective security. In the generation since the 9/11 terrorist attacks, there is no doubt that U.S. leadership and global commitments have successfully demonstrated the effectiveness—and indeed, the increasing necessity—of financial power in combating the greatest collective security threats we face. From al Qaeda and global terrorism to the proliferation of weapons of mass destruction and the threatening activities of rogue states such as North Korea, Iran, and Syria, the United States has increasingly relied on financial power to protect and advance our national and collective security.

Despite these unequivocal successes in the evolution and application of financial power to help combat our gravest threats, the global AML/CFT community continues to struggle in systematically advancing more fundamental objectives of AML regimes. As John clearly demonstrates, traditional quantitative and qualitative metrics on money-laundering prosecutions and forfeitures present a troubling picture of relative stagnation. More fundamentally, we lack a clear, systemic, and shared understanding of the nature and scope of money laundering risks. These fundamental shortcomings exacerbate increasingly evident challenges of the private sector in applying a risk-based approach to AML/CFT programs and controls.

These concerns are particularly troubling given the ongoing expansion of transnational organized crime and the illicit financing networks that support such activity. Numerous threat assessments and corresponding strategies document the continued growth and reach of these networks and the criminal groups they support. Such growth includes opportunistic convergence and increasing infiltration of legitimate economic activities, strategically important industries, and governing elites in a number of states around the world. This is a grim picture.

Fresh thinking is needed to change this reality and address long-standing cracks in global AML/CFT regimes. In this book, John makes a compelling case to begin necessary AML/CFT reform by focusing on trade-based money laundering. He is incredibly well-suited for this, bringing his career AML/CFT investigative experience together with his expert understanding of global trade controls. John's insights on trade-based money laundering, gained from over three decades of professional experience investigating illicit finance, will be invaluable to the full range of AML/CFT stakeholders seeking to strengthen the counter–illicit financing mission.

The AML/CFT world is ready to listen. As John describes, recent developments across the regulatory, law enforcement, financial intelligence, and counter–illicit financing policy communities indicate a renewed interest in trade-based money laundering. From regulatory guidance and examination to FinCEN advisories and the 2015 U.S. National Money Laundering Risk Assessment, authorities are refocusing on the deep-seated, systemic AML/CFT vulnerabilities presented by various forms of trade-based money laundering. My consulting experience over the past two years has indicated this renewed interest is shared by the private sector, particularly in the global banking industry.

This book will encourage the continuation and intensification of these efforts. It stands alone as a comprehensive and practical guide on trade-based money laundering and value transfer. And it will prove to be an invaluable resource for the global financial community and

AML/CFT authorities as we collectively renew our efforts to better understand and attack money laundering systematically, beginning with trade-based money laundering—truly the next frontier in international money laundering enforcement.

— Chip Poncy

Preface

Not long after the September 11 attacks, I had a conversation with a Pakistani entrepreneur. This businessman could be charitably described as being involved in international gray markets and illicit finance. We discussed many of the subjects addressed in this book, including trade-based money laundering, value transfer, hawala, fictitious invoicing, and countervaluation. At the end of the discussion, he looked at me and said, "Mr. John, don't you know that your adversaries are transferring money and value right under your noses? But the West doesn't see it. Your enemies are laughing at you."

The conversation made a profound impact on me. I knew he was right. Spending the better part of a career as a special agent with the U.S. Customs Service, I conducted investigations both in the United States and overseas. Over the years, I developed sources and expertise in many of the indigenous, ethnic-based, underground financial systems that are found around the world. I knew firsthand that the common denominator in many of these underground financial systems was trade-based value transfer.

At the time of the conversation, the U.S. government and the international community had not focused attention or resources on the misuse of international trade to launder money, transfer value, avoid taxes, commit commercial fraud, and finance terror. It was completely under our radar. Our adversaries—criminals, terrorists, kleptocrats, and fraudsters—were operating in these areas with almost total impunity. And unfortunately, many years after that conversation and the tremendous expenditure of resources to counter illicit finance, trade-based money laundering and value transfer are still not recognized as significant dangers. Perhaps as the Pakistani businessman implied, it is because the subterfuges are "hiding in plain sight."

After I "retired" from a 26-year career in the U.S. intelligence and law enforcement communities, I tried to draw attention to the intertwined threats of what the U.S. military calls *asymmetric warfare*, threat finance, international money laundering, and trade-based value transfer. I wrote two nonfiction books: *Hide & Seek: Intelligence, Law Enforcement and the Stalled War on Terror Finance* (Washington, D.C.: Potomac Books, 2006) and *On the Trail of Terror Finance: What Law Enforcement and Intelligence Officers Need to Know* (Washington, D.C.: Red Cell IG, 2010). I continued my efforts by writing articles, consulting, and speaking before various industry and government groups. Realizing that some are not enthusiastic about whitepapers and PowerPoint presentations, I wrote *Demons of Gadara* (CreateSpace, 2013)—the first novel that revolves around the themes of threat finance and trade-based value transfer. I tried to teach by telling a story.

This book is a continuation. It is designed as a straightforward, accessible, and user-friendly resource that is primarily directed toward anti–money-laundering/counterterrorist finance (AML/CFT) professionals such as compliance officers in financial institutions and money-service businesses. I hope to provide insight into opaque financial systems and trade scams that often impact their work. I believe concerned investigators, analysts, and policymakers in government will also find the book valuable.

Value transfer and underground finance are increasingly popular in academia. I have been particularly pleased to hear from students who share my belief in the importance of this topic and find this new field of study fascinating. This book is not written by an academic but, rather, by someone who has worked and supported value-transfer investigations in various international locations. I will try to convey—in a plain speaking and practical style—some lessons learned by personal experience and observations.

I would like to emphasize that this book is *not* a general AML/CFT primer. I am making the assumption that the reader has working knowledge of money laundering, terror finance, and many of our countermeasures. Instead, this book will focus on trade-based money laundering and value transfer—a specific methodology plus a few representative subsets and variations. Moreover, this book will not go into detail on trade finance. For those readers who feel they need a brief introduction to money laundering and terror finance to better understand some of the challenges and countermeasures surfaced in this book, see Appendix A.

HOW THIS BOOK IS ORGANIZED

Trade-based money laundering and value transfer are very broad topics. Chapter 1 introduces the magnitude of the problem, gives a general definition, and makes clear that the international trading system is abused by money launderers, terrorists, tax cheats, and many who engage in a variety of financial crimes. Chapter 2 provides an overview of basic trade-based laundering techniques that are referenced in succeeding chapters. Case examples and illustrative diagrams are used frequently throughout the book. The trade-based schemes are not United States centric, but rather come from around the world.

Chapters 3, 4, and 5 discuss prominent underground financial systems such as the black market peso exchange, hawala, and fei-chien. Historically and culturally, all of these systems—and others like them—are based on the misuse of international trade. Chapter 6 discusses why and how the international gold trade is prominently used to launder staggering amounts of illicit proceeds. Chapter 7 briefly describes commercial trade-based money laundering, such as diversion, misinvoicing, and transfer pricing. Since trade-based money laundering is so broad, Chapter 8 covers miscellaneous topics that do not neatly fit elsewhere, such as barter trade, the misuse of free trade zones, and others. Chapter 9 discusses how trade is monitored for enforcement purposes and includes insight on innovative countermeasures. Chapter 10 discusses red-flag indicators that can be used by both industry and government to help spot forms of trade-based money laundering and value transfer.

Finally, the conclusion contains recommendations for increasing trade transparency, awareness, and enforcement. And although I try as much as I can to stay away from jargon, acronyms, and technical terms, in order to simplify things for the reader there is a glossary of frequently used terms. In addition, where applicable, chapters contain both abstracts and "cheat sheets" of important points covered.

SOURCING

The sourcing for this book is a mix of personal observation and experience and information in the public domain. Some sections draw from my previous books and articles, updated and adapted as necessary. In certain sections, I borrowed heavily from *On the Trail of Terror Finance: What Law Enforcement and Intelligence Officers Need to Know*. The book was co-authored by Mr. Avi Jorisch. Both the Financial Action Task Force (FATF) and the Asia Pacific Group (APG) have produced valuable studies on trade-based money laundering. Web materials such as statistics, investigations, and guidelines are available but change frequently. Recent case examples are used as well as others that are dated. The reason I included some older cases is because they are in the public domain and still representative of current threats.

I have found that both government and academic reporting on money laundering and related topics are often prone to *circular reporting*, wherein analysis is used and reused often enough to make identifying the original source difficult. I assure the readers that to the best of my ability, I have practiced due diligence in my sourcing, and that this book represents my good-faith effort to make the subject matter as interesting, accurate, well-sourced, and current as possible.

Acknowledgments

Financial institutions, money services businesses, and their anti–money laundering compliance and program officers have long been considered "the first line of defense" in financial crimes. Due primarily to my experiences as a criminal investigator for the U.S. Treasury Department and later during an assignment at the Financial Crimes Enforcement Network (FinCEN), I have been an enthusiastic consumer of the financial intelligence or Bank Secrecy Act (BSA) data they produce. Unfortunately, for a variety of reasons, practitioners in the financial industry do not get the feedback, recognition, and thanks they deserve for the time and resources expended in implementing increasingly robust "know your customer" and industry AML/CFT compliance programs. So I would like to take this opportunity to say "thank you." I appreciate your hard work and understand that most of you enthusiastically work with government to help secure our financial systems. Thus I am encouraged that many recognize that trade and value transfer is the "next frontier" in international money laundering enforcement. I am hopeful that industry and government can partner to develop common sense and non-onerous guidelines and reporting that promote trade transparency.

To my colleagues in the intelligence, defense, and law enforcement communities, I hope this book will help explain the opaque nature of value transfer that is so prevalent in many of the challenges we face. I would like to extend my appreciation for all that you do to keep us safe.

I would also like to convey my heartfelt gratitude to some friends and colleagues who so generously shared their time, knowledge, and expertise in the preparation and review of the manuscript—especially Raymond Baker and the staff at Global Financial Integrity; Lou Bock, retired senior special agent, U.S. Customs Service; David B. Chenkin, managing partner, Zeichner Ellman & Krause LLP; Hector X. Colon, special agent and unit chief/director, NTC-Investigations & TTU, Homeland Security Investigations; Mark Laxer, vice president of Data Mining International, Inc.; Rob Siberski, retired HSI (legacy U.S. Customs) senior special agent; and Dr. John S. Zdanowicz, professor of finance and president of International Trade Alert, Inc.

And, as always, my gratitude to Cristina for her love and support.

About the Author

John A. Cassara retired after a 26-year career in the federal government intelligence and law enforcement communities. He is considered an expert in anti–money laundering and counterterrorist finance, with particular expertise in the growing threat of alternative remittance systems and forms of trade-based money laundering and value transfer. He invented the concept of international "Trade Transparency Units," an innovative countermeasure to entrenched forms of trade-based money laundering and value transfer. A large part of his career was spent overseas. He is one of the very few to have been both a clandestine operations officer in the U.S. intelligence community and a special agent for the Department of Treasury.

His last position was as a special agent detailee to the Department of Treasury's Office of Terrorism Finance and Financial Intelligence (TFI). His parent Treasury agency was the Financial Crimes Enforcement Network (FinCEN). Mr. Cassara was also detailed to the U.S. Department of State's Bureau of International Narcotics and Law Enforcement Affairs (INL) Anti-Money Laundering Section to help coordinate U.S. interagency international anti-terrorist finance training and technical assistance efforts.

During his law enforcement investigative career, Mr. Cassara conducted a large number of money laundering, fraud, intellectual property rights, smuggling, and diversion of weapons and high technology investigations in Africa, the Middle East, and Europe. He also served two years as an undercover arms dealer. He began his career with Treasury as a special agent assigned to the Washington field office of the U.S. Secret Service.

Since his retirement, he has lectured in the United States and around the world on a variety of transnational crime issues. He is an industry adviser for SAS, the analytics company. Mr. Cassara has authored or co-authored several articles and books. See www.JohnCassara.com.

CHAPTER 1

The Next Frontier

The Financial Action Task Force (FATF) has declared that there are three broad categories for the purpose of hiding illicit funds and introducing them into the formal economy. The first is via the use of financial institutions; the second is to physically smuggle bulk cash from one country or jurisdiction to another; and the third is the transfer of goods via trade.[1] The United States and the international community have devoted attention, countermeasures, and resources to the first two categories. Money laundering via trade has, for the most part, been ignored.

The United States' current anti–money laundering efforts began in 1971, when President Nixon declared the "war on drugs." About the same time, Congress started passing a series of laws, rules, and enabling regulations collectively known as the Bank Secrecy Act (BSA). The BSA is a misnomer. The goal is financial transparency by mandating financial intelligence or a paper trail to help criminal investigators "follow the money." Today, primarily as a result of the BSA, approximately 17 million pieces of financial intelligence are filed with the U.S. Treasury Department's Financial Crimes Enforcement Network (FinCEN) every year. The financial intelligence is warehoused, analyzed, and disseminated to law enforcement agencies at the federal, state, local, and increasingly the international levels.

The worldwide community slowly followed the U.S. lead. In 1989, the G-7 created the FATF. The international anti–money laundering policy-making body championed 40 recommendations for countries and jurisdictions around the world aimed at the establishment of anti–money laundering (AML), and after September 11, counterterrorist financing (CFT) countermeasures. These included the passage of AML/CFT laws, the creation of financial intelligence, *know your customer* (KYC) compliance programs for financial institutions and money services businesses, the creation of financial intelligence units (FIUs), procedures to combat bulk cash smuggling, and other safeguards.

The FATF's initial recommendations were purposefully imprecise in order to accommodate different legal systems and institutional environments. In its infancy, the FATF was also Western centric, focusing on money laundering primarily through the prism of the West's "war on drugs," where large amounts of dirty money were found sloshing around Western-style financial institutions. The FATF and its members almost completely ignored other forms of non-Western money laundering. Unfortunately, the FATF's early myopia had serious repercussions. Terrorist groups and criminal organizations continue to take advantage of what Osama bin Laden once called "cracks" in the Western financial system.[2]

As FATF evolved and the international community responded to growing financial threats, including the finance of terror, its nonbinding recommendations became increasingly precise. Its recommendations and interpretive notes have undergone periodic updates. In 1996, 2003, and 2012, its standards were significantly revised. The FATF's membership expanded, and today FATF-style regional bodies are found around the world.

Yet outside of FATF's 2006 trade-based money laundering "typology" report and similar studies conducted by FATF-style regional bodies (a study of particular note was conducted by the Asia Pacific Group in 2012), trade-based money laundering and value transfer have, for the most part, been ignored by the international community. This despite the FATF's above declaration that trade is one of the three principal categories of laundering money found around the world. For a variety of reasons, it has not been possible to achieve consensus on the extent of the problem and what should be done to confront it. And there continues to be an ongoing debate about whether financial institutions have the means and should assume the responsibility to help monitor international trade and trade finance as it relates to money laundering.

In 2014, *The Economist* called trade "the weakest link" in the fight against dirty money.[3] I agree with the assessment but believe it will change. Governments around the world—simultaneously pressed for new revenue streams and threatened by organized crime's use of money laundering, corruption, massive trade fraud, transfer pricing, and the associated threat of terror finance—are slowly moving to recognize the threat posed by *trade-based money laundering* and value transfer. (Note: TBML will be used in this book as the accepted acronym.)

 So what is TBML? The FATF defines the term as the "process of disguising the proceeds of crime and moving *value* through the use of trade transactions in an attempt to legitimize their illicit origins."

The key word in the above definition is *value*.[4] To understand TBML, we must put aside our linear Western thought process. Illicit money is not always represented by cash, checks, or electronic data in a wire transfer, or new payment methods such as stored-value cards, cell phones, or cyber-currency. The value represented by trade goods—and the accompanying documentation both genuine and fictitious—can also represent the transfer of illicit funds and value. This book will provide many examples of the *how* and *why*.

THE MAGNITUDE OF THE PROBLEM

To estimate the amount of TBML in the United States and around the world, we must first examine the magnitude of international money laundering in general. Those estimates are all over the map. In fact, the FATF has stated, "Due to the illegal nature of the transactions, precise statistics are not available, and it is therefore impossible to produce a definitive estimate of the amount of money that is globally laundered every year."[5]

However, the International Monetary Fund has estimated that money laundering comprises approximately 2 to 5 percent of the world's gross domestic product (GDP)[6] or approximately $3 trillion to $5 trillion per year. In very rough numbers, that is about the size of the U.S. federal budget! The United Nations Office on Drugs and Crime (UNODC) conducted a study to determine the magnitude of illicit funds and estimates that in 2009, criminal proceeds amounted to 3.6 percent of global GDP, or approximately $1.6 trillion being laundered.[7] So how much of that involves TBML? The issue has never been systematically examined. However, I will use a few metrics to put things in context.

 What is the magnitude of money laundering in general and TBML in particular? The short answer is that nobody knows with precision, but both are *enormous!*

According to the U.S. Department of State's 2009 International Narcotics Control Strategy Report (INCSR), it is estimated that the annual dollar amount laundered through trade ranges into the hundreds of billions.[8] In fact, the State Department has concluded that TBML has reached "staggering" proportions in recent years.[9]

Global Financial Integrity (GFI), a Washington, D.C.–based non-profit, has done considerable work in examining trade-misinvoicing. It is a method for moving money illicitly across borders, which involves deliberately misreporting the value of a commercial transaction on an invoice and other documents submitted to customs (see Chapter 7). A form of trade-based money laundering, trade-misinvoicing is the largest component of illicit financial outflows measured by GFI. After examining trade data covering developing countries, GFI concluded that a record $991.2 billion was siphoned from those countries in 2012 via trade misinvoicing![10] In its 2014 study, GFI finds that the developing world lost $6.6 trillion in illicit financial flows from 2003 to 2012, with illicit outflows alarmingly increasing at an average rate of more than approximately 9.4 percent per year.[11] See the illustration in Figure 1.1 for the 2002–2012 trade-misinvoicing outflows. Of course, much of this hemorrhage of capital originates from crime, corruption, fraud, and tax evasion.

In the United States, the UNODC estimated proceeds from all forms of financial crime, excluding tax evasion, was $300 billion in 2010, or about 2 percent of the U.S. economy.[13] This number is comparable to U.S. estimates.[14]

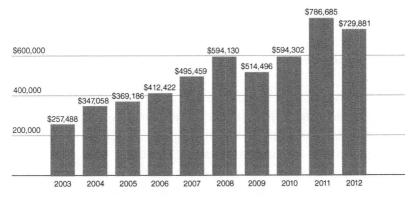

Figure 1.1 Trade-misinvoicing outflows from developing countries 2003–2012[12] (in millions of dollars, nominal)
Source: Global Financial Integrity, http://www.gfintegrity.org/issue/trade-misinvoicing/ (2015).

There are no reliable official estimates on the magnitude of TBML as a whole. Since the issue affects national security, law enforcement, and the collection of national revenue, it is remarkable that the U.S. government has never adequately examined TBML.

Dr. John Zdanowicz, an academic and early pioneer in the field of TBML, examined 2013 U.S. trade data obtained from the U.S. Census Bureau. Using methodologies explained further in Chapters 2 and 9, by examining undervalued exports ($124,116,420,714) and overvalued imports ($94,796,135,280), Dr. Zdanowicz found that $218,912,555,994 was moved out of the United States in the form of value transfer! That figure represents 5.69 percent of U.S. trade. Examining overvalued exports ($68,332,594,940) and undervalued imports ($272,753,571,621), Dr. Zdanowicz calculates that $341,086,166,561 was moved into the United States! That figure represents 8.87 percent of U.S. trade in 2013.[15]

A further complicating factor in estimating the magnitude of TBML involves the factoring of predicate offenses or "specified unlawful activities" involved. Predicate offenses are crimes that underlie money laundering or terrorist finance activity. Years ago, drug-related offenses were considered as the primary predicate offenses for money laundering. Over time, the concept of money laundering has become much more inclusive. Today, the United States recognizes hundreds of predicate offenses to charge money laundering, including fraud, smuggling, and human trafficking. The international standard is "all serious crimes." This is an increasingly important consideration, because in many international jurisdictions, tax evasion is also a predicate offense to charge money laundering. This viewpoint is gaining traction around the world.

Returning to the estimates of the overall magnitude of global money laundering, experts believe approximately half of the trillions of dollars laundered every year represent traditional predicate offenses, such as narcotics trafficking. The other half comes from tax-evading components.[16] In 2012, the FATF revised its recommendations to require that tax crimes and smuggling (which includes non-payment of customs duties) be included as predicate offenses for money laundering. The Internal Revenue Service believes, "Money laundering is in effect tax evasion in progress."[17] In the United States, customs violations including trade fraud is the most important predicate offense involved with TBML.[18] Other primary predicate offenses worldwide for TBML include tax evasion, commercial fraud, intellectual property rights violations, narcotics trafficking, human trafficking, terrorist financing, embezzlement, corruption, and organized crime (racketeering).[19]

The misuse of trade is also involved with capital flight, or the transfer of wealth offshore, which can be very harmful to countries with weak economies. Although many governments have passed laws governing how much currency can be removed from their jurisdiction and what types of overseas investments their citizens can make, individuals and businesses have sometimes been able to circumvent these controls by sending value in the form of trade goods and payment offshore. This was a common tactic during the apartheid era of South Africa and is being done today by wealthy Venezuelans, Pakistanis, Russians, Iranians, Chinese (see Chapter 5), and many others. For example, much private wealth in Iran is also transferred out of the country via *hawala*. Dubai is a favored destination. As we will see later in this book, in the regional hawala networks, trade is the favored network to provide countervaluation between brokers. Wealth is also being siphoned via various forms of commercial trade–based money laundering, such as misinvoicing and transfer pricing. And, of course, trade-based value transfer is often an integral component in various forms of corruption, such as concealing illegal commissions.

 Including all its varied forms, the argument can be made that TBML and value transfer is perhaps the largest and most pervasive money-laundering methodology in the world! And in comparison to the volume of international trade, successful enforcement efforts are practically nil.

Another way of looking at TBML from the macro level is to examine global merchandise trade, which is only the trade in goods, not services or capital transfers or foreign investments. We will discuss it in more detail in the next chapter. Global merchandise trade is in the multiple of tens of trillions of dollars every year. For illustrative purposes, if only 5 percent of global merchandise trade is questionable or somehow related to the multiple forms of TBML discussed in this book, we are talking about well over one trillion dollars a year in tainted money and value!

So if we factor tax evasion, including customs fraud, into the TBML equation, as well as capital flight, forms of informal value transfer systems as described in Chapters 3, 4, and 5, and commercial TBML such as trade misinvoicing as described in Chapter 7, the magnitude is enormous. It could very well be the largest money laundering methodology in the world! And, unfortunately, it is also the least understood and recognized.

HOW ARE WE DOING?

Once again, it is necessary to first look at our success/failure rate versus global money laundering as a whole. Reliable statistics are hard to find and sometimes dated. Yet the data that do exist present a bleak picture. It important to remember that in anti–money laundering efforts, the bottom-line *measurables* (a term used frequently within the U.S. government) are not the number of suspicious transaction reports filed (SARs) or the politically popular but vague term of *disruption*. Rather, the metrics that matter are the number of arrests, convictions, and illicit money identified, seized, and forfeited. Despite periodic positive public pronouncements from the Department of Treasury and various administrations, here are a few sobering numbers:

- According to the United Nations Office of Drug Control (UNODC), less than 1 percent of global illicit financial flows are currently being seized and frozen.[20]

- Per data collected by the Office of the U.S. National Drug Control Policy, Americans spend approximately $65 billion per year on illegal drugs. According to the Drug Enforcement Administration (DEA), only about $1 billion is seized.[21]

- According to Raymond Baker, a longtime authority on financial crimes, using statistics provided by U.S. Treasury Department officials concerning the amount of dirty money coming into the United States and the portion caught by anti–money laundering enforcement efforts, the numbers show enforcement is successful 0.1 percent of the time and fails 99.9 percent of the time. "In other words, total failure is just a decimal point away."[22]

 Information suggests that in the United States, money launderers face a less than 5 percent risk of conviction.[23] And according to the U.S. State Department,[24] buttressed by my personal observations, the situation in most areas of the world is even worse.

▼ The bottom line is that for a money launderer to be caught, convicted, and to have his or her assets identified, seized, and forfeited, the money launderer has to be very stupid or very unlucky.

Trying to narrow the numbers down to cover TBML is even more difficult. Statistics on the detection of TBML are very limited, and most international jurisdictions do not distinguish TBML from other forms of money laundering. Moreover, in most countries, trade data are collected by customs. Their mandate is primarily the collection of revenue via the collection of taxes, fines, and penalties. Thus, many customs services do not have the legal directive to take enforcement action, nor the training or competence to combat TBML.[25]

So considering that experts believe TBML is one of the three largest money laundering categories, it is found around the world, and simultaneously, it is one of the most opaque, least-known and understood, and most underenforced money laundering techniques, we are not doing very well at all.

Moreover, according to the U.S. Department of Treasury, TBML has a "more destructive impact on legitimate commerce than other money laundering schemes."[26] Trade fraud puts legitimate businesses at a competitive disadvantage, creating a barrier to entrepreneurship, and crowding out legitimate economic activity. TBML often robs governments of tax revenue due to the sale of underpriced goods, and reduced duties collected on undervalued imports and fraudulent cargo manifests.[27] Commercial TBML causes massive societal losses—particularly in the developing world.

Simply put, TBML is the "next frontier" in international money laundering enforcement.

NOTES

1. FATF, *Trade-Based Money Laundering* (Paris: FATF, June 23, 2006), p. 1, available online: http://www.fatf-gafi.org/media/fatf/documents/reports/Trade%20Based%20Money%20Laundering.pdf.

2. Osama bin Laden interview by a reporter working for *Dawn* magazine, 2001. See http://www.globalresearch.ca/interview-with-osama-bin-laden-denies-his-involvement-in-9-11/24697.

3. "Uncontained," *The Economist* (May 3, 2014); available online: http://www.economist.com/news/international/21601537-trade-weakest-link-fight-against-dirty-money-uncontained.

4. FATF, *Trade-Based Money Laundering*, p. 1.

5. FATF, FAQ, "What Is Money Laundering?" available online: http://www.fatf-gafi.org/pages/faq/moneylaundering/.

6. United Nations Office on Drugs and Crime, "Estimating Illicit Financial Flows Resulting from Drug Trafficking and Other Transnational Organized Crimes," p. 5, available online, http://www.unodc.org/documents/data-and-analysis/Studies/Illicit_financial_flows_2011_web.pdf.

7. Ibid.

8. U.S. Department of State, Bureau for International Narcotics and Law Enforcement Affairs, *International Narcotics Control Strategy Report (INCSR) Volume II, Money Laundering and Financial Crimes* (February 27, 2009), available online: (http://www.state.gov/j/inl/rls/nrcrpt/2009/vol2/116537.htm).

9. U.S. Department of State, Bureau for International Narcotics and Law Enforcement Affairs, *International Narcotics Control Strategy Report (INCSR) Volume II, Money Laundering and Financial Crimes* (March 2014), available online: http://www.state.gov/j/inl/rls/nrcrpt/2003/vol2/html/29910.htm.

10. Clark Gascoigne, "New Study: Crime, Corruption, Tax Evasion Drained a Record US $991.2bn in Illicit Financial Flows from Developing Economies in 2012," *Global Financial Integrity*, December 15, 2014; available online: http://www.gfintegrity.org/press-release/new-study-crime-corruption-tax-evasion-drained-a-record-us991-2-billion-in-illicit-financial-flows-from-developing-economies-in-2012/.

11. Ibid.

12. "Trade Misinvoicing Outflows from Developing Countries: 2002–2011," Global Financial Integrity, available online: http://www.gfintegrity.org/issue/trade-misinvoicing/.

13. United Nations Office on Drugs and Crime, *Estimating Illicit Financial Flows Resulting From Drug Trafficking and Other Transnational Organized Crimes*, October 2011.

14. *National Anti–Money Laundering Risk Assessment* (Washington, D.C.: U.S. Department of Treasury, 2015), p. 11, available online: http://www.treasury.gov/resource-center/terrorist-illicit-finance/Documents/National%20Money%20Laundering%20Risk%20Assessment%20%E2%80%93%2006-12-2015.pdf

15. Analysis given to the author by Dr. John Zdanowicz via June 30, 2015, email.

16. Raymond Baker, "Dirty Money and Its Global Effect, International Policy Report," a Publication of the Center for International Policy, January 2003, p. 2.

17. IRS website, available online: http://www.irs.gov/uac/Overview-Money-Laundering.

18. A 2014 conversation by the author with Homeland Security Investigations (HSI) officials involved with the Trade Transparency Unit (TTU) initiative.

19. "Asia Pacific Group (APG) Report on Trade-Based Money Laundering," July 20, 2012, p. 38, available online: http://www.fatfgafi.org/media/fatf/documents/reports/Trade_Based_ML_APGReport.pdf.

20. UNODCP, available online: http://www.unodc.org/documents/data-and-analysis/Studies/Illicit_financial_flows_2011_web.pdf.

21. DEA, "Money Laundering," available online: http://www.justice.gov/dea/ops/money.shtml.

22. Raymond W. Baker, *Capitalism's Achilles Heel* (Hoboken, NJ: John Wiley & Sons, Inc., 2005), p. 173.

23. Champion Walsh, "Study Faults U.S. Policies on Money Laundering, Terror Funds," Dow Jones Capital Markets Report via *Dow Jones* (December 14, 2004).

24. "A review of country reports shows that far too many countries that boast solid AML/CTF standards and infrastructures do not enforce their laws. This is true in all corners of the world and for both developed and developing countries alike. In many instances, the lack of enforcement is due to lack of capacity, but in some cases it is due to a lack of political will." INCSR (Washington, D.C.: U.S. State Department, 2009), available online: http://www.state.gov/documents/organization/120055.pdf.

25. APG, p. 73.

26. *National Anti–Money Laundering Risk Assessment*, p. 29.

27. Ibid.

CHAPTER **2**

Trade-Based Money Laundering Techniques: Invoice Fraud

n traditional money laundering involving the transfers of money, criminals seek to *wash, launder,* or *legitimize* illicit funds. Generally, they use a variety of techniques to first *place* dirty money in financial institutions in ways that do not trigger the financial transparency reporting requirements briefly described in Chapter 1. They next *layer* the money by frequently moving it between accounts or wiring it from bank to bank, often through multiple jurisdictions. Finally, criminal organizations *integrate* the laundered money back into the economy by purchasing real estate, businesses, investing in the stock market, and so on. The above three stages of money laundering are designed to make it difficult for investigators to follow the money trail. (See Appendix A for an overview of the three stages of money laundering.)

In TBML, criminals likewise seek to legitimize funds. They do so by genuinely or fraudulently buying and selling trade goods using a variety of techniques that very effectively transfer value in ways that sometimes bypass financial intelligence reporting requirements. Trade is also used in placement, layering, and integration.

In 2010, total global merchandise trade was approximately $31 trillion.[1] The enormous size of global commerce increases the probability of TBML. Just like in traditional money laundering when criminals mix or *comingle* illicit money with licit money via financial institutions, the same holds true in international trade. The large volume of international commerce masks the occasional suspect transfer. It is the sheer magnitude and noise of global trade that presents the primary challenge to law enforcement and customs services around the world in their attempts to detect and counter TBML.

In addition to the massive trade volume and the mixing of the occasional illicit transaction with the overwhelming percentage of legitimate trade, there are other factors that combine to make it very difficult for authorities to monitor suspicious trade transactions:

- There are innumerable, complex types of trade finance deals found in the business world.

- Tax avoidance and capital flight generally involve the transfer of legitimate funds across borders, making it very difficult to distinguish intent.

- Underground financial systems that rely heavily on trade are, by their very nature, nontransparent.

- At all levels of industry and government, there is limited understanding and resources to detect suspicious trade transactions.

- Criminals, fraudsters, and tax cheats use a variety of techniques and schemes in the misuse of trade.

- Corruption is the great facilitator in many forms of TBML.

TBML is generally considered a *complex money-laundering methodology*. Its components cut across sectorial boundaries and national borders. To distinguish TBML and value transfer from the legitimate activities of international trade is sometimes quite difficult. And TBML is often combined with other common money-laundering techniques, such as the layering of financial transactions, the use of offshore shell companies, the use of bulk cash, and various underground financial systems.

HOW DOES TBML WORK?

 TBML generally begins with the invoice!

In its primary form, TBML revolves around invoice fraud and associated manipulation of supporting documents. When a buyer and seller work together, the price of goods (or services) can be whatever the parties want it to be. There is no invoice police! As Raymond Baker—one of the world's foremost experts in financial crimes—succinctly notes, "Anything that can be priced can be mispriced. False pricing is done every day, in every country, on a large percentage of import and export transactions. This is the most commonly used technique for generating and transferring dirty money."[2]

The primary techniques used for invoice fraud and manipulation are:[3]

- Over- and underinvoicing and shipments of goods and services

- Multiple invoicing of goods and services

- Falsely described goods and services

Other common techniques related to the above include:

- *Short shipping:* This occurs when the exporter ships fewer goods than the invoiced quantity of goods, thus misrepresenting the true value of the goods in the documentation. The effect of this technique is similar to overinvoicing.

- *Overshipping:* The exporter ships more goods than what is invoiced, thus misrepresenting the true value of the goods in the documentation. The effect is similar to underinvoicing.

- *Phantom shipping:* No goods are actually shipped. The fraudulent documentation generated is used to justify payment abroad.

INVOICE FRAUD

Money laundering and value transfer through the over- and under-invoicing of goods and services is a common practice around the world. The key element of this technique is the misrepresentation of trade goods to transfer value between the importer and exporter or settle debts/balance accounts between the trading parties. The shipment (real or fictitious) of goods and the accompanying documentation provide cover for the transfer of money.

First, by underinvoicing goods below their fair market price, an exporter is able to transfer value to an importer while avoiding the scrutiny associated with more direct forms of money transfer. The value the importer receives when selling (directly or indirectly) the goods on the open market is considerably greater than the amount he or she paid the exporter.

For example, Company A located in the United States ships one million widgets worth $2 each to Company B based in Mexico. On the invoice, however, Company A lists the widgets at a price of only $1 each, and the Mexican importer pays the U.S. exporter only $1 million for them. Thus, extra value has been transferred to Mexico, where the importer can sell (directly or indirectly) the widgets on the open market for a total of $2 million. The Mexican company then has several options: it can keep the profits; transfer some of them to a bank account outside the country where the proceeds can be further laundered via layering and integration; share the proceeds with the

U.S. exporter (depending on the nature of their relationship); or even transfer them to a criminal organization that may be the power behind the business transactions.

To transfer value in the opposite direction, an exporter can overinvoice goods above their fair market price. In this manner, the exporter receives value from the importer because the latter's payment is higher than the goods' actual value on the open market.

 INVOICE MANIPULATION MADE SIMPLE!

To move money out:

■ Import goods at overvalued prices or export goods at undervalued prices.

To move money in:

■ Import goods at undervalued prices or export goods at overvalued prices.

For example, Figure 2.1 shows the fluctuating value associated with thousands of refrigerators exported from Country A to Country B via a series of shipments. The darker shade represents the declared value of the refrigerators upon export from Country A, and the light

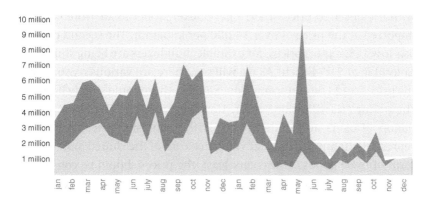

Figure 2.1 Comparative imports and exports of refrigerators[4]

Copyright © 2012. SAS Institute Inc. All rights reserved. Reproduced with permission of SAS Institute Inc., Cary, NC, USA. From http://www.sas.com/news/sascom/terrorist-financing.html.

shade represents their declared value upon arrival in Country B. The horizontal line represents the time period over which these shipments occurred. The vertical line represents the value expressed in dollars. In this case, the refrigerators were overinvoiced. The export data came from the "shippers export declaration" (SED) that accompanies the shipments. The import data came from the importing country's customs service. Obviously, the declared export price should match the declared import price. (There are some recognized but comparatively small pricing variables. In addition, the quantity and quality of refrigerators should also match—which occurred in this case.) The difference in price between the dark and light shades represents the transfer of value from the importer to the exporter. In this case, the transfer actually represented the proceeds of narcotics trafficking.

The reader can see at the end of the chart the shaded colors start to converge. The colors or values between imports and exports begin to match because data were compared, anomalies noted, and joint enforcement action taken by the two countries involved. Trade transparency was achieved. The comparative stability at the end of the chart reflects true market conditions.

Table 2.1 lists genuine examples of abnormal prices of trade goods entering and departing the United States. The information is from a study conducted by Dr. John Zdanowicz analyzing U.S. trade data. For example, plastic buckets from the Czech Republic are imported with the declared price of $972 per bucket! Toilet tissue from China is imported at the price of over $4,000 per kilogram. The second column lists low U.S. export prices; for example, bulldozers are being shipped to Colombia at $1.74 each! As we will see, there are various reasons why the prices could be abnormal. For example, there could simply be a data "input" or "classification" error. However, recalling the above explanation of over- and underinvoicing, the abnormal prices could also represent attempts to transfer value in or out of the United States in the form of trade goods. At the very least, the prices should be considered suspicious. Only analysis and investigation will reveal the true reasons for such large discrepancies between market price and declared price.

I once investigated an international criminal network involved in the transshipment of garments and textiles into the commerce of the United States in violation of quota laws. The conspiracy involved

Table 2.1 Examples of Abnormal U.S. Trade Prices[5]

High U.S. Import Prices	Low U.S. Export Prices
Plastic buckets from Czech. Rep. $972/unit	Live cattle to Mexico $20.65/unit
Briefs and panties from Hungary $739/dozen	Radial truck tires to the United Kingdom $11.74/unit
Cotton dishtowels from Pakistan $153/unit	Toilet bowls to Hong Kong $1.75/unit
Ceramic tiles from Italy $4,480 sq. meter	Bulldozers to Colombia $1.74/unit
Razors from the United Kingdom $113/unit	Missile launchers to Israel $52.03/unit
Iron bolts from France $3,067/kg	Prefab buildings to Trinidad $1.20/unit
Toilet tissue from China $4,121/kg	Forklift trucks to Jamaica $384.14/unit

an international network of brokers and manufacturers. They were involved in trading tens of millions of dollars' worth of garments. The garments were manufactured in China and India but the country-of-origin labels on the garments and accompanying documentation made it appear that they actually originated in countries located in the Middle East and East Africa. Working with an industry source, I obtained information on this transnational fraud scheme including the recovery of a document, which was the proverbial "smoking gun."

The document was sent from the primary suspect, a Dubai-based trade broker, to a garment manufacturer in the Middle East, his co-conspirator in the transshipment scheme. The document advertised the conspirators' trade-based laundering services, including "reexport charges," "relabeling charges," and fees for "unstuffing and reloading containers." The freight forwarder also listed charges for creating bills of lading, customs duties, port fees, and document-handling fees. A notation on the document also stated, "Suggest you send us some blank invoices on company letterhead." With fraudulent invoices and supporting documentation, conspirators on opposite sides of the world commit customs fraud at a minimum. They can also transfer value in the form of trade goods. Unfortunately, there is little risk of detection.

A TALE OF TWO INVOICES

According to Bheki Khumalo, a money-laundering officer of the Financial Intelligence Unit of the Central Bank of Swaziland, " … most of the invoices that are presented to customs officials do not reflect the true value of the goods presented. How many times have we seen people buying goods in South Africa and asking for two invoices? One is for their accounts and the second one for the tax man."[6]

Another technique used to transfer money under the guise of trade is to issue multiple invoices for the same international trade transaction. This is done to justify multiple payments for the same shipment of goods. Although fictitious pricing can be involved, unlike the over- and underinvoicing, there is no need for the importer or the exporter to misrepresent the price of the good on the commercial invoice. And to add further complexity to the scheme, sometimes the fraudsters use different financial institutions to make payments.

For example, as part of the analysis into the laundering of a massive amount of proceeds from narcotics sales in the United States as part of Operation Polar Cap (see below), I investigated gold dealers in Europe and the Middle East. They issued multiple invoices for the same shipment of gold. The invoices facilitated the international payment of laundered drug money from accounts in the United States.

 OPERATION POLAR CAP

Although Operation Polar Cap came to fruition in 1989, it remains one of the largest international money-laundering investigations in history. Many schemes were used in this complex case, including forms of TBML. Some of the techniques still are in use today. The drug money belonged to the Medellin cartel. Called "La Mina" the laundering scheme processed nearly $1.2 billion in drug money. Operation Polar Cap—conducted jointly by the DEA, FBI, IRS, Customs, and state and local law enforcement—led to the first conviction of a foreign financial institution, Banco de Occidente/Panama, for violating U.S. money-laundering laws. More than 100 arrests were made, and some $105 million in assets were seized, including currency, bank accounts, real estate, jewelry, gold, and vehicles.

La Mina involved the buying and selling of gold, both real and fictitious. The multiagency investigation uncovered multiple laundering schemes. The earliest phase of the criminal operation involved the delivery of bulk drug money to collaborating gold dealers in Los Angeles, Houston, and New York. Elsewhere, gold-plated lead bars, misinvoiced and declared as solid gold, were shipped from Uruguay to manufacturers in the United States, giving the appearance of a legitimate gold import business (even though Uruguay did not mine or manufacture gold). Meanwhile, the drug money was packed in boxes that were declared as gold and shipped to a cartel-controlled jewelry retailer in Los Angeles. The cash was then deposited into banks as the proceeds of legitimate jewelry sales. The "*placed*" funds were then *layered* via wire transfer to cartel-controlled bank accounts in New York. The laundering continued as the funds were then transferred through Panama and other overseas accounts, including many in Europe.[7]

Suspect actors involved in TBML and other types of financial fraud may keep false sets of books. I once conducted a joint investigation in Italy with the Italian Guardia di Finanza (GdF), or fiscal police. The suspect was engaged in TBML via the fraudulent invoicing of shipments of gold jewelry from Italy to the United States. The investigation was a spinoff of Operation Polar Cap. The analysis of business records included GdF search warrants served at the subject's business and residence. At the business, they found a set of fictitious business records, including fraudulent invoices. This was the set of books the suspect kept to show the authorities. In the simultaneous search of the suspect's residence, they found the true set of books.

 Follow the money and value trail. But be aware of document fraud and multiple sets of books!

On another occasion, I was in the Middle East conducting a fraud investigation. Once again, fictitious invoicing was involved. During the course of the investigation, copies of the invoices and the supporting shipping documents were obtained. When the investigation was complete, I interviewed the subject in the presence of the local authorities. If the document said one thing, the suspect said another. Finally, when I proved to the suspect that the documents he originated and that we had in front of us were fraudulent, instead of staying quiet or admitting guilt, he offered to get another set of documents within a few hours. They would magically have the correct numbers, signature, amount, certifications, and so on! Thus, because TBML is fraudulent by its very nature, it often involves multiple sets of books and rampant document fraud.

CASE EXAMPLES: INVOICE FRAUD AND MANIPULATION

The best way to understand the variety of the techniques involved with invoice fraud and how it is related to TBML and value transfer is to examine genuine case examples. The following cases originated in diverse locations. Some are recent and some dated. However, even the older cases are exemplary of current schemes. (In my professional experience, criminal organizations continue to use the same methodologies and techniques until there is some sort of successful enforcement action.) In some instances, the identifying information has been omitted or changed. A few of the examples are rather straightforward and deal with some of the techniques already described. Some cases illustrate combinations of money-laundering techniques and are more complex. Case examples involving underground financial systems and other forms of TBML will be included in later chapters.

Case Study 1: False Invoicing Polypropylene Pellets

A narcotics trafficking and money laundering network inflated the value on high-volume shipments of polypropylene pellets exported from the United States to Mexico. Polypropylene is used to make a variety of plastic articles. Eventually, the operation caught the attention of bank compliance officers and they discontinued letters of credit used by the suspected launderers. Law enforcement investigated the network. It is believed the operation was hiding approximately $1 million every three weeks. One individual involved said, "You generate all of this paperwork on both sides of the border showing that the product you're importing has this much value on it, when in reality you paid less for it. Now you've got paper earnings of a million dollars. You didn't really earn that, but it gives you a piece of paper to take to [Mexican authorities] to say: "These million dollars in my bank account—it's legitimate. It came from here, see?"[8]

Case Study 2: Inflated Invoices and Terror Finance

According to Pakistani officials, a madrassa—a fundamental Islamic religious school—was linked to radical jihadist groups. The madrassa received large amounts of money from foreign sources. It was engaged in a side business dealing in animal hides. In order to justify the large inflow of funds, the madrassa claimed to sell a large number of hides at grossly inflated prices. This ruse allowed the extremists to "legitimize" the inflow of funds, which were then passed to terrorists.[9]

Case Study 3: TBML and Export Incentives

A network of co-conspirators based in Argentina engaged in both TBML and fraud against the Argentine government. The conspirators created a company in New Jersey called "Molds, Dies, and Novelties" that imported goods from an Argentine company the conspirators controlled called "Casa Piana." Over a multiyear period, the Argentines exported gold-plated copper medallions worth approximately $95 million. However, the conspirators prepared fraudulent export documentation for Argentine customs showing that the value of the goods was far greater. The medallions were flown from Buenos Aires to New York's JFK International Airport and imported into the United States. In addition to the medallions, Casa Piana also sent fraudulently described "solid gold" coins that were only coated with gold. They were overinvoiced. The scam enabled the conspirators to collect export incentives for the "locally manufactured" goods.

Many countries offer generous tax incentives to domestic manufacturers for selling their goods and services abroad. And criminals sometimes abuse these tax incentives by overreporting their exports. So in addition to engaging in TBML and value transfer through overinvoicing the coins, the government of Argentina awarded the conspirators approximately $130 million in export incentives![10]

Case Study 4: Vehicles, TBML, and Terror Finance

From approximately 2007 to 2011, at least $329 million was trans-
ferred by wire from the Lebanese Canadian Bank, the Hassan Ayash
Exchange Company, the Ellissa Exchange Company, and other
Lebanese financial institutions to the United States for the purchase
and shipment of used cars. Allegedly, some of the money involved was
from the proceeds of narcotics trafficking. According to investigators,
the car buyers in the United States typically had little or no property
or assets other than the bank accounts used to receive the overseas
wire transfers. After purchase, the cars were primarily shipped to
Cotonou, Benin, where they were housed and sold from large car
parks. See Figure 2.2.

The money exchanges in this scheme were involved with various
TBML techniques, including the misinvoicing of automobiles and consumer goods from Asia. The primary suspect, based in Asia, owned a
wide network of companies dealing in numerous products. The suspect
based his banking operations in Lebanon. The suspect received funds
in his accounts from a Latin American drug kingpin. Proceeds generated in local currency from the sale of the imported consumer goods

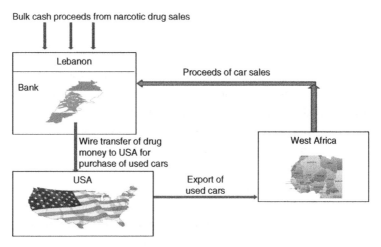

Figure 2.2 Export of used cars from the United States
*Source: http://www.fatf-gafi.org/media/fatf/documents/reports/Trade_Based_ML_
APGReport.pdf, p. 57.*[11]

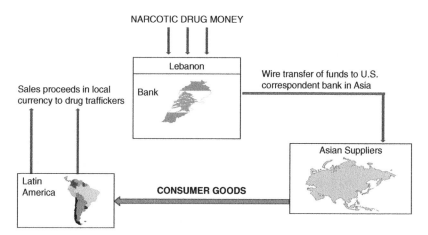

Figure 2.3 Purchase of consumer goods[14]
Source: http://www.fatf-gafi.org/media/fatf/documents/reports/Trade_Based_ML_APGReport.pdf, p. 58.

were deposited in individuals' accounts in the local banks. Per Chapter 3's explanation of the Black Market Peso Exchange, this allowed for the repatriation of narcotics proceeds for the Latin American drug producers.[12] See Figure 2.3. The exchanges also used their foreign money transmitter businesses to process millions of dollars on behalf of narcotics traffickers and money launderers. They attempted to hide the source of the funds by comingling and layering the transactions across a variety of international businesses and financial accounts.[13]

A significant portion of the cash proceeds from the car sales was transported to Lebanon by a Hezbollah-controlled system of money couriers, cash smugglers, hawaladars (see Chapter 4), and currency brokers. A network of money couriers controlled by Oussama Salhab, an alleged Hezbollah operative living in Togo, transported tens of millions of dollars and euros from Benin to Lebanon through Togo and Ghana. Salhab and his relatives also controlled a transportation company based in Michigan that was frequently used to ship cars to West Africa, as well as other entities involved in the scheme. Cash transported from West Africa was often routed through the Beirut airport, where Hezbollah security safeguarded its passage to its final destination.[15]

Case Study 5: TBML and Iranian Sanctions

Because of sanctions, much of Iran's foreign currency has been locked in overseas escrow accounts. The Iranian regime could only use local currency to buy local products. Front companies in Turkey were conduits for Iranian attempts to access the frozen funds. Turkish front companies issued fraudulent invoices for transactions for goods such as food and medicine that were permitted to be shipped to Iran under humanitarian grounds. For example, a Turkish prosecutor's report details a 2013 invoice involving a Turkish luxury yacht company selling nearly 5.2 tons of brown sugar to Iran's Bank Pasargad, with delivery to Dubai. Turkey's state-owned Halkbank facilitated the transaction. The sugar was invoiced at the price of 1,170 Turkish liras per kilo or approximately $240 per pound![16]

Case Study 6: Teddy Bears Used to Launder Drug Money

Angel Toy Corporation based in Los Angeles received a large amount of illicit cash generated from a narcotic trafficking organization based in Colombia. In some cases, couriers affiliated with the drug traffickers dropped off the cash at the toy company's store in Los Angeles. In other cases, cash deposits were made directly into the company's bank account, sometimes by individuals located as far away as New York. During the four-year investigation, more than $8 million in cash deposits were traced into Angel Toy Corporation's accounts; not a single transaction was over the $10,000 currency transaction report (CTR) reporting threshold.

Bank accounts of the toy company were used to pay for the import of toys manufactured in China, including teddy bears. Once the toys arrived in the United States, they were exported from Angel Toy Corporation to another toy company in Colombia. Pesos generated by the sales of toys by the Colombian toy company were used to reimburse the Colombian drug trafficker. Five persons, including two owners of Angel Toy Company, were convicted and fined.[17] See Figure 2.4. The Angel Toy Company case is representative of value transfer techniques, including the Colombian black market peso exchange. (See Chapter 3.)

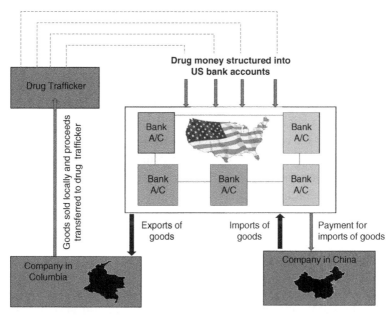

Figure 2.4 Toy company involved with TBML[18]
Source: http://www.fatf-gafi.org/media/fatf/documents/reports/Trade_Based_ML_APGReport.pdf, p. 63.

Case Study 7: Brazilian Paralelo

An investigation of an unlicensed money services business (MSB) in Atlanta resulted in the seizure of substantial funds from several bank accounts. The subsequent investigation revealed that a black market currency exchanger in Brazil, called a *doleiro,* was transferring payments to U.S. bank accounts. The owner of the U.S. accounts would then facilitate third-party wire transfers to U.S. and Asian exporters for commercial goods that were shipped to the South American tri-border area of Brazil, Argentina, and Paraguay. In Brazil, this kind of TBML scheme is known as the *paralelo.* It is designed to avoid high fees and taxes associated with legitimate international wire transactions conducted via the National Bank of Brazil. Criminal organizations use trade-based value to disguise the illicit origins of criminal proceeds. Analysis and investigation documented the illegal transfer of more than $100 million from the triborder area to the United States.[19]

Case Study 8: South Korean Uses Invoice Fraud to Circumvent Iranian Sanctions

According to U.S. State Department reporting, "In 2013, South Korean prosecutors detained and charged a Korean American with the illegal transfer of approximately $1 billion in restricted Iranian money frozen in South Korea pursuant to U.S. and international sanctions. The individual is suspected of making fraudulent transfers in 2011 from the Iranian central bank's won-denominated account at a South Korean bank by using fictitious invoices for payment. The scale and volume of the laundering operation demonstrate the vulnerabilities associated with not fully applying sufficient AML/CFT controls to high-risk customers and jurisdictions."[20]

CHEAT SHEET

- In TBML, criminals also try to *place, layer,* and *integrate* illicit funds. They do so by genuinely or fraudulently buying and selling trade goods using a variety of techniques that very effectively transfer value in ways that sometimes bypass financial intelligence reporting requirements.

- The volume of global merchandise trade (approximately $31 trillion in 2010) increases the probability of TBML.

- The misuse of international trade is also found in tax evasion, transfer pricing, capital flight, customs fraud, commercial fraud, underground financial systems, and various criminal schemes.

- Invoice fraud is the most frequently used form of TBML.

- The key element of TBML is the misrepresentation of a trade good in order to transfer additional value or settle debts between an importer and an exporter.

- The three most common techniques involved with invoice fraud are over- and underinvoicing, multiple invoicing, and falsely described goods.

- The amount shown on an invoice can be whatever the buyer and seller agree upon. "Whatever can be priced can be mispriced."

- Payment for the goods provides cover for the movement of illicit money.
- Illicit actors may create false sets of books and accounting records to match their fraudulent invoices.
- Other documentation used in trade, such as fraudulent bills of lading, are also used to support TBML schemes.

QUESTIONS TO ASK IF A SHIPMENT OF GOODS LOOKS SUSPICIOUS

Questions and observations will vary greatly, depending on the position of the questioner, that is, whether the interviewer works in a financial institution and is involved in trade finance, or perhaps has a position in customs, law enforcement, and so on. A comprehensive list of red-flag indicators is included in Chapter 10.

- What are the items being shipped?
- Where are they manufactured or produced?
- What is the ultimate destination?
- Is the routing logical?
- Is the origin and destination logical or suspect?
- Who is the buyer and who is the seller?
- Who benefits most from the transaction as it appears on paper? (Investigators should direct most of their attention at this party.)
- If one of the parties is obviously losing money on the transaction, investigators should question how they are still in business.
- Who is the shipper, broker, and/or freight forwarder? What is the relationship to the buyer/seller?
- Is this a regularly scheduled shipment of goods?
- Does the content of the shipment match the business of the parties involved with the transaction?
- Are there accompanying documents available? If so, what kind? If possible, request copies of all documents.

▦ Does the content and cost of the shipment match the description in the accompanying documents?

▦ Is the price of the goods in question standard market value? (There will be many variables involved in determining price.)

▦ Are the size, weight, and packaging consistent with the contents?

▦ What kind of payment is involved (e.g., cash, letter of credit, direct wire transfer, barter, etc.)?

▦ What financial institutions are involved?

▦ Is there an extraordinary business relationship between the parties involved (buyer, seller, freight forwarder, brokers, etc.)? Are they part of an identifiable group, network, or family?

▦ Are the parties involved reputable? Have they been engaged in previous verifiable business?

▦ If applicable, is there any law enforcement, financial intelligence, internal, or publicly available derogatory information on any of the parties involved?

NOTES

1. "Asia Pacific Group (APG) Report on Trade Based Money Laundering," July 20, 2012, p. 10, available online: http://www.apgml.org/methods-and-trends/documents/default.aspx?s=date&c=2f18e690-1838-4310-b16a-8112ffa857b1.

2. Raymond W. Baker, *Capitalism's Achilles Heel* (Hoboken, NJ: John Wiley & Sons, 2005), p. 134.

3. Many sources including FATF; "Trade Based Money Laundering" (Paris: FATF, June 23, 2006), available online: http://www.fatf-gafi.org/media/fatf/documents/reports/Trade%20Based%20Money%20Laundering.pdf; and *The Wolfsberg Group Trade Finance Principles 2011*, p. 4, © The Wolfsberg Group, available online: http: http://www.wolfsberg-principles.com/pdf/standards/Wolfsberg_Trade_Principles_Paper_II_(2011).pdf.

4. John Cassara, "Fighting Terror with Analytics," SAS.com magazine, available online: http://www.sas.com/news/sascom/terrorist-financing.html.

5. Dr. John S. Zdanowicz, various examples from Chapter 1 referenced paper, "Trade-Based Money Laundering and Terrorist Financing."

6. Nomile Hlatshwayo, "Trade-Based Money Laundering Digging into Government Coffers," *Times of Swaziland* (July 16, 2010), available online: http://www.times.co.sz/index.php?news=17248&vote=5&aid=17248&Vote=Vote.

7. Information on Operation Polar Cap comes from a variety of sources, including the Drug Enforcement Administration, "1985–1990," in *A Tradition of Excellence*

(Washington, DC: DEA Publications), *Drug Enforcement*, National Institute of Justice, unknown date, available online: https://www.ncjrs.gov/pdffiles1/Digitization/147278NCJRS.pdf; and Robert Powis, *The Money Launderers* (Chicago: Probus Publishing, 1992), pp. 145–190.

8. Tracy Wilkinson and Ken Ellingwood, "Cartels Use Legitimate Trade to Launder Money, U.S., Mexico Say," *Los Angeles Times* (December 19, 2011), available online: http://articles.latimes.com/2011/dec/19/world/la-fg-mexico-money-laundering-trade-20111219.

9. Brett Wolf, "The Hide and Hair of Terrorist Finance in Pakistan," *Complinet* (January 17, 2007).

10. Author knowledge plus Katherine Finkelstein, "Banker Indicted in Fraud Case Said to Have Bilked Argentina," *New York Times* (March 8, 2000), available online http://www.nytimes.com/2000/03/08/nyregion/banker-indicted-in-fraud-case-said-to-have-bilked-argentina.html.

11. APG, *APG Typology Report on Trade-Based Money Laundering*, figure on p. 57, © 2012 Asia/Pacific Group on Money Laundering, available online: http://www.fatf-gafi.org/media/fatf/documents/reports/Trade_Based_ML_APGReport.pdf.

12. Ibid., p. 57.

13. U.S. Department of Treasury, "Treasury Identifies Kassem Rmeiti & Co. for Exchange and Halawi Exchange Co. as Financial Institutions of 'Primary Money Laundering Concern,'" press release, April 23, 2013, available online: http://www.treasury.gov/press-center/press-releases/Pages/jl1908.aspx.

14. APG, p. 58.

15. DEA News: Civil Suit Exposes Lebanese Money Laundering Scheme for Hizballah: press release; December 15, 2011, available online: http://www.dea.gov/pubs/pressrel/pr121511.html.

16. Jonathan Schanzer and Emanuelle Ottolenghi, "Turkey's Teflon Don," *Foreign Policy* (March 31, 2014), available online: http://www.foreignpolicy.com/articles/2014/03/31/turkey_teflon_don_erdogan_elections_corruption.

17. Wilkinson and Ellingwood; and APG, p. 62.

18. APG, p. 63.

19. U.S. Department of State, Bureau for International Narcotics and Law Enforcement Affairs, *International Narcotics Control Strategy Report (INCSR) Volume II, Money Laundering and Financial Crimes* (2008), p. 55, available online: http://www.state.gov/documents/organization/102588.pdf.

20. Ibid., see also South Korea country report (Washington, DC: U.S. Department of State, 2015), available online: http://www.state.gov/j/inl/rls/nrcrpt/2015/vol2/index.htm.

CHAPTER **3**

Black Market
Peso Exchange

olombia's Black Market Peso Exchange (BMPE) is an example of a regional black market financial system based on the misuse of international trade. Its original purpose was to obtain restricted hard currency (U.S. dollars) so Colombian businessmen could import goods (primarily from the United States) for resale and offer them at very competitive prices. Over the years, there were disastrous consequences. Inside Colombia, the BMPE harmed Colombian businesses that played by the rules. The BMPE facilitated trading inefficiencies and inequalities; it also circumvented needed revenue streams for the government. And with the expansion of the Colombian-based drug cartels, the BMPE became a key technique to launder staggering amounts of drug money. Today, the BMPE is one of the largest money laundering methodologies in the United States. And BMPE-like systems are found in various areas around the world.

The BMPE is an example of what is sometimes called an *informal value transfer system*. Other labels include *informal banking, underground banking, parallel banking*, and some are known as *alternative remittance systems*. Occasionally, these regional underground financial schemes are simply lumped together and erroneously labeled *hawala*. (hawala is explained in Chapter 4.)

EXAMPLES OF INTERNATIONAL INFORMAL VALUE TRANSFER SYSTEMS

Note: Names vary based on geographic locations and ethnic groups involved.

- Hawala—India, Afghanistan, East and Southern Africa, Middle East, Americas
- Hundi—Pakistan and Bangladesh
- Fei-chien—China
- Hui kuan—China
- Phoei kuan—Thailand
- Hui—Used by Vietnamese nationals in Australia
- Gift services—Parts of Africa
- Padala—Philippines
- Black market currency exchanges—South America, Nigeria, Iran
- Afghan transit trade—Afghanistan, Pakistan

The above financial systems—and others like them—are regional and ethnic based. I want to emphasize that I am not using "ethnic" in a pejorative sense. On the contrary, the systems are highly developed, sophisticated, and generally very efficient. Many have existed for hundreds of years—long before the advent of modern "Western" banking. Today they are often used by various immigrant groups as a low-cost, indigenous alternative to modern banking.

Many of the underground financial systems such as the BMPE, fei-chien, and hawala operate in a manner where the goods move and the money remains in place. Moreover, the importance of these systems as they relate to this book is that they all have a common denominator (i.e., historically and culturally they all use *trade* as a method of transferring value or balancing the books between brokers). This process of *countervaluation* will be described in Chapter 4.

Although the BMPE is not generally considered an alternative remittance system used by immigrants (such as hawala), it is based on the misuse of trade goods. Similar systems are found elsewhere, so familiarization with the scheme is essential to understanding TBML.

BMPE AND BELL HELICOPTER

An individual approached Bell Helicopter and inquired about purchasing a Bell 407 helicopter. A purchase price was negotiated. Subsequently, red flags should have been waving when Bell received 29 third-party wire transfers from 16 different sources. None of the sources of funding had any previous business relationship with Bell. Later investigation revealed the funds originated via the BMPE.[1]

BACKGROUND OF THE BMPE

The BMPE originated in Colombia years before the drug cartels appropriated it for their purposes. Similar to other money laundering methodologies, tax and tariff avoidance and exchange rate restrictions were the catalysts for an informal value transfer system that evolved into a very effective scheme to wash illicit funds.

Beginning in 1967, Colombia enacted regulations that strictly prohibited citizens' access to foreign exchange. Merchants who wanted to import U.S. trade goods through legitimate banking channels had to pay stiff surcharges above the official exchange rate. The Colombian peso was not free-floating. The government restrictions forced Colombian importers to utilize government-licensed institutions to obtain financing based on the peso. In addition to reporting the details of these transactions to the Ministry of Finance, the banks involved also charged stiff premiums for their services on top of the government's sales taxes and other fees. To avoid these steep add-on costs, importers often turned to underground peso brokers, from whom they could buy U.S. dollars on the black market for less than the official exchange rate to finance their trade, all the while sidestepping government oversight.[2]

By the 1980s, the underground peso situation was taking on a new dimension. As U.S. cities found themselves awash in Colombian cocaine, narco-traffickers and cartels were faced with a logistical problem—namely, how to launder and repatriate the tons of U.S. currency they had accumulated in North America as a result of drug sales. Meanwhile, black market peso dealers needed more and more U.S. dollars to sell to Colombian importers for the purchase of consumer goods, electronics, cigarettes, whiskey, machinery, gold, and so forth. Supply met demand in the form of the BMPE.[3]

By 2004, the Drug Enforcement Administration (DEA) declared that the BMPE was responsible for laundering nearly $5 billion worth of drug money annually.[4] Although recent efforts to control the BMPE by the Colombian and U.S. governments have been somewhat successful, the money laundering methodology still exists between the two countries. An official Colombian estimate is that approximately 45 percent of the country's imported consumer goods are facilitated via the BMPE.[5]

A TYPICAL BMPE VALUE TRANSFER SCHEME

The BMPE cycle begins with drug sales. For example, consider a Colombian drug cartel that has sold $3 million of cocaine in the United States. A representative of the cartel sells these accumulated dollars to a Colombian peso broker at a large discount. In the cartel's view, this discount is an acceptable price of doing business and the cost of laundering its illicit proceeds.

Despite being sold to a Colombian broker, the actual U.S. dollars remain in the United States, where the broker will shortly make use of them. In the meantime, the broker pays the cartel with the $3 million (less fees) worth of clean Colombian pesos, which he has previously purchased at a discount from Colombian businesses that participate in the BMPE. The cartel is now out of the picture, having successfully sold its drug dollars in the United States and having obtained pesos in return.

 The key point to understand is that the drug money never leaves the United States—the value is transferred via trade goods.

To complete the BMPE cycle, the peso broker must take two more steps. First, he directs his representatives in the United States to *place* the purchased drug dollars into U.S. financial institutions, using a variety of techniques designed to avoid arousing suspicion or triggering the financial intelligence reporting (see Figure 3.1 and box, "How Peso

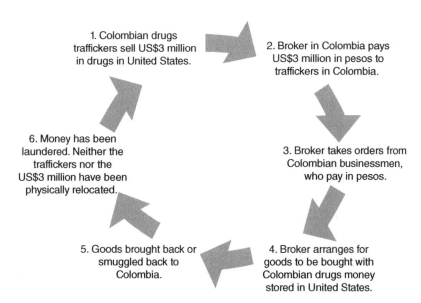

Figure 3.1 The BMPE cycle[6]
Source: Cassara and Jorisch, On the Trail of Terror Finance, *p. 81.*

Exchangers Place Dollars into the U.S. Financial System"). Second, he takes orders from Colombian businesses for U.S. trade goods, arranging for their purchase using the laundered drug money he owns in the United States. American manufacturers and distributors, knowingly or unknowingly, accept payment in drug dollars and export these goods to Colombia. The broker has now laundered the $3 million in drug money he purchased from the drug cartel. Moreover, the new pesos he receives from the Colombian businesses will allow him to conduct future transactions with the cartels.

Each part of the BMPE process moves the money one more step away from narcotics. This sometimes makes it difficult for law enforcement to establish criminal knowledge and intent at later stages of the process.

Although foreign narcotics cartels, organized crime, and overseas businesses are the main players in the BMPE, U.S. companies must take some responsibility for the problem. Unquestioning corporate acceptance of orders for trade goods from questionable sources is a form of willful blindness. For example, in 1997, a Colombian businesswoman cooperated with federal agents and—in disguise—testified before Congress. She stated, "As a money broker, I arranged payments to many large U.S. and international companies on behalf of Colombian importers. These companies were paid with U.S. currency generated by narcotics trafficking. They may not have been aware of the source of the money. However, they accepted payments from me without ever questioning who I was, or the source of the money."[7]

In an undercover pickup operation in the Miami area run by the Tri-County Task Force that culminated in 2011, tens of millions of drug-tainted dollars were laundered in a BMPE scheme centered on computer stores, cell phone outlets, and electronic game distributors. The scheme operated for a number of years and moved drug money out of the United States and into Mexico, Colombia, and other drug-producing countries via trade. The owners of the businesses turned a collective blind eye and professed no knowledge of the narco-money link. "It defies logic and credibility," said Donald Semesky, a former IRS criminal agent with knowledge of the operation. "They don't want to know where the money came from. What they are saying is, 'I didn't see the drugs. Why should I not be able to sell my wares?'"[8]

This attitude and method of business has direct impact on compliance officers in financial institutions and demonstrates the importance of knowing your customer. See Chapter 10 for red-flag indicators.

HOW PESO EXCHANGERS PLACE DOLLARS INTO THE U.S. FINANCIAL SYSTEM

- Typically, a BMPE broker uses runners or *smurfs* to "structure" drug proceeds in the United States. That is, the smurfs are directed to make a series of relatively small deposits in a large number of financial institutions in ways that do not trigger the financial reporting requirements mandated by the U.S. Bank Secrecy Act (see Appendix A for further information).
- Illicit proceeds can also be routinely comingled with the legitimate receipts of an established business.
- Dollars enter via the use of third-party checks.
- Dollars enter via the use of money orders.
- Sometimes bulk cash smuggling techniques are used to physically transport the currency out of the United States and into foreign financial institutions. In Mexico, *casas de cambio* and *centros combiarios* are often used to launder such cash.

Of course, in the Colombian BMPE, it is not just the proceeds of drugs that get laundered but also illicit funds from corruption, weapons trafficking, prostitution, illegal gold mining, and other illegal activities. And the infusion of so much illegal money into Colombia's 2013 $330 billion economy can inflate economic growth numbers by several basis points. According to Luis Edmundo Suarez, head of Colombia's financial intelligence unit (FIU)—the UIAF, "It creates suffering, distorts the economy and alters reference prices."[9] National tax agency head Juan Ortega and some economists feel that the laundered proceeds due to TBML's fake or overstated sales distort a range of official data from inflation to exports and imports. Erroneous data have a ripple effect on everything from government budgets to social programs. Moreover, in Colombia often times the laundered goods are sold at below-market prices. According to Ortega, "For a poor country, the social impact [of unfair competition] is brutal." "It limits growth and destroys opportunity for legitimate business."[10]

According to experienced BMPE industry workers in Colombia, evasion of customs charges is frequently facilitated by the complicity of corrupt customs authorities.[11] In Colombia—as well as other countries struggling with forms of TBML—the pernicious effects of corruption not only enable TBML but also cost the government much-needed revenue and exacerbate social and cultural ethics and values.

EXPANSION OF THE BMPE TO MEXICO AND VENEZUELA

Today—decades after the BMPE was established, and despite the lifting of many of the above-described official Colombian currency controls—narco-traffickers continue to avail themselves of the same underground system, as do many legitimate businesses. In Mexico, Venezuela, and other Latin American countries, organized crime has learned to read from the same BMPE playbook. For example, in June 2010, the Mexican government announced regulations limiting deposits of U.S. cash into Mexican banks.[12] (Subsequently, in June 2014 the government revised the U.S. dollar restrictions so as to ease the impact on legitimate businesses. The impact of the revision is to be determined.)[13] The regulations were later expanded to include purchases of large-ticket goods such as expensive cars, jewelry, and homes, as well as cash deposits made at exchange houses (*casas de cambio*) and brokerages (*casas de bolsa*). The restrictions were put in place primarily to combat the smuggling of illicit bulk cash into Mexico. Yet following the rule of unattended consequences, using variations of the BMPE, narco-trafficking organizations in Mexico have been able to skirt Mexican government limits on the use of how much money Mexicans can deposit.

A number of law-enforcement cases have shed light on the ways the BMPE has been adapted by Mexican narcotics-trafficking organizations. One of the first investigations focusing on TBML between Mexico and the U.S. centered on Blanca Cazares, the alleged queen of money laundering for the Sinaloa cartel. She was indicted in 2008 in Los Angeles for "processing illicit proceeds." One of her techniques was to use the illicit funds from U.S. narcotics sales to import textiles from Asia into the Los Angeles area and then export them to Mexico.[14] The U.S. Department of the Treasury's Office of Foreign Assets Control (OFAC) designated Cazares and 19 companies and 22 individuals in Mexico that were part of her financial network as specially designated narcotics traffickers subject to economic sanctions pursuant to the Foreign Narcotics Kingpin Designation Act.[15]

 CASE EXAMPLE: SAR FILINGS LEAD TO INVESTIGATION OF BMPE

The FBI initiated an investigation after the receipt of a suspicious activity report (SAR) from a bank in New York that identified deposits being structured to avoid Currency Transaction Reports (CTR) requirements. Ultimately, over 80 SARs were filed by New York area banks. They identified 179 deposits in accounts just under $10,000. The investigation revealed that the funds were proceeds from a Colombian drug cartel. The deposited money was regularly withdrawn by means of cashier checks or wire transfers and was used to pay for products to be shipped to Colombia. Ten individuals were arrested and the primary suspect fled overseas.[16]

In 2014, Operation Fashion Police rocked the Los Angeles garment district. A Los Angeles–based maternity clothes wholesaler allegedly received drug proceeds. In the manner described in the BMPE cycle, the dirty dollars were used to pay for product from other nearby garment shops for export orders to Mexico.

One of the clothing exporters allegedly mixed customs fraud into the BMPE conspiracy. "Made in China" labels were removed from thousands of imported garments. (The ruse was very similar to an investigation I worked in the Middle East in the 1990s, described in Chapter 2.) In the Los Angeles case, one of the suspects was paid 50 to 75 cents for each of the altered garments. The fraud saved the co-conspirators from paying taxes on the "Made in China" imports because on paper they appeared to be "American-made," and exempt from customs duties under the North American Free Trade Act (NAFTA).[17]

More than $90 million was seized. It was the biggest one-day seizure of cash in the United States.[18] The large cash seizure demonstrated that the Mexican cartels had successfully adapted the Colombian BMPE methodology in such a way that bulk cash did not have to be smuggled into Mexico. The bulk cash—proceeds from narcotics trafficking, kidnapping, stolen cars, and other illegal activities—stays on the U.S. side of the border.

The collapse of the Venezuelan bolívar under the policies of former President Hugo Chavez and his successors has been striking. Since he took office 1999, the official cost of the dollar in bolívars has risen more than tenfold.[19] And there is a striking imbalance between the official rate and the value of the dollar on the prolific Venezuelan black market. The black market rate factors in supply, demand, and inflation. The centralized government tries to hide both the weak currency and the endemic corruption by setting a fixed, artificial rate. Moreover, price and foreign exchange controls have proven to be a catalyst for corruption—the great facilitator of international money laundering.

 FRAUD AND CORRUPTION

Venezuelan government officials—including the president, the executive vice president, a central bank president, a finance minister, and an interior minister—have all admitted publicly that 30–40 percent of the roughly $53 billion the Venezuelan government spent on imports in 2013 alone were facilitated by overinvoiced or completely fictitious transactions (i.e., schemes to defraud the Venezuela currency commission and by inference the Venezuela government of dollars). An economic consulting firm estimated that from 2003 to 2012, almost $70 billion was stolen through import fraud.[20] Venezuelan government officials have also admitted publicly that corrupt public-sector employees facilitate these transactions in exchange for kickbacks.[21]

In 2003, the government tried to stem capital flight by imposing stringent exchange controls. Ordinary Venezuelan citizens and businesses have faced limits on the amount of foreign currency they can acquire at the heavily subsidized official rate. These restrictions have contributed to depressed economic activity and shortages of consumer goods. To meet the rest of their foreign currency needs, many Venezuelans turned to the black market, where the bolívar has traded at a fraction of its official value.

The Venezuelan government responded to sharp declines in the price of the bolívar on the black market with a series of incremental official devaluations and ever-tighter controls. The adjustments made life slightly easier for the country's beleaguered exporters but did not assist importers or consumers, including those wishing to import popular U.S. goods. As a result, many consumer items practically disappeared from marketplaces. As the Venezuelan central bank became stingier in doling out dollars at the official rate, demand for greenbacks grew on the black market.

Overlapping Venezuela's serious economic downturn was a commensurate upturn in criminality, including narcotics trafficking and money laundering. According to the 2014 congressionally mandated International Narcotics Control Strategy Report (INCSR) Volume II on Money Laundering prepared by the U.S. State Department, Venezuela is a country of "primary concern." The introduction to the Venezuela report notes the following: "Trade-based money laundering remains a prominent method for laundering regional narcotics proceeds. Converting narcotics-generated dollars into Venezuelan bolivars and then back into dollars is no longer attractive for money-laundering purposes given Venezuela's rampant inflation (approximately 50 percent in 2013) and the current bureaucratic challenges for converting bolivars into dollars."[22]

The State Department also reports that some black market traders ship their goods through Venezuela's Margarita Island free port, one of three free trade zones/ports in the country. However, the use of free trade zones for TBML has become less attractive in recent years because the margins gained by laundering money through the government's currency control regime have reduced the incentive to use a free trade zone to avoid import duties.[23]

For example, there are reports that dozens of Venezuelan companies have conspired with Ecuadorian firms to carry out multimillion-dollar operations involving fictitious exports and phantom companies (as well as using bank accounts in Panama, the Bahamas, and Anguilla). The Venezuelan businesses involved made transfers to Ecuador in exchange for fake exports to Venezuela. Many of the cases concerned Venezuelan state contractors involved in construction or importing food. This gave them the justification needed to access dollars at preferential rates via Venezuela's Center for Foreign Trade, also known as Cencoex. Some payments were made in advance, before the merchandise even arrived in Venezuela; there were also Ecuadorian exports with inflated values; multiple invoices for the same shipments; and fictitious shipments of products that never actually made it to Venezuela.[24]

 According to one importer, "In Venezuela, your real business isn't your 'business.' Your real business is what's behind your 'business.'"[25]

The malfunctioning currency system is the catalyst for various schemes used by importers to overinvoice the value of goods shipped into the country in order to obtain dollars provided by the government at artificially low prices. At times, the imports only occur on paper. The suspect importers pocket the fraudulently obtained dollars, bribe officials, and/or sell the scarce dollars for huge profits in the country's black market.

In just a few examples of wildly inflated invoices in Venezuela,[26] weed whackers were imported at $12,300 each. Machinery was imported to kill and gut chickens. The invoice price was $1.8 million. Subsequent investigation disclosed the machinery was a heap of rusted scrap metal. A device was imported to remove kernels from ears of corn. The invoiced price presented to Venezuelan authorities was $477,750. The actual price was about $2,900.

Thus, international businesses (including in the United States) are approached by Venezuela black market currency brokers and their fronts with offers for the purchases of goods in demand in Venezuela. The money-laundering techniques involved are almost identical to those described in Chapter 2 and above, dealing with the Colombian and Mexican BMPE. Unfortunately, some businesses complete the transactions. They knowingly or unknowingly accept cash and other payments that are often comingled with illicit proceeds or are involved with various types of fraud. And despite the warning signs, financial institutions are often the intermediaries.

HSBC FINED $1.256 BILLION—INVOLVEMENT WITH BMPE

In the 2012 deferred prosecution agreement between HSBC Bank and the Department of Justice, it was disclosed that "a significant portion of the laundered drug trafficking proceeds were involved in the BMPE." Investigations identified multiple HSBC Mexico accounts associated with BMPE activity and revealed that drug traffickers were depositing hundreds of thousands of dollars in bulk U.S. currency each day into HSBC Mexico accounts.[27]

THE CHINA CONNECTION

When U.S. government authorities became aware of the BMPE in the mid-1990s, the methodological model was Colombian peso brokers purchasing U.S. manufactured goods using laundered drug proceeds. This still occurs. But investigators have also found that similar black market exchange "shopping centers" are increasingly active in other countries. And there are signs that Chinese manufactured goods are becoming favored instruments in the BMPE and BMPE-like financial systems.

For example, between 2000 and 2008, bilateral trade between China and Mexico grew from less than $1 billion to approximately $18 billion.[28] Although the exponential growth of legitimate Chinese trade has occurred in many areas of the world, there is some evidence that Mexican drug trafficking organizations using illicit proceeds are buying container loads of cheaply made Chinese goods. Using the technique of overinvoicing explained in Chapter 2, low-quality Chinese manufactured items are made to appear on paper as being worth significantly more. By means of the legitimate international financial system, Chinese goods are purchased in Mexico, the United States, Europe, Dubai, the Colon Free Trade Zone, Africa (see Chapter 5), and elsewhere. The purchase launders the illicit proceeds.

There is anecdotal evidence that sometimes cheaply manufactured Chinese goods are never actually claimed after arrival in the importing country.[29] The purchase of the goods serves to launder the drug money. For professional money launderers, that is the price of doing business. Sometimes the end result is that the Chinese products in the unclaimed shipping containers eventually find their way onto the local economy's black market. There are also reports that small Chinese banks are involved with processing enormous numbers of payments for Mexico for trade goods that may or may not actually exist to facilitate the laundering of drug proceeds.[30]

CHEAT SHEET

- The BMPE is an example of an *informal value transfer system*. It is also sometimes categorized as *parallel banking* or *underground banking*.

- The BMPE is a form of TBML and is one of the largest money laundering methodologies in the Western Hemisphere.

- Similar to other trade-based value transfer systems, it operates by transferring money without moving money.

- The BMPE originated in Colombia long before the proliferation of narcotics trafficking. The black market system was developed in order for Colombian businessmen to obtain access to scarce dollars.

- In the BMPE, a black market peso broker buys narcotics proceeds (generally in the United States) at a discount from a narcotics trafficking organization. Using a variety of techniques, the broker then arranges for the cash to be deposited, structured, or placed into financial institutions or money services businesses. The money is used to buy a variety of trade goods that are then exported to Colombia and other Latin American countries.

- The BMPE has expanded and is now frequently found in Mexico and Venezuela.

- In addition to the United States, trade goods used in the BMPE are often purchased from China, Europe, and other suppliers.

- Similar systems to the BMPE are found throughout the world.

NOTES

1. Jeffrey Robinson, "The Black Market Peso Exchange" (April 14, 2012), available online: http://www.jeffreyrobinson.com/blog/?p=62.

2. Much of the material in this section on the BMPE comes from John Cassara and Avi Jorisch, *On the Trail of Terror Finance—What Law Enforcement and Intelligence Officers Need to Know* (Washington, D.C.: Red Cell Intelligence Group, 2010), pp. 77–82.

3. John Cassara, *Hide & Seek: Intellligence, Law Enforcement, and the Stalled War on Terrorist Finance* (Dulles, VA: Potomac Books, 2006), pp. 141–144.

4. Congressional testimony of Karen Tandy, DEA Administrator, March 4, 2004, available online: http://www.justice.gov/dea/pubs/cngrtest/ct030404.htm.

5. Robinson.

6. Cassara and Jorisch, p. 81.

7. The businesswoman was identified only as "Ms. Doe." She delivered her testimony before the House Banking and Financial Services Subcommittee on General Oversight and Investigations, October 22, 1997.

8. Michael Sallah, "A Money Laundering Pipeline to Latin America," *Miami Herald* (June 19, 2015), available online: http://pubsys.miamiherald.com/static/media/projects/2015/license-to-launder/doral.htm.

9. Helen Murphy and Nelson Bocanegra, "Money Laundering Distorts Colombia's Economic Comeback," *Reuters* (May 28, 2013), available online: http://www.reuters.com/article/2013/05/28/us-colombia-moneylaundering-idUSBRE94R03E20130528.

10. Ibid.

11. U.S. Department of State, Bureau for International Narcotics and Law Enforcement Affairs, *International Narcotics Control Strategy Report (INCSR) Volume II, Money Laundering and Financial Crimes* (March 2015), Colombia country report, available online: http://www.state.gov/j/inl/rls/nrcrpt/2015/vol2/index.htm.

12. "Newly Released Mexican Regulations Imposing Restrictions on Mexican Banks for Transactions in U.S. Currency," (June 2010), FinCEN Advisory.

13. U.S. Department of State, Bureau for International Narcotics and Law Enforcement Affairs, *International Narcotics Control Strategy Report (INCSR) Volume II, Money Laundering and Financial Crimes* (March 2015), Mexico country report, available online: http://www.state.gov/j/inl/rls/nrcrpt/2015/vol2/index.htm.

14. Tracy Wilkinson and Ken Ellingwood, "Cartels Use Legitimate Trade to Launder Money, U.S., Mexico Say," *Los Angeles Times* (December 19, 2011), available online: http://articles.latimes.com/2011/dec/19/world/la-fg-mexico-money-laundering-trade-20111219.

15. U.S. Treasury, "Treasury Designates Financial Empire of Key Mexican Money Launderer Blanca Margarita Cazares Salazar" (December 12, 2007), press release available online: http://www.treasury.gov/press-center/press-releases/Pages/hp729.aspx.

16. "SAR Filings Lead to Investigation Involving Black Market Peso Exchange," *FinCEN, SAR Activity Review* (June, 2001), available online: http://www.fincen.gov/law_enforcement/ss/html/069.html.

17. Jamila Trindle, "Drugs, Cash, Luxury Goods, and Maternity Wear," *Foreign Policy* (October 13, 2014), available online: http://www.foreignpolicy.com/articles/2014/

10/13/drugs_cash_LA_FBI_Treasury_money%20laundering_%20cartels_fashion
%20district_Mexico.

18. Ibid.

19. "The Not So Strong Bolivar," *The Economist* (February 11, 2013), available online:
(logs/americasview/2013/02/venezuela%E2%80%99s-currency.

20. William Neuman and Patricia Torres, "Venezuela's Economy Suffers as Import
Schemes Siphon Billions," *International New York Times* (May 5, 2015), available online: http://www.nytimes.com/2015/05/06/world/americas/venezuelas-economy-suffers-as-import-schemes-siphon-billions.html?_r=0.

21. U.S. Department of State, Bureau for International Narcotics and Law Enforcement
Affairs, *International Narcotics Control Strategy Report (INCSR) Volume II, Money Launder-ing and Financial Crimes* (March 2015), Venezuela country report; available online:
http://www.state.gov/j/inl/rls/nrcrpt/2015/vol2/index.htm.

22. U.S. Department of State, Bureau for International Narcotics and Law Enforcement
Affairs, *International Narcotics Control Strategy Report (INCSR) Volume II, Money Launder-ing and Financial Crimes* (March 2014), Venezuela country report; available online:
http://www.state.gov/documents/organization/222880.pdf.

23. U.S. Department of State, Bureau for International Narcotics and Law Enforcement
Affairs, *International Narcotics Control Strategy Report (INCSR) Volume II, Money Launder-ing and Financial Crimes* (March 2015),Venezuela country report; available online:
http://www.state.gov/j/inl/rls/nrcrpt/2015/vol2/index.htm.

24. "How Firms Scammed Venezuela's Foreign Currency System," *Insight Crime*
(May 21, 2015), available online: http://www.insightcrime.org/news-analysis/
how-firms-scammed-venezuela-foreign-currency-system.

25. Neuman and Torres, "Venezuela's Economy Suffers as Import Schemes Siphon
Billions."

26. Ibid.

27. Department of Justice, "HSBC Holdings PLC and HSBC Bank USA N.A. Admit
to Anti-Money Laundering and Sanctions Violations, Forfeit $1.256 Billion in
Deferred Prosecution Agreement" (December 11, 2012), press release, available
online: http://www.justice.gov/opa/pr/hsbc-holdings-plc-and-hsbc-bank-usa-na-
admit-anti-money-laundering-and-sanctions-violations.

28. "Growth Rate of China's Trade with Latin America and Caribbean Decreased in
2008," *People's Daily Online* (English Version), April 3, 2009.

29. Author conversations with authorities in Mexico. Also see Doug Farah, *Money
Laundering and Bulk Cash Smuggling: Challenges for the Mérida Initiative Working Paper
Series on U.S.-Mexico Security Cooperation* (Woodrow Wilson Center for International
Studies and University of San Diego, May 10, 2010); available online: http://www
.strategycenter.net/docLib/20101113_MoneyLaundandBulkCash_Farah.pdf.

30. United States Senate Caucus on International Narcotics Control, *The Buck Stops Here:
Improving U.S. Anti-Money Laundering Practices* (Washington, DC: US Government
Printing Office, April 2013), p. 34.

CHAPTER 4

Hawala: An Alternative Remittance System

There are an estimated 232 million migrant workers around the world.[1] Globalization, demographic shifts, regional conflicts, income disparities, and the instinctive search for a better life continue to encourage ever-more workers to cross borders in search of jobs and security.

Many countries are dependent on remittances as an economic lifeline. The World Bank estimates that global remittances will reach $707 billion by 2016.[2] Western Union, Money Gram, Ria Money Transfer, Dahabshill are just a few of the well-known companies that provide official remittance services for the world's migrants. Of course, banks and nonbank financial institutions are also used. In 2013, some of the top recipients for officially recorded remittances were India (an estimated $71 billion), China ($60 billion), the Philippines ($26 billion), Mexico ($22 billion), Nigeria ($21 billion), and Egypt ($20 billion). Pakistan, Bangladesh, Vietnam, and the Ukraine were other large beneficiaries of remittances. As a percentage of GDP, some of the top recipients were Tajikistan (48 percent), the Kyrgyz Republic (31 percent), Lesotho (25 percent), and Moldova (24 percent).[3]

These are estimates of what is *officially* remitted. *Unofficially*, nobody knows. However, the International Monetary Fund believes, "Unrecorded flows through informal channels are believed to be at least 50 percent larger than recorded flows."[4] So using the above World Bank and IMF estimates, unofficial remittances are enormous!

Sometimes touted as a new phenomenon and a symptom of the emerging borderless world, trade diasporas have existed since ancient times.[5] Informal channels operate outside of the ironically labeled "traditional" channels. It's ironic because for most of the migrants involved, the alternatives to Western-style remittances such as via banks or Western Union are very traditional for them. Two of the largest alternative or informal systems are hawala and fei-chien (see Chapter 5)

 Economists estimate that approximately $100 billion is pumped annually through the global hawala network![6]

Although diverse alternative remittance systems are found throughout the world, most share a few common characteristics.

The first is that they all transfer money (or value) without physically moving it. Another is that they all offer the three Cs: they are certain, convenient, and cheap! And finally, historically and culturally, most alternative remittance systems use *trade* as the primary mechanism to settle accounts or balance the books between brokers.

DEFINITION OF HAWALA

The definition of *hawala* was concisely expressed during the 1998 U.S. federal trial of Iranian drug trafficker and money launderer Jafar Pour Jelil Rayhani and his associates. During the trial, prosecutors termed hawala "money transfer without money movement."[7] That is, a broker on one side of the transaction accepts money from a client who wishes to send funds to someone else. The first broker then communicates with the second broker at the desired destination, who distributes the funds to the intended recipient (less small commissions at both ends). So the money (or value) is successfully transferred from Point A to Point B but the funds are not physically moved.

Hawala (also commonly known as *hundi* in Pakistan and Bangladesh) is an informal value transfer system based on the performance and honor of a huge network of money brokers, which are primarily located in the Middle East, North Africa, the Horn of Africa, and South Asia.

Hawala comes from the Arabic root *h-w-l* (ل و ح), which has the basic meanings "change" and "transform." The modern definition of hawala (حواﻟﺔ) is a bill of exchange or promissory note. It is also used in the expression *hawala safar* (حواﻟﺔ سد فر) or travelers check. The Arabic root *s-r-f* (ف ر ص) has, among other meanings, "pay" and "disburse," and the Arabic word for bank, *masrif*, (ﻑﺻرﻒ), comes from this root. In Iran, *s-r-f* is also the basis for the Farsi words *saraf* (صراﻑ ى), which means a money changer/remitter, and *sarafi* (صراﻑ), which is the name for the business. Afghan hawaladars sometimes refer to themselves as *sarafi*, or *saraf* in the singular.[8]

The primary component of hawala that distinguishes it from most other formal financial systems is trust. This often revolves around the extensive use of family, clan, tribe, or regional affiliations. According to R. T. Naylor, an academic who has studied black markets,

"Typically, entrepreneurial members of a trade diaspora make no distinction between social and economic life. Their business firms are extensions of kinship structure, with leadership that reflects the extended family hierarchy, which can extend across continents."[9] These are the attributes that also make it very difficult for Western law enforcement and intelligence services to penetrate the underground financial networks.

For example, law enforcement agencies in the United States typically do not have many Pashtu speakers, Farsi speakers, Gujarat speakers, and so on. And even if law enforcement recruited an agent to approach an underground hawala network, the very first question might be, "Who is your uncle in the village back in the old country?"

The opaque nature of hawala also explains why it is so attractive to criminal and terrorist organizations. Unlike Western banking, hawala makes minimal use of negotiable monetary instruments; instead, transfers of money are based on trust and communications between networks of brokers.

 ORIGIN OF HAWALA

Although reports on the origin of hawala vary, many think hawala was developed in South Asia centuries ago. Others believe hawala has its origins in classical Islamic law. It is mentioned in texts of Islamic jurisprudence as early as the eighth century. The transfer of debt was not allowed under Roman law but was later widely practiced in medieval Europe, especially in commercial transactions, and was used heavily by Italian city-states, including with the Muslim world. The concept of hawala continued to be developed in common and civil law and can be found in today's French *aval* and Italian *avallo*, which translate into a type of guarantee. Today, hawala is best known as an informal value transfer system.[10]

THE HAWALA TRANSACTION

To illustrate how the hawala remittance process works, we will use a typical example. Ali is an Afghan national and a construction worker in New York City. During the long Taliban occupation of his homeland, he emigrated to the United States. He now earns money that helps support his family. He sends a portion of his salary back to his elderly father, Jafar, who lives in a village outside of Kandahar in southern Afghanistan. To make his monthly transfer—usually about $200—Ali uses hawala. This is very common in Afghanistan. About 30 percent of its population is externally and internally displaced, and remittances from outside of Afghanistan are received by about 15 percent of the rural population.[11]

 HAWALA FEES

Generally speaking, the average cost of transferring funds through an alternative remittance system such as hawala between major international cities is about 2 to 5 percent of the value transferred. (Globally, the cost of sending money through formal remittance companies averages 7.99 percent of the amount sent.[12]) Of course, prices in both the formal and informal remittance industries are influenced by a variety of factors. Hawala networks are most competitive when they operate in areas where banking systems and overt money remittance chains find it difficult, expensive, or high risk to operate.[13]

If Ali went to a bank in New York City to send the money home to his father, he would have to open an account. He doesn't want to do that for a number of reasons. First, Ali grew up in an area of the world where banks are not common. He is not used to them and doesn't trust them. Next, Ali has little faith in governments and wants to avoid possible scrutiny. Many immigrants believe the government is monitoring their immigration status and/or will make them pay taxes. He also doesn't want the U.S. government to screen his money transfers to Afghanistan. In addition, although Ali has lived in New York for a few years, he is still a bit intimidated. His English is marginal. He is only semiliterate (approximately 80 percent of Afghanis cannot read or write) and cannot fill out the necessary forms. Moreover, banks charge their customers assorted transfer fees and offer unfavorable exchange rates. If Ali only earns a little money and is sending $200, bank transfer fees of 15 percent or more are quite substantial! And delivery of a bank transfer to Jafar would pose additional problems. The number of licensed banks in Afghanistan is still quite small. They are used by only about 5 percent of the population. Particularly in a poorly secured area such as Kandahar, Jafar does not want to leave his village home and travel a far distance to a bank.

Hawala is based on trust. Without it, the entire system would collapse.

In light of these problems and concerns, Ali uses a hawaladar in New York City who is a member of his extended clan and family. He feels comfortable dealing with him. The hawaladar also owns and operates a New York City–based "import–export" company. The hawaladar completes the transaction for a lower commission than banks or money services businesses charge. In addition, he obtains a much better exchange rate (the amount of afghanis—the local currency—for dollars). Delivery direct to Jafar's home in the Kandahar area village is also included in the price. In fact, in certain areas of the world, hawala is advertised as "door-to-door" money remitting.

In the New York portion of the hawala transaction, Ali hands over the $200 that he wants to transfer, from which the hawaladar takes his small commission. Ali is not given a receipt because the entire relationship is based on trust. This is a different kind of know your customer (KYC) procedure! For purposes of illustration, particularly if this is a first-time transfer, Ali may be given a numerical or other code, which he can then forward to Jafar. The code is used to authenticate the transaction. But the nature of hawala networks means that codes are not always necessary. As opposed to the often-lengthy formal operating requirements of bank-to-bank transfers, this informal transaction can be completed in the time it takes for the New York hawaladar to make a few telephone calls or send a fax or e-mail to the corresponding hawaladar in his network who handles Kandahar.

 ## A BIT OF JARGON

- Hawala is the system of money transfer without money movement.
- Hawaladars are the brokers who engage in hawala.

Although the word *hawalas* is often used to describe the underground system, the term does not actually exist.

It is important to note that although some transactions are arranged directly, many are cleared or pass through regional hawala hubs such as Dubai, Mumbai, Karachi, and Kabul. So generally speaking, money can be delivered directly to Jafar's home within 24 hours and the transaction will not be scrutinized by either U.S. or Afghan authorities. The above scenario with Ali in New York City could just as easily take place in Minneapolis with its large Somali community, northern Virginia with its large Indian community, or Detroit with its large Arab community.

Similarly, hawala transfers are very common in London, Frankfurt, Dubai, Damascus, Baghdad, Tehran, Karachi, Zanzibar, Durban, the Colon Free Trade Zone, the Tri-Border region of South America, and many other locations around the world. For example, according to the U.S. State Department 2015 INCSR report, in the West African country of Gabon, "There is a large expatriate community engaged in the oil and gas sector, the timber industry, construction, and general trade. Money and value transfer services, such as hawala, and trade-based commodity transfers are often used by these expatriates, particularly the large Lebanese community, to avoid strict controls on the repatriation of corporate profits."[14] The important point is that in all locations, the hawala transfers occur without any physical movement of money (though hawaladars eventually have to settle with each other via methods described in this chapter).

The hawaladars conducting the transactions can offer better prices because they do not have to adhere to official exchange rates, and because they often have representatives in isolated or remote areas where banks do not operate. And for individuals who wish to conduct illicit business, hawala protects their confidentiality. Hawaladars maintain very few records, offering customers near anonymity. They only keep simple accounting records, and even these are often discarded after they settle-up with one another. This means the paper trail is limited or nonexistent, making transactions very difficult to track. Even when records are kept, they are often in a foreign language or code, making them very challenging for Western authorities to decipher.[15]

HOW DO HAWALADARS MAKE A PROFIT?

Hawaladars have many advantages over formal money remitters. They generally do not have to maintain a large bricks-and-mortar storefront. Sometimes the brokers will run the money operation out of their homes; more often, they offer hawala in tandem with other businesses such as import–export companies, clothing stores, money exchange companies, gold and jewelry shops, carpet stores, cell phone/calling card shops, or even from their taxi or tea shop. The money they make from hawala fees reduces their overall operating costs and is easily integrated into normal business activities.

As indicated, many hawaladars also operate as currency exchangers, charging small commissions for the service and, in some cases, profiting from currency speculation or black market currency dealing.[16] For example, restrictions enacted by many governments in South Asia often limit the amount of currency that can be taken out of the country. To get around the restrictions, hawaladars are able to provide "hard currencies" such as dollars or euros in exchange for local currencies such as rupees, dinars, or afghanis. In addition to low overhead, currency speculation is one of the principal reasons why hawaladars can beat the official exchange rates that banks offer. And in some areas, hawaladars also offer short-term lending, trade guarantees, and the safe keeping of funds.[17]

Figure 4.1 represents a prototypical hawala transaction.

1. A person in Country A (sender) wants to send money to a person in Country B (recipient). The sender contacts a hawaladar and provides instructions for delivery of the equivalent amount to the recipient. A small percentage of the amount transferred is the hawaladar's profit.

2. The hawaladar in Country A contacts the counterpart hawaladar in Country B via telephone, e-mail, or fax and communicates the instructions.

3. The hawaladar in Country B contacts the recipient and arranges for delivery of the equivalent amount in local currency (sometimes requiring verification of a remittance code that the sender previously gave to the recipient). The hawaladar in Country B charges a small transaction fee.

4. Per Figure 4.1, funds and value move in both directions between hawaladars in Country A and B. Over time, accounts may have to be balanced. Hawaladars use a variety of methods to settle the books. Historically and culturally, *trade* is the primary vehicle used to provide countervaluation between hawaladars.

Country A  Country B

Figure 4.1 Prototypical hawala transaction

HOW DO HAWALADARS SETTLE ACCOUNTS AND BALANCE THEIR BOOKS?

1. Bank-to-bank wire transfers
2. Cash couriers
3. Trade

Of coming concern:

4. Internet/cyber-currencies
5. Mobile payments

COUNTERVALUATION AND TRADE

Hawaladars eventually have to settle their accounts with each other. Frequently, the close relationships between the brokers help facilitate the settlement. Remember, the key ingredient in hawala is *trust*. So kinship, family, and clannish ties often enable the settlement process. For example, in Afghanistan, intermarriages between the families of hawaladars are common because they help cement confidence between the parties. Brothers, cousins, or other relations often operate in the same hawala networks. They are not going to rip each other off! Lebanese family members that operate in the same hawala networks can be found in Beirut, Dubai, the Colon Free Trade Zone, and various locations in Africa. Yet even though they may be related by family or have tribal ties, they are still in business to make money. Money transfers between hawaladars are not settled on a one-to-one basis but are generally bundled over a period of time after a series of transactions. Payments go in both directions. For example, remittances may flow into South Asia from the United States and Europe, but money and various goods flow back as well. A variety of methods are used to make payments and settle the accounts.

WOULD YOU DO THIS?

Some of us have probably engaged in a hawala-like transaction without realizing it. For example, I do a lot of training overseas. Let's pretend that before the current Syrian civil war, I visited Damascus. I spent a couple of weeks in the country. I missed my wife's birthday! I wanted to bring her a nice gift. So toward the end of my stay, I asked my colleague in the American Embassy if he had a contact where I could buy some gold jewelry. He suggested I visit Omar at the gold souk.

I found a beautiful gold necklace. When Omar and I agreed upon a price, I tried to present payment. He refused my U.S. dollars! He refused Syrian pounds! He refused my credit cards, and he didn't want travelers' checks! "Omar," I asked, "how can I pay you?" "Mr. John," he replied, "I have a daughter. She is going to college in the United States. I have to help support her, but I have a problem sending her money. You have been here for a while now, and you understand the Syrian pound is not convertible and there are restrictions on how much money can be sent out of the country. Besides, I don't want the government to know my personal business. So would you do me a favor? I'll give you my daughter's name and address. When you get back to the States just write her a check for the money that you owe me. I trust you! I've been working with Americans coming from the embassy for years and I've never been taken advantage of."

The above innocent example of something that the reader may or may not agree to do has all the elements of a hawala transaction: It is based on trust. It involves transfer and exchange. It is quick, safe, secure, anonymous, and is often based on family and tribal ties. There is little or no paper trail; it avoids taxation, government scrutiny, and currency exchange controls. The transaction is culturally acceptable. And historically, hawala often involves the trading of gold.

Certainly, most major hawala networks have access to financial institutions, either directly or indirectly. A majority of international hawaladars have at least one or more accounts with formal financial institutions.[18] Bilateral wire transfers between brokers to settle accounts are sometimes used. If a direct wire transfer is made between international brokers, hawaladar A would have to wire money directly to hawaladar B's account to clear a debt. This could be problematic because the banks' foreign exchange rate procedures would be triggered. So in this case, hawaladar A might choose to deposit the funds into B's foreign account.

Direct cash payments are also used to settle debts. This is particularly true in areas of the world that have cash-based economies. Sometimes we forget that hawala networks also operate domestically between states and provinces. For example, in Afghanistan, hawala networks are found in each of the 34 provinces. Periodically, the brokers settle accounts and generally use cash. Hawala couriers have been identified transporting money within Afghanistan and across the border into Pakistan. Cash couriers representing hawala networks also frequently travel from Karachi to Dubai to settle accounts. Moreover, gold is sometimes also used as a medium of settling accounts (see Chapter 6).

Although open source reporting is very sparse, there is reason to believe that some underground remittance networks are using cyber-currencies including bitcoins.[19] This development could potentially have a great impact on the hawala settlement process. It would also further obfuscate the money trail for authorities. Similarly, mobile payments or M-payments—particularly via the use of cell phones—are an increasingly popular vehicle for the remittance of wages, transfer of money, purchase of goods and services, and the payment of bills. The ubiquitous cell phone now acts as a virtual wallet and has brought twenty-first-century financial services directly to the developing world's large unbanked population. Unfortunately, M-payments can also be used to structure or place illicit proceeds via the purchase of M-payment credits. This is sometimes called *digital smurfing*. And it is believed M-payments could be used in the settling of accounts between underground money remitters including hawaladars.[20] There are also reports that informal banking schemes including M-payments have been used to help fund the terrorist group the Islamic State of Iraq and al Sham (ISIS).[21]

As we have seen, from the earliest times—before modern banking and contemporary monetary instruments—trade-based value transfer was used between hawala brokers to settle accounts and balance their books. And the use of trade remains widespread. Settling accounts through import–export clearing is somewhat similar to bilateral clearing using bank transfers, but it uses the import–export of trade goods. That is why many import–export concerns are associated directly or indirectly with hawaladars. If a debt needs to be settled, hawaladar

A could simply send goods to hawaladar B such as gold, electronics, or myriad other trade items. Or at the end of a reporting period, if an outstanding balance exists between, for example, hawaladar A in Somalia and hawaladar B in Dubai, B can use a Japanese bank account to purchase cars for export to Somalia. Once the cars arrive, they would be transferred to A to settle the debt and/or sell them for profit. The transaction would clear the debt between the two hawaladars.[22]

 HAWALA SERVES A NEED

In 2001, before the September 11 terrorist attacks, I had a conversation in the United Arab Emirates with Central Bank officials. We discussed hawala. A Somali national was an adviser to the Bank. He told me, "Mr. John, I know hawala has a bad reputation. But you must understand it serves a need. It is the poor man's banking system."

Chapter 1's discussion of basic TBML techniques such as invoice fraud and manipulation is also in the hawaldars' playbook. As the reader recalls, to move money out, a hawaladar or his agent will import goods at overvalued prices or export goods at undervalued prices. To move money in, a hawaladar or his agent will import goods at undervalued prices or export goods at overvalued prices. This type of procedure is called *countervaluation*. Most other worldwide alternative remittance systems or informal value transfer networks are similarly based on trade. That is why a close examination of trade could be the back door to penetrating hidden hawala networks and is an additional reason why TBML should be the next frontier in AML/CFT enforcement. Trade transparency as a countermeasure will be discussed in Chapter 9.

AN ABUSED FINANCIAL SYSTEM

I want to emphasize that the overwhelming majority of people that use hawala and similar systems are *not* criminals or terrorists—they are simply trying to send or remit legitimately earned money. These transactions are sometimes called "white" hawala. Similar to Ali in the example above, a migrant worker chooses to use an alternative remittance system for both personal and practical reasons.

Most governments do not have any desire to interfere with hard-working migrants who simply wish to send a portion of their wages back to their home country to help support their loved ones. Unfortunately, despite hawala's legitimate role as an alternative remittance system, the system is abused by criminals and terrorists who wish to transfer money and value securely, cheaply, and without transparency. Similar to the BMPE described in Chapter 3 and the Chinese flying money system described in Chapter 5, hawala as the informal value transfer system is abused. Although criminal transactions—often called "black" hawala—constitute only a very small percentage of total hawala transfers, they still add up to an enormous amount of money.

 IS HAWALA LEGAL?

The short answer is, it depends on the jurisdiction. In just a few examples, hawala is illegal in Saudi Arabia. Hawala is also illegal in India, but it is quite popular and plays a large role in India's robust economy. Unlicensed hawala/hundi operators are illegal in Pakistan, but it is estimated that they account for over half of total remittances. Some support the finance of terror.[23] Hawala is legal in the UAE and Afghanistan, but hawaladars must register and file STRs. Few do. Similarly, in the United States hawala is legal. It is classified as a money services business, or MSB. As such, hawaladars must register with Treasury's FinCEN and they are expected to file SARs. They are also required to be registered in almost all of the 50 states.

Even the mostly "white" nature of hawala poses a challenge. Just like money transfers via banks, money services businesses, or even sending value through trade, it is necessary to sift through the statistical noise of a lot of hawala transactions to find the occasional suspect or black hawala transfer. One prominent hawaladar and gold trader in Dubai I once spoke with said that in his experience, it would be necessary to examine 1 million to 1.5 million white hawala transactions to find one black transfer. Although this is undoubtedly a self-serving statement, and experience has shown in areas of Afghanistan and other problematic regions that there are hawaladars who specialize in illicit transfers, it highlights some of the obstacles to successfully monitor hawala networks and to employ effective countermeasures.

As the Dubai source put it, governments can make all of the laws they want in an effort to regulate hawala, but the people will simply go around them and continue to use alternative banking, "until there is no longer a need for the service."[24]

HOW TO RECOGNIZE HAWALA

Both black and white hawala transactions are generally off the authorities' radar screens. In this respect, hawala represents one of the major "cracks inside the Western financial system" that Osama bin Laden once emphasized.[25] As indicated, I believe a concerted international effort to promote trade transparency could be the back door into hawala and many sister underground financial systems. But even without trade transparency, there are some ways to better identify the system and its abuses.

In general, some hawala networks are quite open while others are opaque. Many hawaladars operate in plain view in cities and town throughout the Middle East and Africa, particularly within *souks* (markets). Sometimes a particular city street or area of a souk will have a concentration of hawaladars and other types of financial businesses. Typically, they will advertise themselves as "money remitters," "money changers," "foreign exchange dealers," and "door-to-door" money delivery services. The word *hawala* itself is rarely used. In some areas (including the United States), the shop titles are displayed in both English and the native language. Certain businesses are more likely than others to be involved with hawala. While the following is not an exhaustive list, the following types of establishments have been known to offer hawala or similar services:

- Import–export or trading companies
- Travel and related services
- Jewelry dealers (particularly buyers and sellers of gold)
- Foreign exchange companies
- Sellers of rugs and carpets
- Used car sales
- Telephone/calling card sales
- Ethnic restaurants

Hawaladars sometimes operate out of their homes, attracting customers by word of mouth or relatively inexpensive forms of advertising such as flyers or signs in shop windows. Again, the word *hawala* will not be used in most cases. For example, a hawala advertisement in New York City might look similar to that shown in Figure 4.2.

"Following the money" in hawala investigations is very difficult. By their very nature, the transactions are underground and there is generally very little financial intelligence or other paper trail to follow. In most areas, customer identification is not required and formal recordkeeping is rare. Yet, most hawaladars maintain ledgers to record transactions, sometimes even in computerized spreadsheet form. Hawala bookkeeping emphasizes keeping track of how much money is owed and to whom. The sample ledger in Figure 4.3 is representative of the kind of record that might be kept. (Note that these ledgers are usually handwritten, and it is not uncommon for the native language to be used.)[27]

The first column indicates the date of the transaction. The second column shows the name of the hawala broker to whom the debt is owned; partial names (e.g., "Raj") or codes (e.g., "BJ") are often used. In this example, the names are Indian. The third column is the amount of the debt. This ledger reflects a tendency to do business in multiples of 100,000, so it would not be uncommon to see notations like "1.5" for 150,000. The fourth column indicates the dollar/rupee exchange

MUSIC BAZAAR AND TRAVEL SERVICES AGENCY

- Travel specials to Dubai, Pakistan, Bangladesh, Sri Lanka, India
- Great rupee deals
- Large movie selection
- Latest Bollywood hits on CD and DVD
- International calling cards
- Cellular activations (trade-ins welcome)
- Conveniently located in Jackson Heights

(718) 555-1111 ask for Yasmeen

Figure 4.2 Sample hawala advertisement[26]
From John Cassara and Avi Jorisch, On the Trail of Terror Finance: What Law Enforcement and Intelligence Officers Need to Know *(Red Cell IG, 2010).*

16/6/15	Raj	100000	37.6	2659.57	N-1202
16/6/15	Vinood	250000	39.25	6369.42	N-1203
16/6/15	Nitin Bhai	350000	42.3	8274.23	B-8146
17/6/15	BJ	50000	38.75	1290.32	N-1204
17/6/15	Jaafar	300000	39.25	7643.31	B-8147
17/6/15	Raj	150000	39.75	3773.58	N-1205
18/6/15	Nabhi	380000	42.2	8293.83	L-2160
18/6/15	Singh Trading	200000	38	5263.15	५२ त

Figure 4.3 Sample hawala ledger
From John Cassara and Avi Jorisch, On the Trail of Terror Finance: What Law Enforcement and Intelligence Officers Need to Know *(Red Cell IG, 2010).*

rate in effect for the transaction. The fifth column is the value of the transaction in dollars. The sixth column reflects the manner in which the payment was made. Notations such as "N-1203") usually represent a bank and a check number. (N could be "National Bank," B could be "Basic Bank," and L could be "Local Bank.") In many locations in the Middle East and South Asia, however, checks are not used, and payments/deposits are in cash. In such cases, a remittance code may be designated. In the sample ledger, the notation ५२ त in the Singh Trading row is "52 T" in Hindi. This represents 52 tolas of gold, possibly paid to a local goldsmith or jeweler instead of being remitted via a bank (see Chapter 6 for more on gold transactions).

COUNTERMEASURES

After September 11, a buzz developed in the worldwide media about terrorist finance. There were published stories about al Qaeda's alleged exploitation of gold, diamonds, tanzanite, and even the honey trade. Articles were written about the abuse of charities and donations from wealthy individuals in the Middle East to finance terror. But perhaps the biggest "discovery" for both the media and government agencies and departments was hawala. Talking heads and so-called experts gave interviews and were asked to testify on Capitol Hill about the threat of hawala and other alternative remittance systems that might be exploited by our adversaries. Congress wanted a solution, or at least the appearance of a solution, for an underground system that doesn't have a solution.[28]

Hawala—and similar alternative remittance systems—are here to stay. They are not going away because they fill a need. Moreover, hawala is intertwined with complex issues such as macro and micro economics, currency exchange controls, the devaluation of currencies, tax avoidance, capital flight, illiteracy, underground trading networks, and the promotion of banking services to non-banked populations. New laws, rules, and regulations in the United States and other jurisdictions are not going to solve the problem. Certainly, the last 10 years have proven that the registration and licensing requirements of hawaladars are mostly cosmetic.[29]

In short, there is no silver bullet to prevent the misuse of hawala. Yet we should not stop trying to develop and implement countermeasures or ways to identify suspect hawala transactions. We know trade is still the most widespread method of settling accounts between hawaladars and other underground financial brokers. As I have urged elsewhere, a systematic examination of suspect trade anomalies could provide insights into hawala networks.

 ## FACTORS IMPACTING A POSSIBLE HAWALA "SOLUTION"

- Currency and exchange controls
- Currency devaluations
- Literacy
- Movement away from cash-based economies
- Tax reform
- Low-cost overt alternatives
- Licensing and registration of hawaladars
- Increased awareness by compliance officers
- Increased SAR filings
- Advanced analytics
- Outreach to ethnic groups that use hawala
- Law enforcement initiatives
- The development of low-cost and transparent "new payment methods" such as cell phones
- Trade transparency

CASE EXAMPLES: HAWALA

The following are a few examples of "black" hawala. They are representative of cases that use hawala both to launder criminal proceeds and also finance terror.

Case 1: Manhattan Foreign Exchange

On March 20, 2003, law enforcement agents in New York arrested four individuals in connection with a Pakistani unlicensed money services business called Manhattan Foreign Exchange. Run from the basement of a Kashmiri restaurant in midtown Manhattan,[30] the business was one of New York's largest hundi remitters to Pakistan, transferring more than $33 million to the country during a three-year period, mostly drug proceeds.[31] The criminal organization also sold fake U.S., Pakistani, Canadian, and British passports and travel documents.[32]

Shaheen Khalid Butt, the Kashmiri owner, was charged with money laundering, currency reporting violations, conspiracy, and immigration fraud charges.[33] Over the course of the investigation, law enforcement bugged the basement of the restaurant and videotaped couriers dropping off bags of cash.

Case 2: Shidaal Express

In November 2013, a federal judge in San Diego sentenced three Somali immigrants for providing financial support to al-Shabaab—a designated terrorist organization. Evidence presented during the trial showed the defendants conspired to transfer funds to Somalia through a hawala operation known as the Shidaal Express. Among those involved in the conspiracy were Basaaly Saeed Moalin, a cabdriver, Mohamed Mohamed Mohamud, the imam at a popular mosque frequented by the city's immigrant Somali community, and Issa Doreh, who worked in the hawala operation that was the conduit for moving the illicit funds. Moalin had direct ties with al-Shabaab and one of its most prominent leaders—Aden Hashi Ayrow. At the trial, the jury listened to dozens of the defendants' intercepted telephone conversations, including many between Moalin and Ayrow. In those calls, Ayrow begged Moalin to send money to al-Shabaab, telling Moalin that it was "time to finance the jihad."[34]

Case 3: Health-Care Fraudsters Send Funds to Iran

In March 2013, Hossein and Najmeh Lahiji, a naturalized U.S. citizen and his wife, were indicted for medical billing fraud in Texas, and for sending the illicit proceeds to Iran via hawala. The Lahijis transferred the illicit funds through Espadana Exchange, an unlicensed money remitting business. During the investigation, evidence was obtained that allegedly showed the co-conspirators defrauding multiple health-care benefit programs by submitting false and fraudulent claims, including instances where Dr. Lahiji submitted claims for urology services allegedly performed when in fact he was traveling outside the United States.[35]

Case 4: Somali Remittances

In Somalia, there is an absence of regulated commercial banks. As a result, informal remittance companies are the primary conduits for moving funds into and out of Somalia. Trade goods are often used to settle accounts between hawaladars. In one case, a Somali trader buys commodities from Dubai for resale in Somalia. To finance the trade, the Somali trader contacts a local remittance company in Mogadishu. The trader gives cash to the local remittance agent. (Most transactions are dollar-based, but other currencies are used as well.) A commission is charged for the exchange. The trader asks that the funds be transferred to his foreign bank account located in Dubai.

The local agent of the remittance company contacts a hawaladar also located in Dubai and asks that the funds be transferred to the Dubai-based bank account identified by the Somali trader. The Dubai bank issues a letter of credit so that goods can be purchased. The desired goods are purchased in Dubai and the vendors have no idea—nor do they care—that the origin of the funds is actually the result of a hawala exchange. The trade goods are then shipped to Somalia and sold by the trader. A percentage of the profit is kept and the balance is used to pay suppliers, and the cycle is repeated.[36]

Case 5: Financial Intelligence Instrumental in Hawala Investigation

In 2002, the FBI opened an investigation into the activities of a hawaladar in the western United States. A tip from a citizen complaint prompted a query of the BSA database. The query yielded 30 SARs and 13 CTRs, which were instrumental in identifying numerous bank accounts used in the hawala operation. Over a five-year period, the subjects, all Iraqi immigrants, wired in excess of $4 million from a U.S. bank to accounts in Amman, Jordan. From there, most of the money was illegally smuggled into Iraq. Additional funds were sent to Syria, Saudi Arabia, Iran, UAE, Chile, Ukraine, and Denmark.[37]

Cases 6 and 7: Examples of Hawala and Terror

According to transcripts from the trial of Mohammed al-Owahali, an al-Qaeda member serving a life sentence for his role in the 1998 U.S. embassy bombing in Nairobi, funding for the attack was received through a hawala office in the city's notorious Eastleigh district, a predominantly Somali neighborhood.[38] And according to the indictment of Faisal Shahzad, the Pakistani American who attempted to detonate a bomb-laden SUV in New York's Times Square in May 2010, hawala transfers were used to finance that plot as well. Shahzad reportedly received approximately $12,000 from the Pakistani Taliban to carry out the attack.[39]

CHEAT SHEET

- The magnitude of unofficial remittances is enormous, easily surpassing multiple hundreds of billions of dollars a year.
- Hawala is one of many worldwide alternative remittance systems. It is commonly found in South Asia, parts of Africa, the Americas, and the Middle East.
- Hawala can be defined as "money transfer without money movement."
- The overwhelming majority of hawala transactions are benign and involve the remittance of wages.

- Hawala is based on tust. It works primarily because of family, clan, or tribal associations.

- Transfers of money and value take place based on communications between members of a network of hawala brokers, called hawaladars.

- Attractive elements of hawala are that it is certain, convenient, and cheap. Clients also feel comfortable working with a financial system they trust and understand.

- Accounts between hawaladars are periodically settled through banks, cash couriers, and trade. New settlement techniques such as cyber- and mobile payments are on the horizon.

- Hawala brokers frequently operate other businesses. Some of the most common include currency exchange houses, import–export shops, cell phone/calling card shops, gold jewelers, and various kinds of business brokers.

- Hawala is widespread even in jurisdictions where it is technically illegal.

- Hawaladars generally keep temporary books or an informal ledger to track their transactions.

- Hawala countermeasures have proven ineffective in part because the service is interwined with regional issues such as illiteracy, currency devaluations, nonconvertibility of currency, excessive taxation, corruption, lack of inexpensive financial services, and trade and value transfer.

NOTES

1. International Labor Organization; available online: http://www.ilo.org/global/topics/labour-migration/lang--en/index.htm.
2. World Bank, "Developing Countries to Receive Over $410 Billion in Remittances in 2013, Says World Bank," press release (October 2, 2013), available online: http://www.worldbank.org/en/news/press-release/2013/10/02/developing-countries-remittances-2013-world-bank.
3. Ibid.
4. Dilip Ratha, "Remittances, Funds for the Folks Back Home," International Monetary Fund; available online: http://www.imf.org/external/pubs/ft/fandd/basics/remitt.htm.
5. R.T. Naylor, *Wages of Crime: Black Markets, Illegal Finance, and the Underworld Economy* (New York: Cornell University Press, 2002), p. 144.

6. Gretchen Peters, *Seeds of Terror: How Heroin Is Bankrolling the Taliban and al Qaeda, Thomas Dunne Books* (New York: St. Martin's Press, 2009), p. 170.

7. The information in this section is primarily from John Cassara and Avi Jorisch, *On the Trail of Terror Finance: What Law Enforcement and Intelligence Officers Need to Know* (Washington, DC: Red Cell IG, 2010), chapter 7, p. 113–135.

8. Much of this section was taken from *On the Trail of Terror Finance*; in turn the material originated primarily from Patrick Jost and Harjit Singh Sandhu, *The Hawala Alternative Remittance System and Its Role in Money Laundering* (Lyon, France: Interpol General Secretariat, January 2000); available online: http://www.treasury.gov/resource-center/terrorist-illicit-finance/documents/fincen-hawala-rpt.pdf.

9. Naylor, p. 144.

10. Princeton law, available online: http://www.princeton.edu/~achaney/tmve/wiki100k/docs/Hawala.html.

11. Samuel M. Maimbo, "The Challenges of Regulating and Supervising the Hawaladars of Kabul," in *The Regulatory Frameworks for Hawala and Other Remittance Systems*, International Monetary Fund, 2005, p. 47.

12. Cleofe Maceda, "UAE Remittances: Who Sends Home the Most Money?" *Gulf News* (January 15, 2015), available online: http://gulfnews.com/business/your-money/uae-remittances-who-sends-home-the-most-money-1.1446403.

13. Mohammed El Qorchi, Samuel M. Maimbo, and John F. Wilson, "Informal Funds Transfer Systems: An Analysis of the Informal Hawala System," International Monetary Fund, 2003, p. 7.

14. U.S. Department of State, Bureau for International Narcotics and Law Enforcement Affairs, *International Narcotics Control Strategy Report (INCSR) Volume II, Money Laundering and Financial Crimes* (March 2015), Gabon country report, available online: http://www.state.gov/j/inl/rls/nrcrpt/2015/vol2/index.htm.

15. See Financial Crimes Enforcement Network (FinCEN), Advisory Issue 33 (March 2003), available online: http://www.fincen.gov/news_room/rp/advisory/pdf/advis33.pdf.

16. Patrick Jost and Harjit Singh Sandhu.

17. "The Role of Hawala and other Similar Service Providers in Money Laundering and Terrorist Finance," FATF, October 2013; available online: http://www.fatf-gafi.org/media/fatf/documents/reports/Role-of-hawala-and-similar-in-ml-tf.pdf.

18. Samuel M. Maimbo, *The Money Exchange Dealers of Kabul: A Study of the Hawala System in Afghanistan* 3 (World Bank, Working Paper No. 13, 2003), note 62, 7.

19. This is mostly conjecture. However, there are some articles that indicate the probability of its occurrence, such as "Bitcoins May Be Used by Hawala Traders: Official," *The Times of India* (December 29, 2013), available online: http://timesofindia.indiatimes.com/city/ahmedabad/Bitcoin-may-be-used-by-hawala-traders-Officials/articleshow/28067184.cms.

20. For additional information on the growing use of M-payments in the developing world, see John Cassara, "Mobile Payments, Smurfs, and Emerging Threats," SAS, available online: http://www.sas.com/en_sg/insights/articles/risk-fraud/mobile-payments-smurfs-emerging-threats.html). Also, I call the reader's attention to M-Hawala—a growing mobile payments provider in Afghanistan; see http://mhawala.af/.

21. Matt Levitt, "The Islamic State's Backdoor Banking," The Washington Institute, (March 24, 2015), available online: http://www.washingtoninstitute.org/policy-analysis/view/the-islamic-states-backdoor-banking.

22. Maimbo, page 6, box 1.

23. U.S. Department of State, Bureau for International Narcotics and Law Enforcement Affairs, see Pakistan country report, available online: http://www.state.gov/j/inl/rls/nrcrpt/2015/vol2/239097.htm.

24. Author conversation in Dubai, October 2001.

25. Opening statement of Subcommittee Chairman Evan Bayh (D-Ind.) hearing on "Hawala and Underground Terrorist Financing Mechanisms," U.S. Senate Committee on Banking, Housing, and Urban Affairs, November 14, 2001; available online: http://www.gpo.gov/fdsys/pkg/CHRG-107shrg81714/html/CHRG-107shrg81714.htm.

26. The advertisement has been reproduced in many publications, including *On the Trail of Terror Finance*, p. 126. See endnote vii.

27. The ledger (with modifications) has been reproduced in many publications, including *On the Trail of Terror Finance*, p. 127. See endnote vii.

28. Cassara, *Hide & Seek: Intelligence, Law Enforcement, and the Stalled War on Terror Finance*," p. 180. In large part, the theme of *Hide & Seek* covers shortsighted government policy and the "culture of the bureaucracy" that still prevents us from taking effective action on terror finance.

29. See Cassara and Jorisch, *On the Trail of Terror Finance*, pages 128–133.

30. Benjamin Weiser, "Federal Prosecutors Charge Man in Money Laundering Scheme," *New York Times* (March 22, 2003), available online: http://www.nytimes.com/2003/03/22/nyregion/federal-prosecutors-charge-man-in-money-laundering-scheme.html.

31. "Terror Finance Schemes Busted," *Fox News* (March 24, 2003), available online: http://www.foxnews.com/story/2003/03/24/terror-finance-schemes-busted/.

32. John Solomon, "Feds Launch New Raids against Financing Schemes," Associated Press, March 22, 2003; available online: http://www.theintelligencer.com/archives/article_537eb0da-41ca-5a26-aa1d-9ee76f53eb1e.html.

33. Khalid Hasan, "Kashmiri Held for Money Laundering Out on Bail," *Daily Times* (March 23, 2003).

34. "Three Somali Immigrants Sentenced for Providing Support to Foreign Terrorists," FBI (November 18, 2013), available online: http://www.fbi.gov/sandiego/press-releases/2013/three-somali-immigrants-sentenced-for-providing-support-to-foreign-terrorists.

35. "Healthcare Fraudsters Sent $1.1 Million to Iran," *Money Jihad* (March 26, 2013), available online: http://moneyjihad.wordpress.com/2013/03/26/health-care-fraudsters-sent-1-1-million-to-iran/.

36. International Narcotics Control Strategy Report Volume II, *Money Laundering*, Bureau of International Narcotics and Law Enforcement Affairs, U.S. Department of State, March 2003, p. 151.

37. "Numerous SARs and CTRs Instrumental in Hawala Investigation," FinCEN SAR Activity Review (November, 2003), available online: www.fincen.gov/law_enforcement/ss/html/043.html.

38. Matt Brown, "The Wired Money That Funds Terror," *The National* (May 5, 2008).

39. "Shahzad Pleads Guilty to NYC Bomb Attempt," *CBS News*, (June 21, 2010), available online: http://www.cbsnews.com/news/shahzad-pleads-guilty-to-nyc-bomb-attempt/.

CHAPTER 5

Chinese Flying Money

once gave a presentation to Italian law enforcement officials about hawala. As per the discussion in Chapter 4, I initially explained that hawala was probably invented in South Asia centuries ago long before the advent of Western banking. One Italian wagged his finger and objected. He declared that, "Hawala was invented in Italy!"

"What do you mean?" I asked.

"Don't you remember your history? Back in the Renaissance, Italy as we know it today didn't exist. It was composed of a number of city-states such as Venezia, Firenze, Milano, Pisa, Roma, Napoli, and many others. There was active commerce between them, but they didn't have modern banking. Roads were poor and unsafe. Robberies were common on the highways. Piracy was a risk at sea. If a businessman in Venezia wanted to send money to another businessman in Napoli as compensation for the purchase of goods, he would not want to risk sending gold coins as payment. So the city-states developed a system of commerce where debts were covered by value transfer and exchange. It was very efficient. The money stayed in place, but payment was made. They didn't call it hawala. But it was the same system."

The reason why an introduction to a chapter on Chinese informal money transfer system begins with a shared anecdote about hawala in Renaissance Italy is because for all intents and purposes, modern Chinese underground financial systems also have their origins in antiquity and are quite similar to other "alternative" underground financial systems found around the world. And once again trade is the common denominator.

AN ANCIENT SYSTEM

It is believed that *fei-chien*, sometimes known as "flying money," was invented during the T'ang Dynasty (618–907 AD). The Chinese underground financial system is also known as *hui kuan*—"to remit sums of money" (Mandarin Chinese), *phoei kwan* (Teochew Chinese), or *chiao hui*—"overseas remittances." At the time, there was a growing commodity trade within China. Some historians believe it was the rice trade and others the tea trade that were the catalysts for the new financial system.[1] As opposed to modern-day practice, the transfer schemes were not invented as an underground method of evading the grasp of authorities but rather it was a tool to facilitate taxation.

Merchants sold their goods and then brought their revenues to provincial "memorial offering courts," where taxes due the central government would be collected. In turn, the merchants would be issued certificates for the remaining value of the commodity sales. When the merchants returned to their home provinces, they would present the certificates to the provincial government for payment. Thus, the fei-chien system became an efficient way of payment via trade-based value transfer. Completing transactions in this way simultaneously spared the merchants and government the risk of transporting large sums of money.[2]

Over the centuries, the system continued to evolve. Chinese workers increasingly began to migrate to other provinces and then overseas. Their families back home generally needed financial support. Expatriate Chinese businesses (particularly those that specialized in gold) began to develop side businesses of remitting money back to China.

Strong Chinese family bonds are incorporated into *guanxi*, which is an overarching social system of rules that govern relationships and social behavior. Guanxi is the guarantor of both secrecy and the integrity of the parties to the transaction. Violate its prescriptions and find yourself a social outcast, essentially shunned in all circles.[3] Guanxi is an integral component of fei-chien. In other words, similar to the explanation of hawala in Chapter 4, an essential element of fei-chien is trust.

In the Chinese diaspora, remittances were often sent home to loved ones via rice merchants who traveled throughout Asia and beyond. Over time, the rice trade evolved into much of the region's shipping and commercial routes. The young Chinese postal service soon took advantage of the transportation networks, merchant shops, and shipping schedules and began sending letters and remittances through these carriers. When government-controlled postal services and officially registered banks came into existence, they were accompanied by comparatively high fees, insuring a continuing role for underground bankers in Asian societies. For example, Teochew Chinese families that were in the informal remittance business in Thailand also founded the major banks. And many of the banks remain in the hands of powerful families, which helps to explain today's special relationships between some Asian banks and major money-moving organizations.[4]

 CHITS AND CHOPS

Many correlate the use of *chits* and *chops* with Chinese underground financial systems. The chit was introduced by British colonialists in China, who borrowed the term (diminutive of "chitty") from Hindi (*chitthi*). It was generally used as a note or certificate often given to a servant as payment. The employee then presented the chit to a shop keeper for the purchase of goods and payment was later made by the employer's representative.

The chop evolved into a kind of receipt. It has taken many forms including a seal made of wood or ivory. The chop is often dipped into ink or wax and impressed on a document, including cards and currency. It is sometimes used in funds transfers as a sign of legitimacy.[5]

In fei-chien transfers today, a coded phone call or e-mail message are often used.[6]

THE MODERN ERA

Global Financial Integrity estimates that between 2002 and 2011, illicit financial outflows from China were approximately $1.08 trillion.[7] There are many economic, social, and political reasons for Chinese capital flight. However, there is an increasing personal finance incentive. Chinese banks pay paltry returns on savings. In past years, bullish equity markets and the real estate boom have offered the growing Chinese middle class investment and saving options. Yet those options are teetering, making investment overseas a viable alternative. Savvy Chinese also like to park some of their assets in the West. However, one stumbling block to foreign investments is that the Chinese central government mandates capital controls, which limit Chinese citizens to taking out about $50,000 a year.[8]

Popular ways to send money outside China are via the misuse of the international gold trade (see Chapter 6), gambling, casinos, and junkets (particularly via Macau), the special relationship with Hong Kong, and allegations that some Chinese banks provide special services to select customers to funnel money abroad. Some Chinese use friends' and family members' transfer quotas to get the money they need over the border.[9] Overseas business investments, trade-based value transfer, and its corollary fei-chien are also heavily used.

 A Chinese investor said he doesn't really worry about limits on sending money abroad. "The Chinese are known for finding all sorts of channels for sending their money out of the country."[10]

Similar to demand meeting availability in the narcotics-fueled expansion of the black market peso exchange discussed in Chapter 3, the Chinese informal banking system of yesteryear has taken on both new breadth and sophistication. It offers cheap, efficient, swift, and low-risk cross-border fund transfers of hundreds of millions of dollars each day. Black market banks in China and overseas never advertise their services. Similar to hawala storefronts, they operate ostensibly as tea shops, cellphone vendors, or snack kiosks. Generally, they attract clients by word of mouth. Their service is to provide cash for cash. They can move much faster and more efficiently than regulated Chinese banks.[11] According to one fei-chien broker, "We have a relative in Hong Kong who does business in Mainland China. Once a week, he visits us to pick up renminbi (Chinese currency) for his import business, and in return he maintains a pool of Hong Kong dollars for us across the border. He is family, so we trust him. We avoid the official exchange rates, and everyone is happy."[12]

Although the informal networks are found throughout China, they seem to be particularly active in Guangdong province; a coastal province in southeast China bordering Hong Kong and Macau. Individuals and businesses in the region and elsewhere depend on "flying money" to get around strict government currency controls and to safeguard their assets.[13] Even ranking government officials use the service. According to one money broker, government apparatchiks "bring us sacks of cash in Zhuhai because they are afraid that security cameras at cash deposit terminals will record their faces. Or one of their underlings does it, and they ask us to give them Hong Kong dollars in Macau."[14]

Guangdong in the Pearl River Delta hosts a number of cities and trading and manufacturing centers that are also major underground finance conduits with Hong Kong, Macau, and global underground financial networks. Despite Chinese government controls on capital inflows and outflows and the prohibition of informal financial banking and remittances, the underground networks are flourishing.

 According to an underground broker in Zhuhai, "It's very simple. You give me renminbi here. Then we deliver Hong Kong dollars to you in Macau. We can move tens of millions each day."[15]

HOW DOES IT WORK?

When I was assigned to Treasury's FinCEN, I once gave a briefing on hawala to visiting officials from Taiwan. There is little publicly available information on Chinese underground finance, and I wanted to know how it operates. At the end of the presentation, one of the officials stated, "Generally, hawala and fei-chien operate the same way." So per our discussion and subsequent research, the following are some similarities between hawala and fei-chien. Figure 5.1 is a simplified diagram of a basic fei-chien transfer.

- Both systems have existed for centuries.
- Both are based on trust.
- For the most part, both are generally benign and commonly used today for the remittance of wages.
- Both underground financial systems are also abused by criminals, tax cheats, and as a means of capital flight and the repatriation of profits.
- Both hawala and fei-chien are international in scope.

- Family and clan relationships are often involved.
- Both are based on the concept of money transfer without money movement.
- They are safe and secure.
- They offer inexpensive money transfer in comparison to their formal counterparts.
- Both systems offer quick and efficient transfers.
- There are few paper trails.
- They avoid taxation and government scrutiny.
- For the most part, they avoid official financial transparency reporting requirements.
- They are little understood outside their natural constituencies.
- Both avoid currency and exchange controls.
- They are culturally acceptable.
- Both systems often use front companies such as import–export firms.
- Historically and culturally, both often used gold to settle accounts between brokers.
- Today, accounts are often settled via bank transfers, cash couriers, and trade.
- Over- and underinvoicing, countervaluation, and invoice fraud are all common techniques to transfer value.

Transactions and capital flow both directions. Using the previous example, the fei-chien brokers in Hong Kong and New York have to periodically settle their accounts. Similar to hawala, this is accomplished via bulk cash (U.S. dollars), bank transfers, and trade-based value transfer. For example, Chinese firms working with fei-chien brokers can send money out of China by underinvoicing exports and overvaluing imports. They may, for example, sell $10,000 worth of garments abroad, show an invoice for $8,000 to authorities, and keep the remainder overseas. Chapter 7 will further discuss forms of commercial laundering and mispricing via trade and services.

2. Wang gives the fei-chien
   Hong Kong broker the money and
   in turn receives a playing card with a
   chop. He trusts the broker, as they have a
   familial relationship.

1. Wang in Hong Kong
   wants to send $1 million
   Hong Kong dollars of illicit
   proceeds to his cousin in
   New York City.

3. The fei-chien broker in Hong Kong
   directs his counterpart (perhaps a member of
   the same family) to pay the
   equivalent in U.S. dollars
   (approximately $129,000) upon
   presentation of the chop. A coded telephone
   call or e-mail might also be used for
   authentication.

4. The money is paid to Wang's
   cousin in NYC (less commissions at
   both ends). The money did not
   physically leave Hong Kong.

Figure 5.1 Fei-chien flying money diagram

 TRIADS AND TONGS

According to the FBI, Chinese social organizations called *tongs* have been operating in the United States since the early 1900s. Many evolved into organized crime rings and have been joined by other groups with ties to East and Southeast Asia. They are "highly sophisticated in their criminal operations and have extensive financial capabilities."[16] Chinese triads (underground societies) are criminal enterprises primarily based in Hong

Kong, Taiwan, and Macau. They are often involved with extortion, murder, kidnapping, illegal gambling, prostitution, loan sharking, alien smuggling, narcotics trafficking, and intellectual property rights violations. Their illicit proceeds are sometimes laundered via fei-chien.

According to the most recent FATF mutual evaluation report on China, the FATF evaluators and the Chinese officials they interviewed agree that there are four primary money-laundering methodologies in China:

1. Illicit funds are laundered via bulk cash smuggling.

2. Dirty money is laundered through the legitimate financial system such as banks, cash transactions, account payments, loans, and other financial transactions.

3. Proceeds are transferred by importing or exporting over/underpriced goods, or falsifying/counterfeiting import–export contracts, shipment bills, customs declarations, and other related documents (i.e., trade-based money laundering).

4. Money is laundered through the underground banking system.[17]

Of course, as we have seen, methods three and four are intertwined. What is important to note is that the Chinese themselves acknowledge the threat posed by TBML and its link to underground finance.

CHINESE PRESENCE IN AFRICA

During my travels to Africa, I have observed the growing Chinese presence and suspect Chinese business practices. Over the last decade, there has been a proliferation of Chinese traders in African markets. In fact, it is believed more Chinese have gone to Africa in the past 10 years than Europeans in the past 400![18] Many come to work via China state-owned companies. But after their contracts end, many stay behind and are issued host-country passports.

To put the magnitude of the China and Africa relationship in perspective, trade between the parties was a stunning $160 billion in 2011—as opposed to a mere $12 million in 1950! China is Africa's largest trading partner. The trade is relatively balanced.[19] Africa sends primarily minerals and raw materials back to China.

 Although updated estimates are not available, approximately 10 years ago Asian law enforcement officials believed the Chinese underground banking system handled more money transfers to and from China than are sent via the official banking system.[20]

The small, ubiquitous Chinese shop is the opaque underbelly of China's presence in Africa.[21] The shops are found throughout the continent in large cities and small rural towns. The "mom-and-pop" standalone stores offer just about everything for the typical African consumer, including clothes, electronics, and small appliances. The African people generally welcome the availability of the low-cost products, but complain bitterly about the low quality of poorly made and sometimes counterfeit goods. Many observers feel it is a form of recycled exploitation with Africa providing raw materials for Chinese industry and China providing modern-day consumerism for all.

Exacerbating the situation, Chinese traders seal themselves in insular communities and have very little social interaction with their African hosts. Moreover, Africa has become a needed outlet for Chinese entrepreneurs and economic citizenship is often available—for a price. Some feel that many Chinese settling in Africa have questionable ties and agendas. And, unfortunately, the Chinese business community in Africa functions in a nontransparent mode. Little or no information is available regarding supply chains, financing, and banking. Most China shops operate on a cash-only basis and tax avoidance is rife. Once again, corruption is the great facilitator.

The situation is assuredly abused. The China shop is perfectly situated to facilitate TBML, capital flight from China, and the underground repatriation of profits made in Africa back to China. Underground banking is a lifeline for import–export businesses that are frustrated by strict financial regulations in China and by African host countries that impede the efficiency of commerce. And without fei-chien networks, Chinese workers in Chinese sweatshops would have great difficulty in sending money home and merchants would face additional expenses repatriating profits.

Unfortunately, there is very little reporting on these issues, either by governments or the media, and there are no known criminal investigations. African security services, financial crimes police, and customs services uniformly suffer from lack of expertise and capacity. U.S. law enforcement and intelligence services are also woefully lacking in knowledge of Chinese underground financial systems.

The Chinese/African model is also found in the Americas, Europe, and Central and Southeast Asia. The Chinese fei-chien value transfer system uses trade goods to provide countervaluation between brokers. The networks are shrouded in secrecy and remain far outside of Western experience. The U.S. Department of State shares these views. In the 2015 INCSR report, the State Department urges that "China should cooperate with international law enforcement to investigate how indigenous Chinese underground financial systems and trade-based value transfer are used to circumvent capital restrictions for illicit outbound transfers and capital flight, and receive inbound remittances and criminal proceeds for Chinese organized crime."[22]

Via personal interviews, anecdotes, and observation, I have come to the conclusion that Chinese underground banking via value transfer (both outbound and inbound) is a phenomenon of growing importance. It must be understood and addressed in the next frontier of TBML.

CASE EXAMPLES

Case 1: Fei-Chien and Hawala

According to the DEA, "A Chinese trafficker enlisted the services of ethnic Indian hawala dealers to transfer hundreds of thousands of dollars from New York City to Bangkok. The trafficker brought the cash to the Indian gem trading company on Fifth Avenue. The hawala dealer contacted a counterpart in Bangkok, who made the money available at a gem trading company. The trafficker's associate in Bangkok then was notified and told to pick up the money at the gem store."[23]

Case 2: Underground Money Shops' Role in Drug Money Laundering

In 2005, 15 defendants involved in a transnational drug trafficking case, jointly investigated by the Chinese and Malaysian police, were convicted of drug manufacturing and trafficking and money laundering by the Intermediate People's Court of Quanzhou, Fujian. A drug dealer called "Cai C" transferred the drug proceeds from underground money shops in the Philippines to their counterparts in Quanzhou, Jinjiang, and Shishi, China. Relatives of "Cai C" opened accounts with their own names in local Chinese banks. Most of the illicit money was used for the purchase of vehicles and the election of a local village chief.[24]

Case 3: Underground Banking and Immigrant Smuggling

A Chinese businesswoman in New York's Chinatown known as "Sister Ping" was also a *snakehead*—a Chinese immigrant smuggler. She charged up to $40,000 per person to smuggle migrants on the dangerous and suffocating voyage from China to New York in the hold of a rogue vessel. She also owned restaurants, a clothing store, and real estate in Chinatown. According to testimony at her 2005 trial, from a humble-looking Chinatown storefront, she also oversaw a large multinational underground financial empire that stretched from New York to Thailand, Singapore, Hong Kong, and China. She admitted to being the busy chief executive of an "underground or unofficial bank" for immigrants. The illegal Chinese migrants used her to remit their American earnings to support relatives back in China and sometimes to smuggle them into the United States. According to the New York State Banking Department, Sister Ping never held a banking license.[25]

Case 4: Triads Use Underground Finance in Russia's Far East

According to Asian organized crime expert Bertil Lintner, the equivalent of hundreds of millions of dollars was transferred in just one year from China to the Russian Far East—mostly through the Chinese underground banking system. The funds were invested in casinos, hotels, restaurants, hostess bars, illegal logging and fishing ventures, and other businesses. Chinese triad gangs control many of the same businesses. Many Russian gangsters work for the Chinese syndicates expediting business deals or as security guards in gaming houses. Timber, fish, and illicit proceeds are transferred to China, costing Russia tax revenue.[26]

Case 5: Used-Tire Trade Masks TBML and Trafficking in Endangered Wildlife

The African continent is one of the fastest growing markets for the global tire industry and China has emerged as a leading exporter of both new and used tires to many African countries. There are growing imports of low-quality second-hand tires, which soon wear out on Africa's rough roads. Some have accused China of "dumping" tires in Africa.[27] Against this backdrop, Country X in Africa imports cheaply made or "used" tires from Asia—primarily from China. Similar to the kind of BMPE scheme described in Chapter 3 with Mexico buying cheaply made goods from China as a ruse to send payment abroad, the tires enter Africa. They could be overinvoiced. Payment is made and money is laundered or possibly simply repatriated back to China. Another possibility is that upon arrival the African importer labels the tires as "defective" and has them "returned." In that case, there is no duty on the return of the tires. There are incidents where contraband (including endangered wildlife products) is hidden among the tires in 40-foot containers for shipment to China. Or the containers with "returned" tires to China are simply cycled back to Africa in a kind of carousel scheme whereby they are purchased and overinvoiced yet again and more money is laundered or repatriated.[28] The involvement of Chinese underground finance in these schemes is not known but the investigations continue.

Case 6: Underground Banking Links Korea and China

According to 2015 U.S. Department of State reporting, "South Korean officials have uncovered numerous underground banking systems being used by South Korean nationals, North Korean defectors, and foreign national workers from China and Southeast Asian and Middle

Eastern countries. Reports indicate North Korean defectors living in South Korea are sending more than $10 million per year to family members in North Korea through illegal banking systems between South Korea and China."[29]

Case 7: Chinese TBML in Poland

According to 2015 U.S. Department of State reporting, "[Polish] authorities continue to report that Asian (primarily Chinese and Vietnamese) organized criminal elements are increasingly remitting profits from tax evasion and the sale of counterfeit goods via money transfers and couriers. The majority of Asian organized crime activity occurs at the Chinese Trade Center located in Wolka Kosowska, approximately 25 kilometers from Warsaw. There are also smaller Asian shopping centers located in Rzgow (near Lodz) and Jaworzno (near Katowice) where organized crime activity is suspected. The principal scheme involves the extreme undervaluing of imported goods through the falsification of invoices, which are used to determine the customs value of products and the applicable value added tax (VAT). The sale of counterfeit goods and illegal drug trafficking are also suspected at these markets."[30]

Cheat Sheet

- Fei-chien and similar Chinese underground financial systems are sometimes known as *flying money*.
- The informal financial system was invented during the T'ang Dynasty (618–907 AD).
- Today, it essentially operates the same way as hawala and similar worldwide alternative remittance systems.
- Modern fei-chien has taken on new breadth and sophistication.
- Historically and culturally, fei-chien is trade-based value transfer.
- Money is transferred but not physically moved.
- Fei-chien is insular, indigenous, secretive, and based on trust.

▪ To show ownership, the recipient of a fei-chien transfer will sometimes use an authenticated *chop* or token as a sign of legitimacy. Coded telephone calls and e-mails are also used.

▪ Chinese underground financial systems are used to remit wages, engage in capital flight, avoid taxes, launder criminal proceeds, repatriate profits, and avoid currency exchange controls.

▪ Fei-chien is not easily recognized, and there is little government or open source reporting on the underground financial system.

NOTES

1. Leonides Buencamino and Segei Gorbunov, "Informal Money Transfer Systems: Opportunities and Challenges for Development Finance," United Nations, November 2002, p. 3.

2. Ibid.

3. S. Carroll, "Anti-Money Laundering Laws and the Quasi-Banker: A Report on Alternative Banking in Australia," AUSTRAC, 1995, p. 41.

4. Drug Enforcement Administration, "Asian Money Movement Methods." The author has only a paper copy of this undated report, believed to have been written in the mid-1990s.

5. Buencamino and Gorbunov.

6. Bertil Lintner, "Triads Tighten Grip on Russia's Far East," *Asia Pacific Media Services Limited*, first appearing in *Jane's Intelligence Review* (September 2003), available online: http://www.asiapacificms.com/articles/russia_triads/.

7. Clark Gasgoigne, "Global Financial Integrity" (September 23, 2014), available online: http://www.gfintegrity.org/chinas-illicit-outflows-2002-2011-us1-08-trillion/.

8. Alex Frangos, "The Mechanics of Moving Cash Out of China," *Wall Street Journal* (October 19, 2012); available online: http://blogs.wsj.com/chinarealtime/2012/10/19/how-hong-kongs-legal-system-enables-china-cash-flight/.

9. "China Cracks down on Money Leaking Out of Its Borders," *Australian Business Review* (August 15, 2014), available online: http://www.theaustralian.com.au/business/latest/china-cracks-down-on-money-leaking-out-of-its-borders/story-e6frg90f-1227025396290?nk=84c339cf9ec5c301a2e5bcd33b02fc55.

10. "The Flight of the Renminbi," *The Economist* (October 27, 2012), available online: http://www.economist.com/news/china/21565277-economic-repression-home-causing-more-chinese-money-vote-its-feet-flight.

11. Brendon Hong, "Inside China's Underground Black Market Banks," *The Daily Beast* (February, 26, 2014), available online: http://www.thedailybeast.com/articles/2014/02/26/inside-china-s-underground-black-market-banks.html.

12. Ibid.

13. James Pomfret and Matthew Miller, "Insight—Despite Curbs, China's Vast Hot Money Triangle Flourishes," Reuters (May 19, 2013), available online: http://www.reuters.com/article/2013/05/19/us-china-laundering-triangle-insight-idUSBRE94I0CB20130519.

14. Hong.

15. Pomfret and Miller.

16. FBI, "Asian Criminal Enterprises," available online: http://www.fbi.gov/about-us/investigate/organizedcrime/asian.

17. "Mutual Evaluation Report on Anti-Money Laundering and Combating the Financing of Terrorism, Peoples Republic of China," Financial Action Task Force (2007), p. 8, available online: http://www.fatf-gafi.org/media/fatf/documents/reports/mer/MER%20China%20full.pdf.

18. "The Chinese in Africa, Trying to Pull Together," The Economist (April 20, 2011), available online: http://www.economist.com/node/18586448.

19. Terence McNamee, "Africa in Their Words—A Study of Chinese Traders in South Africa, Lesotho, Botswana, Zambia and Angola," The Brenthurst Foundation, 2012; available online: http://www.thebrenthurstfoundation.org/files/brenthurst_commisioned_reports/Brenthurst-paper-201203-Africa-in-their-Words-A-Study-of-Chinese-Traders.pdf.

20. Lintner.

21. McNamee.

22. U.S. Department of State, Bureau for International Narcotics and Law Enforcement Affairs, International Narcotics Control Strategy Report (INCSR) Volume II, Money Laundering and Financial Crimes (March 2015), China country report, available online: http://www.state.gov/j/inl/rls/nrcrpt/2015/vol2/index.htm.

23. Drug Enforcement Administration.

24. The Role of Hawala and Other Similar Service Providers in Money Laundering and Terrorist Finance," Financial Action Task Force (October, 2013), p. 38, available online: http://www.fatf-gafi.org/media/fatf/documents/reports/Role-of-hawala-and-similar-in-ml-tf.pdf.

25. Julia Preston, "Prosecutors Say Defendant in Immigrant Smuggling Case Ran an Underground Empire," New York Times (May 23, 2005), available online: http://www.nytimes.com/2005/05/23/nyregion/23ping.html?pagewanted=print&_r=0.

26. Lintner.

27. "The Market for Tyres in East Africa," Africa Business Pages, available online: http://www.africa-business.com/features/tyres.html.

28. February 26, 2015, e-mail exchange between the author and Gretchen Peters, researcher, analyst, and author of Seeds of Terror: How Heroin Is Bankrolling the Taliban and Al Qaeda (New York: St. Martin's Press, 2009).

29. U.S. Department of State, Bureau for International Narcotics and Law Enforcement Affairs, International Narcotics Control Strategy Report (INCSR) Volume II, Money Laundering and Financial Crimes (March 2015), South Korea country report, available online: http://www.state.gov/j/inl/rls/nrcrpt/2015/vol2/index.htm.

30. Ibid., see Poland country report.

CHAPTER **6**

Misuse of the International Gold Trade

The transfer of value through the misuse of the international gold trade is one of the oldest and most pervasive forms of international money laundering in the world. And in terms of total monetary value, some of the largest money laundering schemes in history have involved gold. Because of its unique nature—it is both a commodity and a de facto bearer instrument—it is often used to both store and transfer funds. Gold is used in all three stages of money laundering: placement, layering, and integration. It is attractive to both criminal and terrorist organizations. Gold also plays an important role in alternative remittance and underground financial systems such as the black market peso exchange, hawala, and fei-chien. In short, there is nothing else like it out there.[1]

As the reader has seen, just about any commodity can be used in TBML. I could launder money with a shipment of apples! However, if a criminal organization wanted to launder lots of dirty money or transfer significant value via trade, gold is one of the favored commodities. Its intrinsic value is high and so is its value to mass. It is a very efficient laundering vehicle.

WHY GOLD IS SO POPULAR WITH MONEY LAUNDERERS

To fully understand why gold's unique properties make it so popular with money launderers, one must consider a wide variety of factors.

Gold Has Been a Haven of Wealth Since Antiquity

Since the dawn of recorded history, in diverse locales and cultures, gold has symbolized wealth and guaranteed power. Its possession has obsessed men and nations, destroying some cultures while helping others expand their influence.

The oldest gold objects discovered thus far were the products of the ancient Thracian civilization, dating from 4000 BC. They were found at a burial site in Varna, Bulgaria.[2] Archaeological digs suggest that the use of gold as a measure of wealth was initiated in the Middle East, where the first-known civilizations began. Egyptian tombs from the third millennium BC have been discovered with gold jewelry. The Egyptians obtained gold via trade with the Nubians of Ethiopia, as well as from their own mines. In West Africa, people traded gold for salt from the Sahara Desert in the north. The Persian Empire, in what is now Iran, made frequent use of gold in artwork as part of the Zoroastrian religion, while the Roman Empire used gold coins as currency. In fact, the acquisition of gold was the main focus of some of the Roman conquests, such as Rumania. Gold has also been important in the cultures of South Asia, China, and Central and South America. Finally, gold was one of the main reasons behind the early European exploration of the Americas. In the Inca civilization, gold was considered the blood of the sun. Gold exploration and mining were also keys to the development and settlement of the American West.

Gold Is a Readily Acceptable Medium of Exchange Anywhere in the World

Early in my career, while working for the U.S. intelligence community, I began training for a covert overseas assignment. I was to be inserted into one of the most remote areas of Africa to link up with a liberation group fighting a Soviet proxy government. In case I ran into trouble and would have to make my way to a nonhostile area, I was outfitted with boots that had gold coins secreted in the insoles. The assignment never materialized. But the reason for this anecdote is that it provides an excellent illustration that gold is recognized as a de facto bearer instrument anywhere in the world. In that sense, it is better than the paper dollar. Gold is an internationally recognized form of currency—even in far-flung and isolated lands.

In Times of Uncertainty and Civil Strife, Gold Is Often More Reliable Than National Currencies

I once traveled to Kuwait shortly after Saddam Hussein's Iraqi army was forcibly expelled by coalition forces. At the time, there were many stories of Kuwaiti citizens who had fled their country during the invasion and occupation. Prior to leaving, they had desperately tried to exchange their dinars and dollars for gold. These actions had many historical precedents. In times of economic or political uncertainty, gold generally increases in value as people seek out the comparative stability it offers. Today, in certain parts of the world, individuals continue to stockpile gold holdings in case they find it necessary to flee.

Indeed, gold is a much better insurance policy, bribe factor, and source of transportable wealth than currency. With it, people can carry much more value on their person than they could via even large-denomination currency, whether they are using specially designed smuggling vests, small bags, or other means. Perhaps most important, gold is accepted at almost any destination—the same might not be true of some national currencies.

Gold Prices Are Fixed Daily in Markets Worldwide, and Gold's Value Is Relatively Constant Over Time

The price of gold is set in international trading markets, and as with most commodities, it fluctuates daily. Yet if gold is selling for $1,200 per ounce in New York, it will sell for the same price in London, Zurich, Tokyo, Dubai, or Johannesburg. The daily price can easily be determined, whether one is consulting financial markets, the Internet, a major newspaper, or visiting an Arabian gold souk (market).

In addition, although the price of gold varies over time, its value remains relatively constant. This is due to the fact that its supply is limited and generally fluctuates no more than a few percentage points annually; the gold in circulation continues to be recycled. Thus, it is the value of the dollar that changes, which in turn affects the price of gold. Because money launderers are businesspeople, they are attracted to the relative constancy that gold offers.

 DID YOU KNOW?

According to the American Museum of Natural History, the total amount of gold ever mined is 152,000 metric tons, or enough to fill 60 tractortrailers. And all of the gold that has ever been refined could be placed into a cube measuring 65.5 feet or 20 meters per side![3]

The Weight and Quality of Gold Can Be Assured

Gold is mined in every continent but Antarctica. Russia, South Africa, the United States, Canada, Australia, and Peru are some of the top producing countries. Gold is generally manufactured into bars and other forms in more limited gold centers, including Switzerland, London, and Dubai. There are strict international standards and safeguards regarding the purity, sizing, and quality of this manufactured gold.

Solid gold bars must be 99.99 percent pure. These bars are sometimes referred to as *four-nine* gold. Depending on the market, the so-called "good delivery bars" are formed into 35.27-ounce kilo bars, about the size of a small brick, which are particularly popular in Western countries and the Middle East. In South Asia, 10-*tola bars* (an Indian unit of weight) are popular; these 3.75-ounce pieces are approximately the size of a candy bar. Wafer-thin *tael bars* are primarily found in the Far East and are manufactured in various shapes and sizes (the tael is an ancient Chinese weight approximately equal to 1.2 ounces).

Gold Offers Easy Anonymity

When investigating traditional money laundering, authorities try to "follow the money" via a paper trail. Financial intelligence can be generated from bank records, identifiers found on currency, electronic codes associated with wire transfers, and numerous other sources. Gold, the commodity, lacks such identifying records. Gold coins, and even gold bars, may have serial or manufacturing numbers that are easily removed. Chemical analysis is generally unable to conclusively trace its origin. Although trade data are generally available (see Chapter 9), matters are complicated because gold's form is readily altered. In other words, there are very few effective ways to follow a disguised or laundered "golden trail."

 GOLD OR DIAMONDS?

I once had a conversation with a source who was involved in the international gold and diamond trades. He told me that diamonds are attractive to money launderers because they are the most condensed form of physical wealth in the world. And they are easy to smuggle. However, he explained that the price of uncut or raw diamonds is somewhat subjective. That's not the case with gold. If you have "four-nine" gold in Europe, the price is the same as "four-nine" gold in the United States or the Middle East. Since money launderers and criminal organizations are attracted to certainty, my source said that generally speaking gold is the favored medium to launder money.

Gold Is Generally Immune to Asset Freezes

Given the proliferation of asset freezing and seizing efforts, criminal and terrorist organizations are often reluctant to deposit liquid assets in financial institutions. Many have realized that it is much more secure to simply hoard assets such as gold outside the formal financial system. For example, in 2007, as part of one of the largest money laundering seizures in history, the Colombian National Police and DEA discovered more than $80 million worth of cash and gold in private residences and businesses, buried in the ground, stashed in private safes, or hidden elsewhere.[4] In 2008, when the European Union threatened new sanctions against Iran, $75 billion worth of Iranian assets were moved from European banks, and some of these funds were reportedly converted to gold.[5] And in a 2009 law enforcement operation targeting a marijuana distribution ring that brought large quantities of the drug from Canada to Saratoga County, New York, authorities found 172 gold bars, 161 gold coins, and a 100-ounce silver bar in one of the conspirators' homes. The items were purchased with money from the drug trade.[6]

There Is a Tremendous Demand for Gold in Various Cultures around the World

Gold plays important cultural roles in much of the world. Throughout their histories, India, China, the Middle East, and Latin America have all treasured gold. It continues to be in high demand whether as jewelry, savings, a type of bearer instrument, a hedge against unexpected currency devaluations, an escape from the tax collector, a means of transporting wealth, or as part of religious/cultural ceremonies such as weddings.

China recently surpassed India as the largest consumer of gold. In 2013, Chinese consumers had purchased a record 1,066 tons of gold, 32 percent more than a year earlier.[7] Historically, Saudis are the world's largest spenders on gold per capita.[8] For example, it is not unusual at Saudi weddings for the bride to be draped with kilos of gold jewelry.

HOW IS GOLD MANIPULATED TO LAUNDER MONEY AND TRANSFER VALUE?

Gold has unique properties that make it fairly easy to manipulate and thus uniquely attractive to money launderers around the world.

Depending on the Need, Gold Can Be Altered in Form

Gold's unique characteristics allow its form to be altered. For example, brokers and traders can change gold bars into various forms of jewelry. Moreover, it is not uncommon for gold to be melted or smelted and poured into special molds. As in the case of Operation Meltdown[9] in New York City (described in the Case Examples section below), the gold was disguised as machine parts, tools, nuts and bolts, belt buckles, and other items. Once cast, these fake golden parts require only a coat of black spray paint and grease, making them much easier to smuggle across borders. Similarly, the Jordanian Customs Bureau told me that there have been instances of gold being smuggled in the form of license plates. The smugglers melted the gold, put it in a license plate mold, painted it to resemble a commonly issued vehicular plate, and simply drove it across the border.[10] Although there are some small expenses associated with the schemes, the alteration of the gold is an acceptable cost of doing business for the illicit actors.

Gold also has myriad industrial uses that facilitate changing the form of gold and give paper justification for illicit transfers. For example, there are often strict controls on gold exports, particularly in countries that mine their own gold. But in some TBML schemes, the conspirators switch from four-nine gold to gold "scrap," which bypasses controls. While scrap gold theoretically lessens the value of the shipment (see Figure 6.1), the new classification works in the favor of those who want to disguise illegally mined artisan gold.[11] Gold scrap is a frequent TBML commodity.

Electronic gold or "e-gold" has been used by criminals laundering illicit money via online accounts. E-gold is yet another way to alter the form of gold. As a result, in the United States the government has

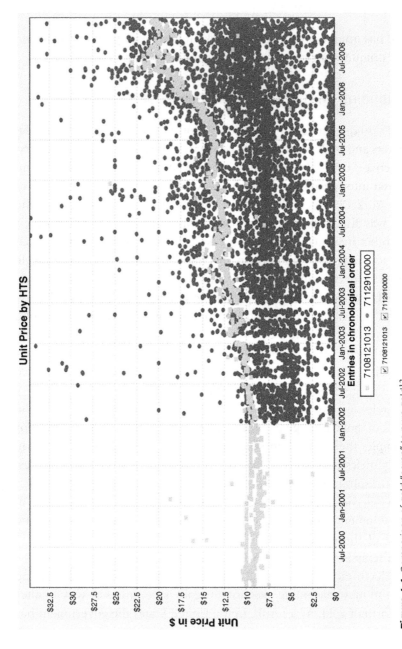

Figure 6.1 Comparison of gold "scrap" to pure gold[12]

moved to ensure that e-gold businesses are licensed and operate under the same regulations as money services businesses.

Figure 6.1 represents the import of solid "four-nine" (99.99%) pure gold in comparison with gold scrap. The horizontal line represents time and the vertical line represents value. The data are taken from a comparison of harmonized tariff schedule entries representing the importation of gold into the United States from various countries in Central and South America. Gold scrap is not defined with precision and invites fraud. Suffice it to say its value and gold content do not approach "four-nine" gold. That being the case, why is the United States importing massive quantities of gold scrap at prices higher than gold bullion? Perhaps criminal organizations are seeking to launder the proceeds of crime by overinvoicing multiple shipments of scrap to send payment out of the country?

Gold Brokers Can "Layer" Transactions That Further Confuse the Paper Trail

As described in Appendix A, layering is simply a method of disguising a money trail via a series of transactions. In traditional money laundering using financial institutions, this is often accomplished by the use of multiple wire transfers from one location or jurisdiction to another. This tactic can be used with gold as well. For example, criminal organizations involved directly or indirectly in the gold business often have "gold accounts" in banks or trading houses, as well as silver accounts, dollar accounts, and local currency accounts. To muddy the trail, they can shift value from one account or institution to another and from one jurisdiction to another. They can even combine this practice with the previous tactic of altering gold's physical form. This type of activity makes it very difficult for criminal investigators to follow the value trail.

Gold Is Susceptible to Double Invoicing, False Shipments, and Other Fraudulent Schemes

Chapter 2 offered an explanation of trade fraud and examples of fictitious invoicing and related schemes. Although most commodities can be used in such schemes, gold is particularly attractive to trade-based money launderers. Because its high value can be condensed into a comparatively small size, gold can be used to launder or transfer larger amounts of value in a single transaction, contrary to other items such as foodstuffs or textiles. Since money launderers generally want the largest return for their efforts, gold's unique properties make it the commodity of choice in various fraudulent schemes.

For example, Colombia's official annual gold exports are reported to be approximately 75 tons although the industry only produces 15 tons.[13] Could the difference be fictitious sales?

Figure 6.2 illustrates how massive quantities of gold were exported from two neighboring countries "into the commerce of the United States" (customs terminology). (*Note:* The graph was created from real data, but many of the details of this case constitute privileged information so the details are omitted.) Neither of these neighboring countries mine or produce gold in notable amounts. According to the U.S. Customs special agent who investigated the case, the spike in exports represented drug proceeds cycling through the region in the

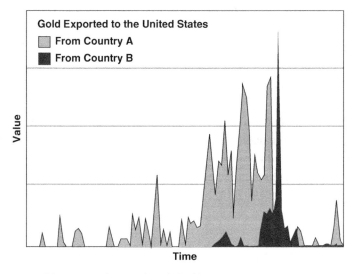

Figure 6.2 Gold exports and money laundering[14]
Source: Cassara and Jorisch, On The Trail of Terror Finance: What Law Enforcement and Intelligence Officers Need to Know *(Washington, DC: Red Cell Publishing, 2010).*

form of gold. As explained in Chapter 2, multiinvoicing is a common TBML technique.

The graph's horizontal axis represents time while the vertical axis represents the value of gold being exported to the United States. The data make clear that when authorities cracked down on the illicit gold trade in Country A and made arrests, the criminal organization responsible for this activity simply relocated to neighboring Country B (additional arrests were eventually made in Country B as well, confirming the shift indicated in the graph).

Gold Is Easily Smuggled

Gold smuggling in various forms has been chronicled around the world. Because of its unique characteristics, it can be altered in form to fit a smuggler's needs. As described previously, it can be melted or smelted into various shapes and sizes, disguised, and smuggled across borders. It can also be concealed on a person, within baggage, or hidden in a shipping container. There are special gold smuggling vests outfitted for smugglers that allow them to transport hundreds of thousands of dollars of gold on their person—much more value than actual paper currency. Some gold bars are even manufactured with special rounded corners and edges so as not to rip courier bags (or sensitive body cavities).

In certain areas of the world, illegal gold mines are also a major problem. For example, in Latin America the last decade has seen a tremendous boom in illegal gold mining that in some cases has eclipsed the cocaine trade as the leading source of criminal income. Guerilla groups such as the Urabeños and the Revolutionary Armed Forces of Colombia (FARC) have set up their own mining operations or charge miners "fees" to operate in territory they control. The gold is then smuggled out of the country or combined with licit production. According to the Colombian Ministry of Defense, in 2014 authorities seized approximately 740 kilos of illegal gold. In 2010, no gold was seized at all.[15] Similar schemes involving gold, illegal mining, smuggling, and money laundering have taken place in Mexico and Peru.[16]

GOLD JEWELRY SMUGGLING FUNDS TERROR

Analysts have observed that Chechen mujahedeen have smuggled gold from various points in Asia to the Arabian Gulf for profit. Their method of transporting gold is simple: instead of bullion, they carry coins and jewelry. In many cases, individual couriers or travelers are fitted with necklaces, earrings, and other pieces—not as a fashion statement, but as an easy method of transporting value from one country to another.[17]

Gold smuggling has been curbed in some regions. However, pilfering and smuggling from mines is still a concern in South Africa, Ghana, and other locations. Although the gold trade in the Indian subcontinent was liberalized in the mid-1990s, Dubai still maintains a shadowy reputation as an international gold smuggling center. In fact, the waterway winding through the port of Dubai has been dubbed "Smugglers Creek" because of its multitude of rarely inspected dhows that ply the Arabian Sea, Indian Ocean, and waters of eastern Africa.

In the United States, customs authorities have investigated cases in which drug proceeds are used to purchase gold from American vendors. The gold is then smuggled across the border into Mexico in the same manner as illicit bulk cash.

In most jurisdictions, gold is exempt from traditional cross-border currency reporting requirements. Vietnam, Italy, Saudi Arabia, Jordan, Taiwan, and Ukraine are among the few countries that mandate the declaration of gold as a form of currency. For example, travelers entering or leaving Vietnam must fill out a cross-border currency declaration form if they are transporting the equivalent of more than approximately $5,000 or more than 300 grams of gold.[18] A customs official opined that almost every woman crossing a customs terminal, anywhere in the world, is carrying gold. He said, "Monitoring this flow of funding can be implemented only through amendments to laws and regulations, including forcing customs declarations for personal precious jewelry. Even then, only a minor portion will be reported."[19]

Gold Is Often the Commodity of Choice in Underground Financial Systems

As per the discussions in Chapter 4 on hawala and Chapter 5 on fei-chien, gold has long been one of the principal means for brokers dealing in underground finance to balance their books. In fact, a 1998 study by the British Commonwealth Secretariat on the misuse of hawala found that "gold smuggling linked to invoice manipulation plays an important role in the settling of accounts between hawaladars."[20] At the time, the Secretariat concluded that if gold (and silver) smuggling were somehow curtailed, 80 to 90 percent of hawala transactions would cease.[21] Although underground financial systems are increasingly diversified today, TBML and value transfer based on the misuse of the international gold trade are still essential.

According to the U.S. Department of State's 2015 INCSR report, in Taiwan, "Jewelry stores increasingly are being used as a type of underground remittance system. Jewelers convert illicit proceeds into precious metals, stones, and foreign currency, and generally move them using cross-border couriers. The tradition of secrecy in the precious metals and stones trade makes it difficult for law enforcement to detect and deter money laundering in this sector."[22]

POSSIBLE QUESTIONS FOR GOLD DEALERS

The following questions may prove helpful to authorities and compliance officers during the course of inquiries dealing with questionable gold transactions. Many are only appropriate for dealers outside the United States, and some are geared toward gathering intelligence.

- Where do you get your supply of gold/gold jewelry? (Include both foreign and domestic sources.)
- Do other local gold dealers generally get their supply from the same source(s)?
- Do you deal in "raw" gold or "worked" gold?
- Do you import or export "gold scrap"?

- How do you keep your records? (Inventory is probably in grams and kilos.)
- Do you have foreign trading partners?
- Do you make jewelry here?
- What types of gold do you sell, and what kinds of customers buy each type?
- Who are your best customers? Why?
- Do clients sell gold here? Why?
- Do people in this area use gold as a form of savings?
- Do you work with individuals involved with remittance systems?
- Are there underground gold markets in this area?
- There are reports that gold is commonly smuggled in and out of the country. Why does this happen?
- Does the government impose taxes or fees on the gold trade? Raw gold? Worked gold?
- Do the gold dealers here have a guild or union?
- Could I meet a guild official?
- Do local gold dealers feel secure? Why/why not?
- Do criminal organizations deal in gold in this area?
- Have you ever been approached by somebody suspicious offering to purchase large amounts of gold for cash?

CASE EXAMPLES

Over the years, there have been some major money laundering investigations involving the misuse of the international gold trade. Chapter 2 contains a summary of Operation Polar Cap—one of the largest such cases in history. The following are some additional examples.

Case Study 1: The Magharian Brothers

The first major case that brought attention to gold's role in international money laundering was the late 1980s investigation targeting

Barkev and Jean Magharian.[23] Operating from hotel rooms in Zurich, these Armenian Lebanese brothers laundered an estimated $1 billion in drug proceeds through gold dealers and Swiss banks with the help of a Bulgarian government connection.

The Magharians were part of an international currency and gold smuggling network. Under their direction, money from drug sales in the United States and elsewhere was smuggled in suitcases to Turkey where it was delivered to gold shops. Acting as a parallel banking system, the shops then forwarded cash to Bulgaria. The security services of the communist Bulgarian government facilitated the shipment of cash to Zurich, where it was deposited into banks by Lebanese and Syrian couriers. Operatives then purchased gold from a Swiss precious metals dealer, transported it to Bulgaria, and smuggled it into Turkey. Once safely in the gold bazaars, it was used to pay the drug traffickers.[24] The trail continued into the boardrooms of the three largest Swiss banks and even to the highest levels of the Swiss government.[25] The Magharian brothers were eventually indicted in California for conspiracy to launder drug money and in New York for selling cocaine.[26]

Case Study 2: Illegal Gold Mining and Tax Fraud in South Africa

According to Global Financial Integrity, South Africa is the fifth largest producer of gold. The gold mining sector represents about 2 percent of the South Africa GDP.[27] Yet there is a growing problem with underground mines in South Africa that are serviced by thousands of illegal gold miners. Many of them are illegal immigrants from neighboring countries. In addition to the criminally mined gold, South African authorities are concerned about the large associated tax fraud.

The South African government doesn't charge value-added tax (VAT) on mined gold. However, like many countries, it does charge tax on processed or "worked" gold. Some of those who traffic in illegally mined gold recognized an opportunity. They disguise the gold as second-hand "scrap" gold. According to the Financial Transparency Coalition, they employ "invoice writers," create false identities, and use trade misinvoicing tricks to produce false documentation that is adequate to pass audits from the tax authorities. They then claim back VAT they never paid. Official corruption is assuredly involved. So South African taxpayers end up paying 14 percent VAT over and above what they lost on the illicit gold itself![28] And not only is the scheme a fraud against the South African treasury, but illegal mining can cause severe environmental degradation. It has also generated gang warfare over turf, robbery, theft, and prostitution.[29]

Case Study 3: Gold Smuggling into Colombia

According to official Colombian statistics, in 2013 Colombia exported 58 metric tons of gold and in 2012 exported 77 metric tons. It is believed more than half of the gold exported may have been smuggled into the country and treated on the books as local production. It is estimated that as much as $3.3 billion of gold was smuggled into Colombia from Venezuela, Panama, Mexico, and Chile. Some of the contraband gold was allegedly sent via trading firms and bought at inflated prices with drug money.[30]

Case Study 4: Operation Meltdown

In a 2003 case, ICE investigators discovered that money launderers were converting the proceeds of narcotics sales to gold. The launderers visited gold jewelers in the greater New York City area and purchased jewelry in various forms. They then melted the gold and recast it into a wide range of common materials such as wrenches, nuts, bolts, belt buckles, and trailer hitches. Sometimes the golden objects were painted and covered with a layer of grease. The disguised gold was then shipped to Colombia to be sold and converted back to cash. "Operation Meltdown" resulted in 23 arrests along with the seizure of 140 kilograms of gold and $1.5 million in cash.[31]

Case Study 5: Fake Gold Sales

A two-year investigation by Colombian law enforcement officials focused on a gold export company. The company reportedly used fake gold sales to launder 2.3 billion pesos (approximately $1 billion). Investigators found that many of the thousands of alleged providers of gold that did business with the suspect company didn't even exist or were registered in the names of deceased individuals. Some of the companies were reportedly linked to Colombia's largest criminal group.[32]

Case Study 6: Cash-for-Gold-for-Drugs

In a 2015 investigation centered in Chicago, 32 people from the United States and Mexico were accused of being involved in a "cash-for-gold" conspiracy that laundered more than $100 million in U.S. drug proceeds for Mexico's Sinoloa drug cartel. Individuals used cash from narcotics sales to purchase gold scrap and gold jewelry in a multistate area. The gold was later sent to precious metal refineries in Florida and California. The refineries sometimes transferred payments for the gold directly to Mexico.[33]

EXAMPLES OF GOLD AND TERRORISM FINANCING

There have been numerous cases over the years that have highlighted the nexus between gold and terrorist financing. For example, the Taliban, al-Qaeda, and affiliated groups have sometimes included gold in their rare public statements about finance:

- In May 2004, Osama bin Laden himself offered a reward for killing American and coalition military commanders; tellingly, he offered the reward in gold.[34]

- In 2005, cartoons of the prophet Muhammad were printed in a Danish newspaper. The resulting publicity caused outrage in the Muslim world. In February 2006, the Taliban offered 100 kilograms of gold to anyone who killed the individuals responsible for the "blasphemous" cartoons.[35]

- On January 4, 2005, an al-Qaeda gold smuggler faced trial by a U.S. military tribunal for his role in gold smuggling and money transfer operations in Afghanistan.[36]

▓ In 2014, there were reports that the terror group ISIS or Islamic
State stole assets from the Mosul Central Bank including gold
bullion.[37]

▓ In 2015, ISIS announced plans to create a Central Bank and use
a gold-based currency.[38]

Besides Islamic extremist groups, there are many other examples
of the terrorist-gold nexus. For example, in the United States, the
Posse Comitatus, a militant right-wing extremist group, believes that
the income tax is illegal and that the dollar is not legal tender. As a
result, the group created a system of barter houses where members
could convert cash into silver bullion and gold coins without any
records being kept of the transactions.[39] In Japan, members of the
Aum Shinrikyo cult entered the Tokyo subway system and released
sarin, a powerful nerve agent—the deadliest assault in the group's
campaign of terror. When law enforcement officers subsequently
raided the cult's headquarters, they found 22 pounds of gold.[40]

CHEAT SHEET

▓ Gold is an intrinsic part of diverse cultures around the world.

▓ Because of gold's unique characteristics and uniformly recognized value, gold has been used frequently in global money
laundering and terrorist financing activities.

▓ Gold is a favored commodity in TBML and value transfer.

▓ Gold prices are fixed daily; its constant value is relatively pre-
dictable, and there are gold markets worldwide.

▓ Gold offers anonymity. Its form can be readily altered as needed.
It is frequently smuggled across borders.

▓ Gold is susceptible to double invoicing, false shipments, and
other fraudulent schemes.

▓ Gold plays an important role in underground financial systems
such as hawala and fei-chien.

▓ Gold is an international medium of exchange that is largely
immune to Western-style financial transparency reporting

requirements and countermeasures such as sanctions, asset freezing, and designations.

NOTES

1. Author's note: Most of the material in this chapter comes from personal experience, observation, source debriefs, and investigations. The narrative was developed
   over the years and was consolidated in *On The Trail of Terror Finance: What Law
   Enforcement and Intelligence Officers Need to Know* (Washington, DC: Red Cell Publishing, 2010), chapter 6, pp. 91–111. Per permission of my co-author Avi Jorisch,
   much of that material is reproduced in this volume with updates and additional case
   examples.

2. Veselin Toshkov, "Archaeologists dig up oldest town in Europe," *National Post*
   (November 1, 2012), available online: http://news.nationalpost.com/2012/11/01/
   archaeologists-unearth-oldest-town-in-europe.

3. American Museum of Natural History, "Gold Fun Facts," available online: http://
   www.amnh.org/exhibitions/past-exhibitions/gold/eureka/gold-fun-facts.

4. U.S. Department of State, Bureau for International Narcotics and Law Enforcement
   Affairs, *International Narcotics Control Strategy Report (INCSR) Volume II, Money Laundering and Financial Crimes* (2007), Introduction, available online: http://www.state
   .gov/j/inl/rls/nrcrpt/2007/vol2/index.htm.

5. Parisa Hafezi and Fredrik Dahl, "Iran Withdraws $75 Billion from Europe," Reuters
   (June 16, 2008), available online: http://www.reuters.com/article/2008/06/16/us-
   iran-assets-withdrawal-idUSDAH63024720080616.

6. Keshia Clukey, "Loot Seized from Pot Ring Goes to Law Enforcement," *Times Union*
   (September 9, 2014), available online: http://www.timesunion.com/local/article/8-
   9M-to-Capital-Region-in-drug-seizure-case-5741858.php.

7. Shu-Ching Jean Chen, "China's Secret Vaults: Where Is all the Missing Gold?"
   Forbes Asia (March 18, 2014), available online: http://www.forbes.com/sites/
   shuchingjeanchen/2014/03/18/chinas-secret-vaults-where-is-all-the-missing-
   gold/.

8. Timothy Green, *The World of Gold* (London: Rosendale Press, 1993).

9. "Operation Meltdown," Immigration and Customs Enforcement; available online:
   http://www.ice.gov/doclib/news/library/reports/cornerstone/cornerstone1-3.pdf.

10. Author conversation with Jordanian authorities in Amman, 2008.

11. Daniela Guzman, "Scrap Metal, Free Trade Zones, and Lack of Accountability for
    Refineries of Fuel Gold Laundering Schemes," ACFCS (March 12, 2015).

12. The data and information about this case was given to the author by a representative
    of ICE.

13. Helen Murphy and Nelson Bocanegra, "Money Laundering Distorts Colom-
    bia's Economic Comeback," Reuters (May 28, 2013), available online:
    http://www.reuters.com/article/2013/05/28/us-colombia-moneylaundering-
    idUSBRE94R03E20130528.

14. The data and information about this case were given to the author by U.S. Customs.
    The graphs were recreated and originally published in *On the Trail of Terror Finance*,
    p. 99.

15. James Bargent, "Colombia's Illegal Mining Crackdown May Be Too Little, Too Late," *Insight Crime* (January 13, 2015), available online: http://www.insightcrime .org/news-briefs/colombia-illegal-mining-crackdown-may-be-too-little-too-late.

16. Elyssa Pachico, "Crime Ring Laundered $1 Billion in Colombia Gold Exports," *Insight Crime* (January 19, 2015), available online: http://www.insightcrime.org/ news-briefs/crime-ring-laundered-a-billion-in-colombia-gold-exports.

17. Joseph Farah, "Financial Squeeze Pushes al-Qaeda South of the Border," *World Net Daily* (March 8, 2004).

18. Vietnam Online, Customs Regulations, available online: http://www.vietnamonline .com/visa/customs-regulations.html.

19. Farah.

20. Commonwealth Secretariat, "Money Laundering: Special Problems of Parallel Economies," paper presented at the Joint Meeting of Commonwealth Finance and Law Officials on Money Laundering, London, June 1–2, 1998, p. 16.

21. Ibid.

22. U.S. Department of State, Bureau for International Narcotics and Law Enforcement Affairs, *International Narcotics Control Strategy Report (INCSR) Volume II, Money Laundering and Financial Crimes* (March 2015), Taiwan country report, available online: http://www.state.gov/j/inl/rls/nrcrpt/2015/vol2/index.htm.

23. Steve Greenhouse, "Zurich Journal: In a Clean Land, Even Dirty Money Gets Washed," *New York Times* (April 4, 1989).

24. R.T. Naylor, *Wages of Crime* (London: Cornell University Press, 2002), p. 201.

25. Ibid.

26. Greenhouse.

27. Channing May, "Good as Gold? South African's Problem with Illegal Gold Mining is Severe and Growing," Global Financial Integrity (November 20, 2014), available online: http://www.gfintegrity.org/good-gold-south-africas-problem-illegal-gold-mining-severe-growing/.

28. Naomi Fowler, "Exposed: Illegal Gold, Trade Mis-invoicing and Tax Fraud in South Africa," Financial Transparency Coalition (September 26, 2014), available online: http://www.financialtransparency.org/2014/09/26/exposed-illegal-gold-trade-mis-invoicing-and-tax-fraud-in-south-africa/.

29. May.

30. Andrew Willis, "Gold Traders Investigated in Colombian Cocaine Laundering," *Bloomberg* (May 26, 2014), available online: http://www.bloomberg.com/news/ 2014-05-23/gold-traders-investigated-in-colombian-cocaine-laundering.html.

31. "Operation Meltdown."

32. Pachico.

33. "Thirty Two Defendants Facing Federal or State Charges Alleging the Laundering of over $100 Million in Narcotics Proceeds through Cash-for-Gold Scheme," U.S. Attorney's Office Northern District of Illinois Press Release, February 11, 2015, available online: http://www.justice.gov/usao/iln/pr/chicago/2015/pr0211_02.html.

34. Maggie Michael, "Bin Laden Said to Offer Gold for Killings," Associated Press, (May 7, 2006).

35. "Taliban Offers Reward," *Dawn.com* (February 9, 2006).

36. Paisley Dodds, "Accused Gold Smuggler Faces Tribunal," Associated Press (January 4, 2005).

37. Terrence McCoy, "ISIS Just Stole $425 Million, Iraqi Governor Says, and Became the 'World's Richest Terrorist Group," *Washington Post* (June 12, 2014); available online: http://www.washingtonpost.com/news/morning-mix/wp/2014/06/12/isis-just-stole-425-million-and-became-the-worlds-richest-terrorist-group.

38. Kenneth Schortgen Jr., "Terror Group ISIS to Open Central Bank and Prepare for Gold-Backed Currency," *Examiner.com* (January 6, 2015), available online: http://www.examiner.com/article/terror-group-isis-to-open-central-bank-and-prepare-for-gold-backed-currency.

39. Naylor, p. 200.

40. Ibid., p. 206

CHAPTER **7**

Commercial TBML

T BML is generally considered to be a money-laundering methodology that is used to wash the proceeds of criminal activities such as narcotics trafficking, weapons smuggling, the trafficking of persons, and intellectual property rights violations. As we have discussed, TBML is also used in evading taxes and customs duties. TBML schemes are also sometimes used to circumvent restrictions on capital flows. Informal value transfer systems—a subset of TBML—such as hawala and fei-chien are also used.

Unfortunately, commercial enterprises also misuse trade in other suspect ways. International businesses and brokers engage in fraud and deceptive trade practices to obfuscate the money trail and transfer value for profit. Sometimes this takes the form of lowering taxes or claiming government trading incentives. The commercial misuse of trade goes hand-in-hand with the criminal misuse of trade. We cannot succeed in stopping criminals while we turn a blind eye to multinationals using misinvoicing and abusive transfer pricing as they choose. While commercial TBML is not the focus of this book, the reader should be aware of some common techniques such as trade diversion, misinvoicing, and transfer pricing. While some of the schemes may be generally accepted and legal per se, they often have the look and feel of their sister TBML scams.

TRADE DIVERSION

In international economics and finance, there are various types and definitions of trade diversions. For the purpose of commercial trade-based value transfer, trade diversion is considered one of the more sophisticated forms of laundering large amounts of money.[1] Like other forms of trade-based money laundering, commercial trade diversion often relies on hiding in plain sight; suspect or fraudulent transactions are disguised as legitimate, often using well-known firms to accomplish the transfer.

In trade diversion schemes, generally speaking, the conspirators take advantage of the fact that pricing differentials of goods can vary greatly from market to market and from country to country and are often based on narrow regulations and legislation in particular markets. In an international trade situation, a business or broker that offers a lower-cost product for importation into a particular country tends to create a trade diversion away from another importer or local producers whose prices are higher for a similar product.[2] According to the late Donald deKieffer, an international trade attorney who studied trade diversion schemes, "The amount of people who are actually masters of the technique is fairly limited. These individuals, however, move millions of dollars every day in international commerce, largely undetected."[3]

 Trade diversion is considered a gray market activity. The key criterion is that the product is genuine. However, sometimes counterfeit goods are mixed into the shipment. The global risk is growing due to complex international commerce and finance.[4]

The "U-boat" commercial trade diversion scheme is popular in many international locations. Let's use the following hypothetical example where a buyer or a professional "diverter" directly or indirectly approaches a U.S. manufacturer and multinational corporation. Famous consumer brands such as Kraft, Johnson & Johnson, and Procter & Gamble have immediate brand recognition and are sought after around the world, so diverters often seek out these and other well-known companies. The diverters use a veneer of authenticity, often using shell companies and fronts to facilitate the transaction. The lack of transparency and beneficial owner information creates difficulties in later following the paper trail.

The broker/buyer/diverter presents a large and seemingly legitimate order. A sophisticated seller such as a large U.S. multinational will generally insist on an irrevocable letter of credit (L/C)—see Chapter 9. The conspirators in the scheme have relationships with financial institutions that can issue an L/C acceptable to the seller. When asked the destination of the product, the "buyer" most likely will indicate a legitimate market that is not served by the multinational manufacturer. The proposal might be presented in such a way as the buyer/broker will help the manufacturer "break into a new market."

While there is nothing wrong with the above scenario, there are a few alarming possibilities:

1. When the buyer/broker takes control of the goods, the shipment could be diverted to a proscribed destination or sold to a front that acts as a broker for a prohibited end-user such as Iran or North Korea.

2. The goods could be diverted and sold back in the original country of origin—in the current example, the United States.

The first scenario is self-explanatory. The reason the second scheme is sometimes called *U-boating* is that upon purchase, the goods are frequently transshipped via an intermediary location. Rotterdam and Dubai are among the favored diversion locations. The containers are stripped, stuffed, and reloaded (in a manner similar to the method described in Chapter 2). The goods are then shipped right back to the country of origin. In the United States, taxes and tariffs are not paid to import the goods since customs law provides "duty-free treatment for U.S. goods returned."[5] (Many other countries have similar provisions.) A co-conspirator takes possession of the goods and they are sold and distributed at sometimes-steep discounts to prevailing prices. As a result, U.S. manufactured name-brand goods can sometimes be found in the U.S. black and gray markets and suspect distribution channels. They even surface in "big-box" discount stores.

The U-boat scheme requires an international network of conspirators. According to deKieffer, there are dozens of trading companies in Switzerland, Dubai, Singapore, the United Kingdom, and other locations that specialize in these types of transactions. Generally speaking, diversion purchases of the type described above are rarely less than $100,000 and often in the multimillions of dollars.[6]

Trade diversion can have disastrous effects when counterfeit goods are sometimes introduced into the equation. Particularly in the case of pharmaceuticals, it is very difficult to determine the difference between goods acquired in the gray market from those sold via legitimate trade. And illegal pharmaceuticals pose a potential safety hazard, as they often do not pass through a controlled and regulated supply chain. Even in the United States, a highly regulated and protected market, diverted pharmaceuticals have penetrated the supply chain.

Figure 7.1 Pricing arbitrage through diversion

Using a hypothetical example of the sale of ABC medicine manufactured in the United States, per Figure 7.1 the selling price can vary dramatically in different markets. Yet it's the same medicine. This type of pricing arbitrage is unlike the fraudulent invoicing described in Chapter 2. Invoices are not used to launder money or transfer value in the form of a trade good, but rather product is diverted for profit.

The complex international supply chain for medicine provides a platform of opportunity for unscrupulous secondary wholesalers and traders to illegally divert product. Sometimes the medicine is passed through a wide array of other entities before reaching the end provider and patient or a bricks-and-mortar pharmacy.[7] Two cases dramatically illustrate this type of commercial trade-based value transfer.

Example 1: Illegally Diverted Cancer Drug

An online pharmacy network based in Canada was investigated for its involvement in procuring illegally diverted pharmaceuticals. The Canadian company did not use best business practices and began to buy product in far-flung countries that drug safety experts say have lax regulation and problems with counterfeiting. In one case, purchase orders were made for Avastin—a lifesaving drug for some patients with cancer. The orders originated through a U.K. business, with a Barbados affiliate. Reportedly, the Barbados company owned or controlled some of the companies involved with the subsequent diversion.

Product was obtained through a Danish company, which in turn purchased the product from a licensed Swiss company. The cancer drug was originally ordered through an unlicensed Egyptian company, which obtained counterfeit drugs in Turkey using a Syrian broker.[8] In the bastardized supply chain, some of the diverted and counterfeit Avastin ended up in the tightly controlled U.S. distribution network.

Example 2: HIV Drugs Destined for Africa Diverted to Europe

Drug maker GlaxoSmithKline participated in an HIV drug-discount program for developing countries. At the time, Combivar HIV anti-viral medication was selling for approximately $6 a pill in Western Europe. It was to be offered for sale at 80 cents a pill in sub-Sahara Africa.

Glaxo used airfreight companies to ship the medicine to Africa. However, once on the ground, the shipments were sent to multiple companies and then finally to an airfreight service employed by the diverters. In a type of U-turn transaction, the HIV drugs were then flown back to Europe and were introduced by middlemen into the regular supply chain for medicines. The African-destined version of Combivar was identical to the European version, thus mitigating scrutiny. The scheme was finally detected when customs inspectors in Belgium noticed irregularities in a shipment of HIV drugs sent from Senegal.[9]

TRADE MISINVOICING

According to Raymond Baker, the head of Global Financial Integrity (GFI) and a worldwide authority on financial crime, "Trade misinvoicing—a prevalent form of trade based money laundering—accounts for nearly 80 percent of all illicit financial outflows that can be measured using available data."[10]

The rapidly increasing volume of international trade exacerbates the situation. During my career with U.S. Customs, I observed first-hand the never-ending balancing act between efforts to promote commerce on the one hand against security and revenue concerns on the other. Because of the enormous pressures on customs services around the world to process commercial shipments as quickly as possible, trade misinvoicing is a comparatively low-risk endeavor for fraudsters—especially conspirators that only misrepresent their transactions by a moderate amount. If a buyer and seller do not get too greedy, their odds of getting caught are very slim.

 ## "BUT THAT'S WHAT WE DO!"

I once had a conversation with a Dubai-based trader who was under investigation. I discussed with him trade-based money laundering and misinvoicing. At the close of my discourse with him, the trader looked at me with incredulous eyes. He finally said, "Mr. John, money laundering? But that's what we do." Precisely.

On another occasion in Istanbul, I was shopping for a carpet in the Grand Bazaar. After a suitable amount of haggling, the seller and I agreed upon a price. After I paid him, he asked me what kind of receipt I wanted. "What do you mean?" "Well, he replied, I can give you a true receipt, a receipt with a lower amount you can present to your customs, or a receipt with a higher value you can keep for insurance purposes." It goes without saying that the vendor would create his own sales invoice for his tax purposes.

The point of these anecdotes is that sometimes the way of doing business in certain environments is not necessarily considered illegal or immoral. It is simply the way things are done, have been done, and will probably continue to be done. If there is an opportunity to maximize profits, pay fewer taxes, take advantage of the system, and avoid government scrutiny for both buyers and sellers, it makes perfect sense.

So how do companies misinvoice trade goods? In many areas corruption and poor governance come into play, but according to GFI, legal gray areas and financial secrecy are the most important facilitators.[11] An essential component of re-invoicing is sending profits offshore.

 "Re-invoicing is the use of a tax haven corporation to act as an intermediary between an onshore business and his customers outside his home country. The profits of this intermediary corporation and the onshore business allow the accumulation of some, or all, profits on transactions to be accrued to the offshore company."[12]

An excellent explanation of how the re-invoicing process works comes from GFI's Brian LeBlanc. I am quoting his imaginary example:[13]

> Let's assume the following scenario: imagine a hypothetical Zambian exporter of copper arranges a deal with a buyer in the United States worth $1,000,000. Now, let's assume that the Zambian company only wishes to report $600,000 to government officials to circumvent paying mining royalties and corporate income tax.
>
> First, the Zambian exporter sets up a shell company in Switzerland, which (because of anonymity) cannot be traced back to him. By doing so, any transaction the Zambian exporter conducts with the shell company will look like trade with an unrelated party. Thus, even if the Zambian government suspects some wrongdoing, it will be very difficult, or impossible, to tie the Zambian exporter to the shell company in Switzerland.
>
> Second, the exporter then uses the shell company to purchase the copper from the exporter in Zambia for a value of $600,000, $400,000 less than the true value of the copper. An invoice that shows receipt for the $600,000 copper sale is then forwarded on to Zambia tax collectors.
>
> Third, the shell company in Switzerland then re-sells the copper to the ultimate buyer in the United States for the agreed-upon $1,000,000. The importer is instructed to make a payment to the shell company, and the goods are sent directly from Zambia to the United States without ever even passing through Switzerland.
>
> Thus, the Zambian exporter lowered its taxable revenue from $1,000,000 to $600,000. The remaining $400,000 remains hidden in Switzerland where it is untaxed and unutilized for development purposes.

Figure 7.2 helps explain the process visually.

TRANSFER PRICING

There is nothing illegal per se about transfer pricing. Transfer pricing is not used to launder criminal proceeds, but rather to lower taxes

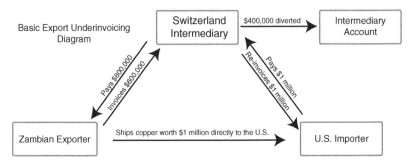

Figure 7.2 Basic export underinvoicing diagram[14]

Source: http://www.gfintegrity.org/press-release/trade-misinvoicing-or-how-to-steal-from-africa

and increase profits. It is a fact of international commerce and occurs millions of times every day. However, *abusive* transfer pricing or the manipulation of the international trading system within the same multinational group to take advantage of lower jurisdictional tax rates represents enormous tax loss in the producing country. The magnitude of transfer pricing is difficult to determine but is believed to be in the hundreds of billions of dollars per year.[15] Transfer pricing is found in both the developed and developing world but most dramatically affects poor countries, robbing them of needed revenue. According to tax expert Lee Sheppard of Tax Analysts, "Transfer pricing is the leading edge of what is wrong with international tax."[16]

 Approximately 60 percent of international trade happens within multinationals—not between. In other words, the trade flows across national borders but stays within the same corporate group.[17]

If two unrelated companies trade with each other across international boundaries, there is generally negotiation on price, resulting in a fair or market-driven charge. This is known as *arm's-length* trading and is considered acceptable for tax purposes. But if two companies jointly owned by a parent multinational group artificially distort the price of the recorded trade to minimize the tax bill, this becomes an issue of concern—particularly when the tax liability is shifted to a low-tax or tax-free haven.

The reader may recall during the explanation of TBML in Chapter 2, that when a buyer and seller are working together, the price of a good (or service) can be whatever the two parties want it to be. Although the above rule of thumb applied to TBML and illicit proceeds, the same applies to commercial transfer pricing.

So how does transfer pricing work?

Per Figure 7.3, Global Inc. is a hypothetical multinational headquartered in Canada. Tax Haven Inc., South Africa Inc., U.K. Inc., and Other Global partner companies are all subsidiaries of Global and part of the same multinational group.

Global Inc. produces a variety of food products and wants to maximize its profit by lowering its tax rates. Per Figure 7.3, South Africa Inc. sells the product to Tax Haven Inc. at an artificially low price. This results in South Africa Inc. having low profits and the government of South Africa receiving little tax revenue. Then Tax Haven Inc. sells the product to U.K. Inc. at a very high price. The sale price per unit between the corporations is almost as high as the final retail price per unit offered for sale in the U.K. This results in U.K. Inc. having a very low tax bill and the U.K. government not receiving much revenue. In contrast, Tax Haven Inc. (part of the Global Inc. multinational family), bought the product at a very low price and sold it at very high price.

Tax Haven Inc.'s profits are enormous. But since it is in a tax haven jurisdiction, it has little tax liability. The end result is that Global Inc. artificially shifted its profits out of both South Africa and the United Kingdom and into a tax haven. Tax revenue was likewise shifted from South Africa and the United Kingdom and converted into higher profits

Figure 7.3 Transfer pricing scheme

for the multinational Global Inc.[18] According to international trade expert Dr. John Zdanowicz, "It is not really necessary to move corporate headquarters to slash taxes and increase profits. What is necessary is to move taxable income."[19]

 ## TRANSFER PRICING AND SOUTH AFRICA

There are reports that mining companies in Africa are the continent's most significant tax dodgers. With approximately 6,000 subsidiaries, many of which are located in tax havens, the big mining companies have ready networks for transfer pricing and misinvoicing—whether legal or not. For example, data on South African diamond production show that the uncut or rough value of South African diamonds in 2011 was $1.73 billion. Yet, according to a Tax Statistics Report, produced by the South African Treasury and Revenue Service, the two largest diamond-producing companies that account for 95 percent of the country's production paid just $11 million in mining royalties from 2010 to 2011.[20] Transfer pricing was largely responsible.

The hemorrhage of needed tax revenue is enormous—particularly in the developing world. There are real societal losses connected to trade misinvoicing and transfer pricing. According to Global Financial Integrity, "For each $1 developing nations receive in foreign aid, $10 in illicit money flows abroad—facilitated by secrecy in the global financial system. Beyond bleeding the world's poorest economies, this propels crime, corruption, and tax evasion globally."[21]

The human costs of commercial trade-based money and value transfer are the strongest arguments for international trade transparency and why this issue must be the next frontier in financial crimes enforcement.

 ## LUXEMBOURG—EXAMPLE OF A TAX HAVEN

Luxembourg has been called a "magical fairyland" for well-known corporations that seek to drastically minimize their tax bills. Pepsi, IKEA, Coach, Abbott Laboratories, Deutsche Bank, and the Abu Dhabi Investment Authority are only a few of the approximately 340 companies that have secured deals in Luxembourg that allow them legally to slash their taxes—in some cases, at tax rates of less than 1 percent on the profits they shifted into the European duchy. In many cases, the Luxembourg subsidiaries of multinationals that handle hundreds of millions of dollars in business maintain only a token presence. For example, the address of 5, rue Guillaume Kroll, is home to more than 1,600 companies.[22]

CHEAT SHEET

- Generally speaking, commercial TBML is not usually considered to be a vehicle used to launder illicit proceeds.

- Commercial TBML is widespread in international commerce and is used primarily to maximize profits and minimize taxes.

- Three prominent forms of commercial TBML are trade diversion, trade misinvoicing, and transfer pricing.

- Like other forms of TBML, commercial trade diversion often relies on hiding in plain sight.

- Participants in these schemes take advantage of the fact that pricing differentials of goods can vary greatly from market to market and from country to country and are often based on narrow regulations and legislation in particular markets. They rely on a type of arbitrage: buying goods cheaply and selling them dearly.

- Trade diversion is considered a gray-market activity. One of its most prominent forms is the U-boat scheme where genuine product is purchased at a very favorable price and is rerouted or diverted from its intended international market and "returned" to the country of production. There is generally no duty on returning goods. The goods are often resold on the black market or fraudulently into suspect distribution channels.

- An essential component of re-invoicing is sending profits offshore.

- Approximately 60 percent of international trade happens within multinationals—not between.

- If two unrelated companies trade with each other, there is generally negotiation on price. This results in a fair or market-driven charge. The process is known as arm's-length trading and is considered acceptable for tax purposes.

■ If two or more companies jointly owned by a parent multinational group artificially distort the price of the recorded trade to minimize the tax bill, this becomes an issue of concern—particularly when the tax liability is shifted to a low-tax or tax-free haven. This is known as transfer pricing.

NOTES

1. Donald E. deKieffer, "Trade Diversion as a Fund Raising and Money Laundering Technique of Terrorist Organizations," *Countering the Financing of Terrorism* (London and New York: Routledge Publishing, 2008), Chapter 7, pp. 150–173. In addition, in 2010 the author had conversations with Mr. deKieffer in Washington, D.C.

2. See: http://www.businessdictionary.com/definition/trade-diversion.html.

3. Ibid., p. 151.

4. "RX-360 Supply Chain Security White Paper—Illegal Diversion of Pharmaceuticals," RX 360—An International Pharmaceutical Supply Chain Consortium, April 30, 2013; available online: http://rx-360.org/LinkClick.aspx?fileticket=UgkgMFRt0ak%3D&tabid=358.

5. U.S. Customs and Border Protection website, available online: https://help.cbp.gov/app/answers/detail/a_id/375/~/duty-on-u.s.-made-goods-returning-to-the-u.s.

6. deKieffer, p. 152.

7. RX-360.

8. RX-360; and Christopher Weaver and Jeanne Whalen, "How Fake Cancer Drugs Entered U.S," *Wall Street Journal* (July 20, 2012), available online: http://online.wsj.com/articles/SB10001424052702303879604577410430607090226.

9. "HIV Drugs for Africa Diverted to Europe," *Washington Post* (October 2, 2002), available online: http://www.hst.org.za/news/hiv-drugs-africa-diverted-europe.

10. "The Economist Highlights the Scourge of Trade Misinvoicing," Global Financial Integrity (May 2, 2014), available online: http://www.gfintegrity.org/press-release/the-economist-highlights-the-scourge-of-trade-misinvoicing/.

11. Brian LeBlanc, "Trade Misinvoicing, or How to Steal from Africa," *Think Africa Press* (May 7, 2014), available online: http://thinkafricapress.com/economy/trade-misinvoicing-how-to-steal-from-africa.

12. Ibid.

13. Ibid.; this section including the definition of "re-invoicing" is used with the generous permission of Global Financial Integrity.

14. Ibid.

15. "Transfer Pricing," Tax Justice Network, available online: http:///www.taxjustice.net/topics/corporate-tax/transfer-pricing/.

16. "Top U.S. Tax Expert in Savage Attack on Transfer Pricing Rules," Tax Justice Network (August 23, 2012), available online: http://taxjustice.blogspot.ch/2012/08/top-us-tax-expert-in-savage-attack-on.html.

17. "Transfer Pricing," Tax Justice Network.

18. Ibid. The example and illustration are similar to the hypothetical explanation found in the referenced article.

19. June 26, 2015, telephone conversation between the author and Dr. John Zdanowicz.

20. Jeff Rudin, "SA Biggest Losers in Transfer Pricing," *Business Report* (June 22, 2014), available online: http://www.iol.co.za/business/opinion/sa-biggest-losers-of-transfer-pricing-1.1707152#.VF4mKmd0zIU.

21. Global Financial Integrity website: http://www.gfintegrity.org/.

22. Leslie Wayne, Kelly Carr, Marina Walker Guevara, Mar Cabra, and Michael Hudson, "Leaked Documents Expose Global Companies' Secret Tax Deals in Luxembourg," *International Consortium of Investigative Journalists (ICIJ)* (November 5, 2014), available online: http://www.icij.org/project/luxembourg-leaks/leaked-documents-expose-global-companies-secret-tax-deals-luxembourg.

CHAPTER 8

More Schemes and Facilitators

A s noted in the preface of this book, TBML and value transfer are very broad topics. Included are a variety of schemes and facilitators that do not fit neatly into a clearly defined category. Yet they are often intertwined throughout TBML. So this chapter is a bit of a "catch-all" and includes some components of TBML that don't tidily fit anywhere else. They are important because they enhance understanding of the overall concept. These miscellaneous items include: barter trade; service-based laundering; free trade zones; the Afghan Transit Trade; the Tri-Border area, and carousel fraud.

BARTER TRADE

The concept of value transfer goes back thousands of years, long before the modern concept of coins, paper money, monetary instruments, or electronic blips in an electronic wire transfer. Historically, all commerce is based on exchange, and originally took the form of barter. One party in a transaction traded, exchanged, or swapped an item or commodity or service for another. Bartering is perhaps the most basic form of trade. "I'll trade you flour for sheepskins." To this day, bartering enjoys many advantages and continues to be practiced around the world—particularly in areas where money is scarce, currency is frequently devalued, there is high taxation, or there are forms of economic and political uncertainty.

Today, barter trade is also growing in developed countries. It is often facilitated by the Internet and social networking sites that readily advertise and match goods and services to exchange. Check out dozens of trading websites that entice clients: "Buy, Sell, List or Trade for FREE!" Modern bartering can be as simple as trading a box of apples for a box of oranges. One could barter a haircut for babysitting service. Somebody could barter a car for a tractor. As was the case thousands of years ago, people exchange things they might have in excess or no longer want for things they feel they need.

Low-level bartering between individuals and small businesses is often off the books. Yet for larger transactions, even though money is not being exchanged, in most jurisdictions there are tax implications for both parties. Generally speaking, the goods or services bartered are supposed to be recorded at fair market value.

The problem, of course, is that criminals also barter. When this occurs, bartering an illicit commodity and transferring value via bartering are forms of TBML. And for the most part, the bartering of illicit goods is completely off the radar screen of authorities. There is no paper trail or financial intelligence reports—our primary financial crimes countermeasure.

Many different types of illegal goods (and services) are bartered. The following are just a few examples of criminal barter trade focusing on narcotics. In some parts of the world, narcotics are not really thought of as something illicit but as simply a type of commodity that can be bought, sold, or traded:

- In certain areas of Afghanistan and Pakistan, the going rate for a kilo of heroin is a color television set.[1]

- In South Africa, methaqualone, also known as mandrax (a recreational narcotic), is exchanged for diamonds.[2]

- In Afghanistan, warlords exchange one commodity they have—opium—for others they want such as SUVs.[3]

- In Canada, drug dealers use diamonds to pay drug suppliers, which are then sold to jewelry stores in small increments to avoid detection.[4]

- In a 2013 investigation in southern Indiana and western Kentucky, it was determined that narcotics obtained from sources in Texas and Mexico were brought to Indiana for distribution. The drugs were bartered or exchanged for weapons that were transported to the Cartel del Golfo in Mexico.[5]

SERVICE-BASED LAUNDERING

Service-based money laundering is exactly what the name implies. Instead of laundering money or transferring value through trade goods, services are used. Similar to TBML, service-based laundering revolves around invoice fraud and manipulation. We are not necessarily talking about the predicate offense of fraud—for example, fraudulent Medicare billing practices—but rather, using services (real or fictitious) as a means to launder money. Many of the same techniques explained in Chapter 2 are employed. Invoices are generated and payment is made. Similar to TBML involving commodities, there could be multiple invoices generated for the same service, over- or underinvoicing, and so on. Common fraudulent service-based laundering scams include accounting, legal, marketing, and natural resource exploration fees.

I once visited Belgrade and authorities told me about a case where organized crime used fraudulent invoices generated from "music concert promotions" as a technique to send illicit funds to Cyprus. Similarly, in the State Department's 2015 INCSR country report on Montenegro, it is reported that "in some cases, off-shore companies send fictitious bills to a Montenegrin company (for market research, consulting, software, leasing, etc.) for the purpose of extracting money from the company's account in Montenegro so funds can be sent abroad. It is a form of service-based laundering."[6]

In TBML, authorities can often track an item or a commodity. They can follow a physical trail. In service-based laundering, an invoice is presented. What authority is able to judge its validity? From an investigative standpoint, it's much more difficult to track a service. And in international transactions, there are difficulties surrounding competence, jurisdiction, and venue. I believe we will be seeing more cases of service-based laundering.

FREE TRADE ZONES

Free trade zones (FTZs) are designated geographic areas outside of normal customs areas and procedures. FTZs and similar districts generally offer duty- and tax-free access and sometimes incorporate a number of other incentives for businesses. They provide a preferential environment for goods and services usually associated with exports.

The number of FTZs has proliferated in recent years. They are often included in economic growth plans for the developing world but are also hubs of manufacturing, trading, and innovation for developed countries. They promote trade, support new businesses, and encourage direct foreign investment. A typical general-purpose zone often provides leasable storage or distribution space to users in general warehouse-type buildings with access to various modes of transportation. Many FTZ projects allow users to construct their own facilities. Some FTZs are also located in regional financial centers and trade and transportation hubs. These features, combined with an unfortunate lack of comprehensive oversight in many of the zones, sometimes attract criminal activity. FTZs can be conducive to TBML and value transfer schemes.[7]

In 2015, there were approximately 4,300 FTZs around the world, and three out of four countries have at least one.[8] Hundreds of billions of dollars' worth of goods are transferred through FTZs every year.[9] In just one example, the Colon Free Zone in Panama, the world's second largest FTZ, generated approximately $31 billion in exports and re-exports in 2012.[10]

Although ownership of FTZs varies, oftentimes public or private corporations operate the facilities or sometimes contract for their operation.

In addition to FTZs, common terms for these areas include *special economic zones, enterprise zones, freeports,* and *export processing zones.*[11] Each type has distinguishing features. In the United States, Customs and Border Protection (CBP) calls these types of facilities *foreign trade zones.*[12]

Under foreign trade zone procedures, the usual formal CBP entry procedures and payments of duties are not required on the foreign merchandise unless it enters CBP territory for U.S. domestic consumption. While in the zone, merchandise is not subject to U.S. duty or excise tax. Certain tangible personal property is generally exempt from state and local ad valorem taxes. Domestic goods moved into the zone for export are considered exported upon admission to the zone for purposes of excise tax rebates and drawback. CBP duty and federal excise tax, if applicable, are paid when the merchandise is transferred from the zone for consumption. Goods may be exported from the zone free of duty and excise tax.[13]

The Financial Action Task Force (FATF) believes that many of the rules and regulations governing FTZs are outdated. The proliferation of FTZs has not kept up with the latest AML/CFT developments and sometimes anti–money laundering safeguards do not apply to businesses and transactions within these special areas.[14]

Goods introduced into an FTZ often undergo various economic modifications such as manufacturing, processing, warehousing, repackaging, and relabeling, as well as storage, marketing, delivery, and transshipment.[15] Although the rules vary, generally the modifications to the product are tax free. The sheer volume in trade and the size and scope of many of the FTZs make it very difficult to effectively monitor incoming and outgoing cargo. Some shipments in and out of the zones must be turned around within 24 hours. The volume and time constraints combine to limit effective monitoring.

As we have seen in previous chapters, TBML schemes often involve false invoicing and other forms of fictitious documentation that misrepresents the contents, quality, or quantity of the goods involved. The scope of customs inspection and control over goods introduced into FTZs vary from one jurisdiction to another. I have personally visited a number of FTZs in the Middle East. I've observed that official oversight varies greatly. Yet particularly in high-risk jurisdictions, it is fair to say that lax safeguards allow opportunities for abuse, including purchases using tainted bulk cash, the processing of counterfeit goods, smuggling, black market operations, and various types of customs fraud and TBML.

THE AFGHAN TRANSIT TRADE

The first time I visited Afghanistan in 2006, I asked a gathering of Afghan bankers, hawala brokers, and businessmen how the Taliban and warlords launder drug proceeds and finance terrorism. Without exception, they said that illicit money was laundered not via Afghanistan's licensed banks, but primarily through trade and its link to regional hawala networks. This should not be a surprise in a country where an estimated 80–90 percent of economic activity is in the informal sector, and where some 80 percent of the population is illiterate.

The heartbreaking political and social situation in Afghanistan requires no explanation. But most do not understand that TBML and value transfer help enable the corruption, poor governance, underground finance, and terror that grip the nation. Entrenched TBML and its corollaries such as underground finance have found a laboratory in South Asia, Iran, and parts of the Middle East.

Before we begin to discuss the misuse of trade and the Afghan Transit Trade and their role in TBML and the finance of terror, a brief review of the role of Afghanistan in the production of narcotics is required.

Opium is one of the few Afghan commodities that outsiders value. According to the U.N. Office on Drugs and Crime (UNODC) and the Afghan counter-narcotics ministry, in 2013 the amount of land under opium cultivation jumped to approximately 209,000 hectares (516,000 acres).[16] Afghanistan produces more than 80 percent of the world's illicit opium.[17] The country is also one of the world's largest suppliers of cannabis—in fact, it produces more drugs overall than Colombia, Peru, and Bolivia combined.[18]

There are estimates that that over one-third of Afghanistan's licit and illicit gross domestic product is derived from the drug trade,[19] with some observers asserting that it makes up as much as half the country's economy. The situation will assuredly become even worse as U.S. and coalition forces complete their withdrawal from the country.

Afghan opium is refined into morphine and heroin by production labs, which are increasingly being established inside Afghanistan's borders. The drugs are often broken into small shipments and smuggled across porous borders via truck or mule caravan for resale abroad. The ancient smuggling routes follow mountainous trails out of Afghanistan into Pakistan, Iran, Turkmenistan, Uzbekistan, and other neighboring countries.[20]

According to the UNODC, approximately 60 percent of Afghanistan's opium is trafficked across the Afghan-Iranian border. Some of the narcotics remain within Iran—a nation with one of the highest rates of addiction in the world.[21] In order to reach lucrative markets in Europe, traditional smuggling routes continue through Iran into Turkey and the Balkans. In addition, more and more Afghan drugs are moving into the increasingly lucrative Russian market via routes that wind through many of Afghanistan's northern neighbors.

Opium gum itself is often used as a currency in Afghanistan, especially by rural farmers. Moreover, opium stockpiles are a store of value in prime production areas. As a result, a type of barter trade has developed whereby drugs are sometimes exchanged for trade goods (see above on barter trade). Although a simplistic formula, drugs are smuggled out of Afghanistan and trade goods come in. So how do many of the goods actually reach the country?

Although Afghanistan is landlocked, it has brokered favorable agreements with several neighboring countries to facilitate the movement of goods. Under a 1965 bilateral treaty with Pakistan called the

Afghan Transit Trade Agreement, Afghan imports or exports moved through the Pakistani port of Karachi are exempt from Pakistani duties or customs tariffs. The treaty was subsequently expanded. In 1974, for example, Iran agreed to allow free transit through its port city of Bandar Abbas, and in 2003 it granted the same status to the port of Chabahar. Access to these port cities through rail or road gives Afghanistan direct access to the Arabian Sea and the opportunity to ship goods internationally.[22]

In 2011, the Afghanistan-Pakistan Transit Trade Agreement (APTTA) expanded trade cooperation between the two countries and attempted to minimize smuggling by maximizing oversight and technical monitoring. Authorities plan on installing tracking devices on transport units and to better utilize customs-to-customs information sharing through data transfer technology. The APTTA establishes the framework in which Afghan businesses can more easily export goods through Pakistan to India, China, and beyond. Afghanistan will also be able to import goods more quickly via Pakistan. Similarly, Pakistan will also be able to export its products to Afghanistan with a streamlined customs and paperwork process. However, implementation and enforcement of the APTTA remains problematic. Massive smuggling continues as does the associated drain on customs revenue.[23]

Notably, the majority of commodities that are traded and smuggled in the Afghan region—such as electronics, construction supplies, automobiles, foodstuffs, and even gold—originate from or transit Dubai. (Hong Kong, Singapore, China, and other international trading centers are used as well, but to a lesser extent.)

Many of the trade goods that enter the transit trade are broken down into smaller shipments to be distributed in Afghanistan or smuggled back into Pakistan, Iran, and other countries for resale on the black market. As a Pakistani customs official told me, "Many times the only part of the shipments that actually leaves Pakistan for Afghanistan is the paperwork." That is, the shipping documents may indicate that the goods are destined for Afghanistan, but sometimes the cargo never actually crosses the border. Pakistani officials also related stories in which goods are taken a short distance across the border—literally just out of view of the authorities—then split into smaller loads and transported right back into Pakistan. They are then sold on the streets of

Islamabad, Karachi, and other cities, including local bazaars such as Peshawar's Karkhano market.

Undoubtedly, most of the Afghan Transit Trade involves legitimate commerce. But illicit trade goods—the ones that help pay for drugs produced in the region and trafficked by terrorist-linked trading syndicates and criminal groups—also enter the subcontinent via the ATT. There are many methods of payment for these goods, including conventional bank-to-bank transfers via letters of credit and other formal financial methods. Yet a substantial percentage of tainted goods destined for Afghanistan are part of the TBML equation discussed previously in this book, including hawala (see Chapter 4).

Many elements in the trade settlement process are intermingled, including smuggling, corruption, countervaluation, legitimate commerce, and so forth. Even exchange-control credits can be used to purchase goods. For example, a trader in the region will sometimes report to exchange-control authorities that certain imports cost more (or certain exports less) than their actual price. The difference or credits can be held abroad and used to pay for additional imports. Moreover, throughout the Arab world and South Asia, cash is often accumulated and purchased by trading syndicates in the form of "guest worker" remittances. Some of the accumulated foreign exchange and currencies from various sources are used to purchase goods from souks (markets) and free trade zones in Dubai and elsewhere.

And even the new APTTA poses challenges. The increase in transit routes within Pakistan offers insurgents the ability to move materials, value, and personnel under the guise of legitimate trade transport. The designated trade routes all pass through key locations where insurgent and terrorist groups operate, particularly Karachi, Quetta, Baluchistan, Chaman/Spin Boldak, the Federally Administered Tribal Areas (FATA), Peshawar, and Torkham. It appears that insurgents are finding creative ways to utilize APTTA's new rule of being able to maintain control of a cargo truck from country of origin to cross-border destination without having to risk unloading trucks at border crossings.[24]

In addition, since the initiation of the new APTTA agreement, it appears that organized smuggling groups have increased their use of Iranian ports of entry.[25] And with the phasing out of Iranian sanctions, this trend will continue to grow. Although there is little data available on money laundering in Iran, the country's underground economy is enormous, spurred in part by attempts to avoid government corruption and restrictive taxation. Indeed, capital flight via trade is a major problem for the Iran government (with Dubai a frequent destination) while currency exchange restrictions encourage the use of hawala rather than formal financial institutions. The ATT/APTTA is therefore a perfect vehicle for Iranian brokers to both circumvent currency controls and export capital by using apparently "legitimate" trade with Dubai. As one analyst noted, "Dubai is Iran's lifeline to the world. American politicians like to bray about Iran's ties to Syria, Iraq, and Lebanon's Hezbollah, but it is Dubai that keeps the ostracized nation functioning."[26] Several hundred thousand Iranians reside in Dubai and more than 10,000 Iranian-run businesses operate in the city-state.[27] A great many are of the proverbial "import–export" variety.

The misuse of the ATT—facilitated by TBML and value transfer—has real-world political ramifications in both South Asia and the Arabian Sea area. It is one more reason why understanding TBML is essential.

LATIN AMERICA'S TRI-BORDER AREA

Argentina, Brazil, and Paraguay meet at a bend in the Parana River bounded by the key border towns of Puerto Iguazu', Foz do Iguaçu, and Ciudad del Este, respectively. The Tri-Border Area (TBA) has long served as a hub of organized crime, smuggling, and narcotics and weapons trafficking. The TBA's thriving cross-border trade is estimated at approximately $5 billion per year between Ciudad del Este and Foz do Iguaçu alone![28] Much of that is off the books. The commercial trade and laundering of illicit proceeds is facilitated in large part by TBML and value transfer.

The TBA first started to grow rapidly in the 1960s and 1970s when tax incentives encouraged large numbers of foreign merchants and businessmen to relocate to the region. Today, the Syrian, Lebanese, and Chinese presence is strong. (See Chapters 5 and 6.) It is believed the Shia Syrian-Lebanese community in the TBA numbers approximately 20,000 to 30,000.[29] Authorities claim that some of the Muslim residents give financial support to groups such as Hezbollah, Hamas,

Islamic Jihad, and al-Qaeda.[30] It is difficult to gauge the amount of funds provided since much of it is transferred via hawala,[31] unlicensed and unsupervised exchange houses, and trade-based value transfer. According to an official in Paraguay's antiterrorist unit, "Terrorists partly finance their operations by remitting dollars from Ciudad del Este to the Middle East."[32]

DO MONEY LAUNDERING OPERATIONS IN THE TBA FUND TERROR?

Between 2003 and 2006, former Manhattan district attorney Robert Morgenthau traced billions of dollars channeled through New York City banks from money-laundering activities in the TBA. Although convinced some money had ties to terrorism, by the end of the investigation Morgenthau admitted he could not make a direct nexus between the $19 billion in laundered money and terrorist activity.[33] According to one investigator involved, "It's hard to say what's going to terrorism and what's good old-fashioned crime and what is legitimate business. It's all intermingled."[34] Generally speaking, the governments of Paraguay, Brazil, and Argentina downplay the TBA/terror link. However, a 2014 U.S. State Department report on money laundering in Paraguay acknowledged that the "[TBA] is well known for arms and narcotics trafficking and violations of intellectual property rights with the illicit proceeds of these crimes a source of laundered funds. Some of these illicit activities have been supplied to terrorist organizations."[35]

Much of the economic activity in Ciudad del Este is the "re-export" trade to Brazil. Merchants import cigarettes, clothing, electronics, and other consumer and luxury items from the United States, Europe, and increasingly China, and then sell them to primarily to Brazilians but also neighboring Argentinians. Paraguay boasts low import tariffs and free trade zones that facilitate the TBA trade.

At the lower end of the "trading" spectrum are tens of thousands of small-time *sacoleiros*, named for their ubiquitous overstuffed shopping bags (*saco* means "bag" in Portuguese). Sacoleiros account for the majority of the 30,000 to 40,000 people who cross the Ponte da Amizade (Friendship Bridge) every day.[36]

It is surprisingly easy to move across the borders of the TBA. People and motorbikes are allowed to cross without travel documents and larger vehicles, watercraft, and smugglers can find ready ways to pass undetected. Many sacoleiros earn a living through illicit international arbitrage, buying low in Paraguay and selling high in Foz do Iguaçu. Ordinary Brazilians also flock in large numbers to the TBA as well, regularly flouting the official $300-per-month duty-free allowance to buy foreign goods in bulk.[37]

There are also larger criminal enterprises at work in the TBA. Buyers with larger orders are sent to Ciudad del Este from far-away Brazilian cities to fulfill transactions placed on the Internet. Generally they charge a commission of 10–15 percent for their travel time and the (slim) risk of being caught by the police. There are also organized criminal networks operating in the Triple Frontier area. One of their most lucrative activities is smuggling large quantities of low-tax cigarettes (genuine and counterfeit) from Paraguay into Brazil.[38]

In the last few years there have been attempts at transparency. In 2009, the "Unified Tax Regime" became law. The objective was to encourage Paraguayan import firms to register, systematize, and document their sales, and register vehicles used in the transport of goods. Tax and customs simplification is also part of the new trading regime. All of this information is housed in a database controlled by Brazil's Receita Federal.[39] However, similar to the APTTA between Afghanistan and Pakistan described above, there are problems with implementation and enforcement. The problems are particularly acute on the Paraguayan side of the border. As is the case elsewhere around the world where TBML flourishes, corruption, weak law enforcement, little regulatory oversight, and the lack of effective customs control are catalysts for criminal activity.

CAROUSEL FRAUD

Carousel fraud or missing trader fraud is the practice of importing goods from a country where they are not subject to value-added tax (VAT), selling them with VAT added, then deliberately not paying the VAT to the government. The fraudster charges VAT on the sale of the goods and instead of paying it to the government simply absconds—taking the VAT with him, hence *missing trader fraud*. It is a form of "carousel" or "merry-go-round" fraud when sometimes goods are cycled between companies and jurisdictions, collecting ever more fraudulent VAT revenues. Sometimes in TBML, *carousel fraud* also refers to the process of cycling trade goods (genuine or fictitious) in-and-out of markets in order to justify payment abroad.

Although a foreign concept to American readers, VAT is a consumption tax assessed on the value added to goods and services. In the countries that apply it, like those in the European Union, consumers pay the VAT tax every time they buy a product or service. Whether it involves a sale to a consumer or another business, VAT taxes involve a lot of paperwork as each company involved must keep track of it when it makes a transaction. It is a very important source of income for the countries involved; for example, France levies approximately 140 billions of euros with the VAT tax, or twice what French citizens pay in income tax.[40]

Unfortunately, trade fraud follows VAT; Canada, Mexico, and the Ukraine are just a few countries where VAT scams regularly occur. According to a 2015 *INCSR* report by the U.S. State Department, "A significant facet of the grey economy in Bulgaria is large-scale tax evasion, particularly of VAT and excise duties. Proceeds from VAT fraud are significant and are largely transferred out of the country to foreign accounts held by offshore companies. They are then returned to Bulgaria and declared as loans, thus creating a legal origin for future use."[41] The State Department reports that in the Czech Republic:

> [F]raud and tax evasion, especially related to the Value-Added Tax (VAT) and excise tax, are reportedly the primary sources of laundered assets in the country. A common tactic for hiding the origin of illicit proceeds is to transfer or layer funds among multiple companies, creating a system of "carousel trading," whereby fictitious invoices, wages, and benefit payments are created. The ultimate goal of the carousel system is to benefit from an unauthorized VAT allowance.[42]

Carousel VAT fraud in the European Union first involves obtaining a VAT registration number in an EU member state for the purposes of trade. (In general, countries that have a VAT system have a threshold or regulations specifying at which turnover levels VAT registration becomes compulsory.) Next, the same goods are traded around artificial supply chains within and sometimes beyond the EU. The goods reenter the original member state on a number of occasions with the intention of creating large unpaid VAT liabilities and associated fraudulent VAT repayment schemes.[43]

The following is an example of a simple VAT carousel fraud operating in the EU:[44]

- Company X in one EU country purchases goods from a supplier in another EU country. The VAT rate is zero.

- After acquiring the goods, Company X supplies them to Company Y, within the same country for a price plus VAT. However, X does *Not* pay the VAT to the EU Member State and becomes a "missing trader."

- Company Y then supplies the goods to another EU member country and claims back the VAT that Y paid for the original purchase of the goods from Company X.

The scheme becomes more complex when Company Y adds "buffers" to the equation, distancing itself from Company X—the missing trader.

Conspirators in carousel fraud often use items that are low bulk and high value, for example, mobile phones, electronics, and computer chips. Similar to other examples of TBML found in this book, conspirators have used invoice fraud and manipulation, buying and selling goods that don't actually exist. In other cases, there have been boxes of dummy items involved.

According to a study by the FATF,[45] career criminals and organized crime groups are attracted to VAT carousel fraud because it generates large profits with a relatively low risk of prosecution. Criminal involvement is the reason why VAT carousel fraud can be considered TBML. For example, organized crime groups in the United Kingdom have conducted violent armed robberies at freight forwarder premises to steal mobile phones for use in carousel fraud. In other cases, criminals hijacked and "stole" their own goods in order to make fraudulent insurance claims, which were then used to finance further carousel fraud. Moreover, illicit proceeds—including those from narcotics trafficking—have been invested in carousel fraud.

Although some governments are addicted to VAT because of the revenue it generates, the VAT tax system is complex, invites fraud, and costs a lot of money to administer. And rising VAT rates have encouraged some companies to avoid the tax rather than pay it. As per Chapter 7, some companies seek to avoid taxes by relocating their headquarters to Luxemburg, for example, where the VAT rate is lower.[46]

CASE STUDIES

Case 1: Customs Fraud in an FTZ

A Belgium company imported textile products from the United Arab Emirates. According to the documentation accompanying the shipments, the goods were either produced or received "significant transformation" in the Sharjah Airport Free Zone. However, it is very unlikely that there is substantive textile production in an airport free zone! The documentation trail and invoice circuit appeared fictitious to investigators. There was admittedly relaxed oversight and enforcement.[47] In fact, Sharjah FTZ advertised its "[intent] to promote and enhance business in an atmosphere free of regulation and red tape."[48]

Case 2: Smuggling via an FTZ

PAUL was involved in smuggling contraband cigarettes manufactured in China into the United States. The cigarettes were imported into an FTZ located in Hawaii, and then diverted to the state of Washington. The claimed destination was a Native American reservation in Idaho. PAUL sold the illegal cigarettes in Washington and structured cash deposits in an attempt to launder the proceeds and avoid payment of taxes to Washington.[49]

Case 3: Afghan Transit Trade Scheme

Because military, law enforcement, and intelligence officials typically do not understand how the ATT is misused, there is little official reporting on the transfer and exchange of value via drugs and trade goods.

The following is a simple scenario based on personal knowledge and interviews by expert Edwina Thompson:[50]

- Drugs are smuggled from Afghanistan into the United Kingdom via Iran, Turkey, and the Balkan countries via the well-known "Balkan Route." Payment is made via bank-to-bank wire transfers from the United Kingdom to Peshawar, Pakistan.

- From Peshawar, continuing payment is fragmented. Part goes to a hawaladar in Helmand, Afghanistan, who credits the criminal or terrorist organization that supplied the drugs.

- The criminal/terrorist organization uses other portions of the payment from afar to finance imports of commodities from Dubai via the ATT.

- The suspect organization either uses these goods directly or can sell them for further profit.

Case 4: TBML in the TBA

Homeland Security Investigations (HSI), as part of a Joint Terrorism Task Force, initiated an investigation into the suspicious exportation of electronic goods from Miami to Ciudad del Este in Paraguay, located in the TBA. In December 2006, Galeria Page, one of the large shopping centers within Ciudad del Este, was named as a specially designated global terrorist (SDGT) entity by the Office of Foreign Assets Control (OFAC). Galeria Page had ties to the terrorist group Hezbollah. Once an individual or business is designated, U.S. entities are prohibited from conducting business with the SDGT or face criminal prosecution.

HSI and its investigating partners determined several Miami-based freight-forwarding companies were illegally exporting electronic goods to Galeria Page. Working with officials in Paraguay, agents discovered the criminals concealed the true destination of the prohibited shipments by using fake invoices containing false addresses and fictitious ultimate consignees on the required export paperwork. In addition, wire transfer payments were routed through various facilities to mask their true origin. As a result of the investigation, the conspirators pled guilty and $119 million of merchandise, primarily high-end electronics, were seized.[51]

Case 5: Carousel Fraud

Examining trade data, fraud investigators of the Dutch Economic Inspection Service of the Fiscal Intelligence and Investigation Service (FIOD) discovered a large VAT carousel fraud. They identified 2,000 personal computer components at Schiphol Airport destined for the United Kingdom. Computer chips and electronics are often favored goods for carousel fraud, as they are small and have high value. The investigation disclosed that the components were originally exported to the United States from the United Kingdom and would be reintroduced to the United Kingdom via the Netherlands. Aiding the Dutch investigation was the discovery that the goods already contained British export stamps.[52]

NOTES

1. Author conversation with Pakistani authorities in Islamabad, 2002.
2. Author conversation with South African officials in Johannesburg, 2004.
3. Author conversation with Afghan officials, Kabul, 2006.
4. Christine Duhaime, "Canada's Diamond Trade Being Used for Money Laundering and Terrorist Financing, Report Finds," Duhaime's Anti-Money Laundering Law in Canada (February 3, 2014), available online: http://www.antimoneylaunderinglaw .com/2014/02/canadas-diamond-trade-being-used-for-money-laundering-and-terrorist-financing-report-finds.html.
5. "Seymour Man Accused of Trading Guns to Mexican Cartel," WBIW News (May 5, 2013), available online: http://www.wbiw.com/local/archive/2012/07/seymour-man-accused-of-trading.php.
6. U.S. Department of State, Bureau for International Narcotics and Law Enforcement Affairs, International Narcotics Control Strategy Report (INCSR) Volume II, Money Laundering and Financial Crimes (March 2015), Montenegro country report, available online: http://www.state.gov/j/inl/rls/nrcrpt/2015/vol2/index.htm.
7. Much of the information in this section originates from "Money Laundering Vulnerabilities of Free Trade Zones," Financial Action Task Force (FATF), March 2010, available online: http://www.fatf-gafi.org/media/fatf/documents/reports/ML %20vulnerabilities%20of%20Free%20Trade%20Zones.pdf.
8. "Not So Special—Special Economic Zones," The Economist (April 4, 2015), available online: http://www.economist.com/news/leaders/21647615-world-awash-free-trade-zones-and-their-offshoots-many-are-not-worth-effort-not.
9. Angela Shah, "Free Trade Zones Attract Criminals," New York Times (November 10, 2010), available online: http://www.nytimes.com/2010/11/11/world/middleeast/ 11iht-m11mtrade.html?_r=0.
10. National Institute of Statistics and Census of Panama (INEC), available online: http:// logistics.gatech.pa/en/assets/special-economic-zones/colon-free-zone/statistics.

11. FATF—Free Trade Zones.
12. "About Foreign-Trade Zones," Customs and Border Protection, available online: http://www.cbp.gov/border-security/ports-entry/cargo-security/cargo-control/foreign-trade-zones/about.
13. Ibid.
14. FATF—Free Trade Zones.
15. Ibid.
16. Margherita Stancati, "Opium Production in Afghanistan Soars to Record Levels," *Wall Street Journal* (May 13, 2013), available online: http://www.wsj.com/articles/SB10001424052702303460004579193992106490318.
17. "Afghan Opium Soars to New High Fueling Taliban," Reuters (November 12, 2014), available online: http://nypost.com/2014/11/12/afghan-opium-crop-soars-to-new-high-fueling-taliban-forces/.
18. David Rohde, "Afghan Opium Crop at Record High," *New York Times* (August 28, 2007).
19. U.S. Department of State, Bureau for International Narcotics and Law Enforcement Affairs, *International Narcotics Control Strategy Report (INCSR) Volume II, Money Laundering and Financial Crimes* (2009), Afghanistan, available online: http://www.state.gov/j/inl/rls/nrcrpt/2009/vol2/index.htm.
20. Syed Saleem Shahzad, "Opium Gold Unites U.S. Friend and Foes," *Asia Times* (September 2, 2005).
21. INCSR 2009 Country Report Iran.
22. Mariam Nawabi, "Afghanistan's Trade Routes," *Development Gateway* (February 3, 2004).
23. Vivian Chiu Cochran, "A Crossroad to Economic Triumph or Terrorism: The Afghanistan-Pakistan Transit Trade Agreement," *Global Security Studies* 4 (1) (Winter 2013), available online: http://globalsecuritystudies.com/Cochran%20APTTA%20.pdf.
24. Ibid.
25. "Decline in Afghan Transit Trade," *Dawn* (April 29, 2013), available online: http://www.dawn.com/news/1025675/decline-in-afghan-transit-trade.
26. Jim Krane, *City of Gold: Dubai and the Dream of Capitalism* (New York: St. Martin's Press, 2009), p. 293.
27. Ibid., p. 292.
28. Christine Folch, "Trouble on the Triple Frontier," *Foreign Affairs* (September 6, 2012), available online: http://www.foreignaffairs.com/articles/138096/christine-folch/trouble-on-the-triple-frontier.
29. Ibid.
30. Rex Hudson, *Terrorist and Organized Crime Groups in the Tri-Border Area of South America* (Washington, D.C.: U.S. Government Printing Office, July 2003).
31. Benedetta Berti, "Reassessing the Transnational Terrorism-Criminal Link in South America's Tri-Border Area," Jamestown Foundation (September 22, 2008), available online: http://www.jamestown.org/single/?no_cache=1&tx_ttnews%5Btt_news%5D=5172#.VJNyp14AA.
32. Hudson.
33. Berti.

34. Joseph Goldstein, "Morgenthau's Crime Reach Extends to South America," *New York Sun* (August 20, 2007), available online: http://www.nysun.com/new-york/morgenthaus-crime-reach-extends-to-south-america/60838/.
35. U.S. Department of State, Bureau for International Narcotics and Law Enforcement Affairs, *International Narcotics Control Strategy Report (INCSR) Volume II, Money Laundering and Financial Crimes* (March 2014), Paraguay country report, available online: http://www.state.gov/j/inl/rls/nrcrpt/2014/vol2/222765.htm.
36. "Good Neighbors: Smuggling across South America's Triple Frontier," Global Initiative Against International Crime, available online: http://www.globalinitiative.net/smuggling-across-south-americas-triple-frontier/.
37. Ibid.
38. Ibid.
39. Folch.
40. "VAT Fraud: The Mysterious Case of the Missing Trader" (August 25, 2014), available online: http://linkurio.us/vat-fraud-mysterious-case-missing-trader/.
41. U.S. Department of State, Bureau for International Narcotics and Law Enforcement Affairs, *International Narcotics Control Strategy Report (INCSR) Volume II, Money Laundering and Financial Crimes* (March 2015), Bulgaria country report, available online: http://www.state.gov/j/inl/rls/nrcrpt/2015/vol2/index.htm.
42. U.S. Department of State, Bureau for International Narcotics and Law Enforcement Affairs, *International Narcotics Control Strategy Report (INCSR) Volume II, Money Laundering and Financial Crimes* (March 2015), Czech Republic country report, available online: http://www.state.gov/j/inl/rls/nrcrpt/2015/vol2/index.htm.
43. "Laundering the Proceeds of VAT Carousel Fraud," Financial Action Task Force (February 23, 2007), available online: http://www.fatf-gafi.org/media/fatf/documents/reports/Laundering%20the%20Proceeds%20of%20VAT%20Caroussel%20Fraud.pdf.
44. Ibid.; example in Annex 1.
45. Ibid.; the examples in this section originate from the FATF typologies paper.
46. Aline Robert, "France's €30 Billion VAT Gap Revealed," *EurActiv* (September 18 2013), available online: http://www.euractiv.com/euro-finance/exclusive-study-vat-gap-france-3-news-530508.
47. "Money Laundering Vulnerabilities of Free Trade Zones," FATF; case study 6.
48. Ibid.
49. Ibid.; case study 9.
50. Edwina Thompson, "The Nexus of Drug Trafficking and Hawala in Afghanistan," in *Afghanistan's Drug Industry, Structure, Functioning, Dynamics, and Implications for Counter-Narcotics Policy*, ed. Doris Buddenberg and William Byrd, UN Office on Drugs and Crime/World Bank, 2006, pp. 155–188.
51. "Homeland Security's Trade Transparency Unit Investigations," *The Cornerstone Report* (Winter 2011), available online: http://www.ice.gov/doclib/news/library/reports/cornerstone/cornerstone7-3.pdf.
52. Jan Libbenga, "Dutch Customs Exposes UK Chip Carousel Fraud," *The Channel* (May 5, 2005), available online: http://www.channelregister.co.uk/2005/05/05/pc_components_carousel_fraud_exposed/.

CHAPTER **9**

Monitoring Trade

STEPS IN THE INTERNATIONAL TRADE PROCESS

An analyst or investigator charged with identifying TBML is fortunate to be assisted by a wide variety of data and documentation generated throughout the international trade process. (Underground informal value transfer systems are sometimes another story!) Trading parties generally follow identified, accepted, and almost sequential steps that create a data and paper trail that can be used in spotting suspicious behavior and anomalies.

As noted in the preface, this book will not delve into the intricacies of trade finance. This includes the issuance of letters of credit, lending to import–export companies, guarantees and pre-export financing, supporting companies in the process of collections, discounting drafts and acceptances, and offering services such as credit and other information on buyers.[1]

The following is a brief overview of a typical trade transaction so the reader can understand where information might be available and the kind of data that are generated for analysis. Of course, the trade process varies, depending on whether it is an arm's-length transaction (as discussed in Chapter 7), and whether they are engaged in an extra-business relationship, have completed previous transactions, or are involved with some sort of trade fraud or TBML conspiracy. The terminology and trading steps also vary somewhat by market. An explanation of additional terms commonly used in the trade process is found in the Glossary.

1. **Export promotion**—Exporters often promote their goods through sales representatives, a variety of media, the web, communications systems, and trade exhibitions, both at home and abroad. Promotion can also take place through commercial officers assigned to embassies, chambers of commerce, trade associations, and other business organizations.

2. **Letter of inquiry**—An interested importer sends a letter of inquiry to the exporter or to the exporter's representative that generally contains a request for a price quote, product specifications, quantity, availability, and delivery details including the destination port.

3. **Offer sheet**—In response to the letter of inquiry, the exporter sends the importer an offer sheet containing the requested information and perhaps a sample product.

4. **Purchase order (P/O)**—If the offer sheet is acceptable, the importer will place an order via a form or letter called a purchase order. It is sometimes called an order sheet.

5. **Invoice**—The exporter prepares an invoice or a sales contract based on the information in the offer sheet and purchase order; details of the purchase contain the identifying information of the product, shipment date, transshipment details if any, inspection, packing and marking details, and cargo insurance. The sales contract is signed by both the exporter and the importer and each side maintains a copy.

6. **Payment**—There are various ways for the importer to make payment. Letters of credit (L/Cs) are among the most secure instruments available. An L/C is a commitment by a bank on behalf of the buyer that payment will be made to the exporter provided that the terms and conditions on the purchase order and contract have been met. Generally, verification occurs through the presentation of all required documents. An L/C is useful when reliable credit information about a foreign buyer is difficult to obtain, but the exporter is satisfied with the creditworthiness of the importer's foreign bank. An L/C also protects the buyer since no payment obligation arises until the goods have been shipped or delivered as promised. Other payment options include cash-in-advance, documentary collections, and open account.

7. **Shipment process**—After receiving LC confirmation, the exporter readies the goods for shipment and, if necessary, retains a shipping company or freight forwarder. A number of documents are prepared by those involved directly or indirectly in the transaction:

   - *Bill of lading*—A document signed by a carrier (transporter of the goods) and issued to a consignor (the shipper of goods) that confirms the receipt of the goods for shipment to a specified destination and company or representative.

A bill of lading is, in addition to a receipt for the delivery of goods, a contract for their transport and their document of title. The bill of lading describes the method of freight, states the name of the consignor and the provisions of the contract for shipment, and directs where and to whom the cargo is to be delivered. There are two basic types of bills of lading. A straight bill of lading is one in which the goods are consigned to a designated party. An order bill is one in which the goods are consigned to the order of a named party. This distinction is important in determining whether a bill of lading is negotiable (capable of transferring title to the goods covered under it by its delivery or endorsement). If the terms provide that the freight is to be delivered to the bearer of the bill, or to the order of the named party, the document of title is negotiable. In contrast, a straight bill is not negotiable.

■ *Shippers export declaration or (SED)*—An SED is a document used in some jurisdictions when the value of the commodity requires an export license for shipment from the country of export to another country. In the United States, the SED is used for developing export statistics and for export control purposes. The SED imparts general information about a transaction, including the parties involved, the date of exportation of the shipment, consignees and agents for the shipment, classifications, weight, and the value of the goods. The SED is signed by the exporter or the authorized agent.

■ *Destination control statement*—This document is required only by certain countries (including the United States) for the export of commodities such as munitions and sensitive technology that requires a license or a license exemption.

■ *Certificate of inspection*—The certificate of inspection is prepared by the seller or an independent inspector designated by the buyer that is a statement providing evidence for the characteristics of the goods.

- *Certificate of manufacture*—This document is from the producer of the goods. It describes the goods, states that the production of the goods is complete, and that the goods are at the buyer's disposal.
- *Insurance document*—This certifies that the goods are insured for shipment.
- *Export license*—A document issued by a government agency authorizing the export of certain commodities to specified countries.
- *Import license*—A document issued by a government agency authorizing the import of certain commodities into the buyer's country.

8. **Clearance**—After receiving the appropriate shipping documents listed above, the importer or consignee secures import clearance by customs in the destination port. The importer will later contact the shipping agent in the destination port to receive the goods.

9. **Delivery**—The shipping agent surrenders the cargo/goods to the importer.

INFORMATION SOURCES

Much useful information and data are generated in the international trade process. In addition to the buyer (importer) and the seller (exporter), the reader can see in Figure 9.1 that there are additional players that can also be valuable information sources. Similar to assembling the pieces of a jigsaw puzzle, the analyst, investigator, or concerned compliance officer assembles as much information as possible to follow the value trail. The intelligence generated provides authorities data to monitor trade and to spot anomalies that could be indicative of customs fraud, TBML, value transfer, and/or underground finance.

Over the course of my career, I found that there are four very broad categories of information that have proved particularly valuable in combating TBML. They are not found in isolation and often overlap. They are used both in examining the non-price characteristics of a transaction (such as investigator and analyst assessments and company know-your-customer policies) and in evaluating the more quantifiable elements and risk of a particular transaction.

1. **Human source information.** As a former intelligence and law enforcement officer, I know firsthand that there is no substitute for human intelligence (humint) to provide inside information regarding a trade conspiracy. Human sources can provide tips that might point an investigator in the right direction, provide documents (officially or unofficially) that facilitate following a money and/or value trail, and perhaps explain the intricacies of the trade process, industry, and parties involved. The ideal is if the source has direct or personal access to a TBML conspiracy. Sources can be found both within and outside of the parties illustrated in Figure 9.1.

2. **Financial intelligence.** Generally speaking, both the importer and the exporter work with a financial institution or institutions. Trade financing documents are produced. Banks and some involved money services businesses also generate financial intelligence. In TBML, the filing of suspicious activity reports (SARs), generally known outside the United States as suspicious transaction reports (STRs), can be very helpful. For example, according

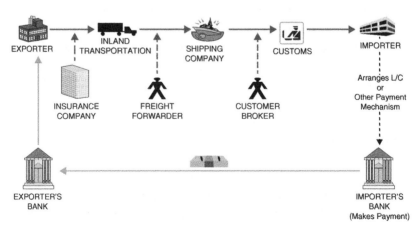

Figure 9.1 Basic trade transaction

to Treasury's FinCEN, "over 17,000 SARs reporting potential TBML activity that occurred between January 2004 and May 2009 reported transactions that involved in the aggregate over $276 Billion."[2]

FinCEN believes that SAR filings on suspected TBML are increasing.[3] However, many financial institutions are just becoming aware of TBML in all of its varied forms, and they may see only a partial bit of information related to a suspect transaction.

As a former consumer of financial intelligence, I whole-heartedly concur with FinCEN's advice that "financial institutions check the appropriate box in the Suspicious Activity Information section of the SAR form and include the abbreviation "TBML" or "BMPE" (or any other identified TBML methodology) in the narrative portion of all relevant SARs filed. The narrative should also include an explanation of why the institution suspects, or has reason to suspect, that the customer is participating in such activity."[4]

3. **Documents generated by the parties involved in the trade transactions.** The parties involved in the international trade process generate paper or electronic documents. Some of the information is restricted, privileged, or available only through the use of a customs or criminal subpoena. However, quite a bit of data are now in the public domain.

In every country, concerned government agencies and departments also track trade. As noted earlier, this is done for a variety of reasons, including national security, revenue, the promotion of commerce, analysis, etc. Much of the data are in the public domain. In the United States, the Foreign Trade Division of the U.S. Census Bureau produces *USA Trade Online* (https://usatrade.census.gov/). A user can access "current and cumulative U.S. export and import data for over 9,000 export commodities and 17,000 import commodities." The data are based on the Harmonized System (see below), and analytic programs allow customers the opportunity to create reports and charts detailing foreign trade variants including: port level detail, state exports and imports, balance of trade, method of transportation, and market level ranking.[5]

Commercial services also are available that allow inquiries from bank compliance officers and other interested parties into a particular commodity's generally accepted price. These services will provide an alert if the sales price represents a significant discrepancy off the global market price of similar goods.

4. **The Harmonized Commodity Description and Coding System**. This is sometimes simply known simply as the Harmonized System, or HS. It was developed by the World Customs Organization (WCO). The HS comprises about 5,000 commodity groups, each identified by a common six-digit code. Countries are allowed to further define commodities at a more detailed level than six digits, but all general definitions must be within the six-digit framework. The HS is supported by well-defined rules to achieve uniform classification. The system is used by more than 200 countries as a basis for their customs tariffs.[6] For purposes of monitoring trade, the data generated is useful for the kind of comparative analysis and the identification of trade anomalies discussed throughout this book.

The HS is also extensively used by governments, international organizations, and the private sector for many other purposes, such as determining trade policies, the monitoring of controlled goods, taxes, transport statistics, price monitoring, quota controls, and various types of research and analysis. The HS is thus a universal economic language. Indeed, more than 98 percent of the merchandise in international trade is classified in terms of the HS.[7]

In the United States, the Harmonized Tariff Schedule (HTS) was enacted by Congress and made effective on January 1, 1989. The HTS replaces the former Tariff Schedules of the United States. Export codes (which the United States calls Schedule B) are administered by the U.S. Census Bureau and Commerce Department and used to collect and publish U.S. export statistics. Import codes are administered by the U.S. International Trade Commission (USITC). However, only the Bureau of Customs and Border Protection (CBP) within DHS is authorized to interpret the HTS, to issue legally binding rulings on tariff classification of imports, and to administer customs laws.[8]

All U.S. imports and exports are documented on CBP form 7501 (Entry Summary) and U.S. Department of Commerce form 7525 (Shipper's Export Declaration—SED).

The HTS is based on the HS administered by the WCO. The 4- to 6-digit HS product categories are further subdivided into 8-digit rate lines unique to the United States that provide further specificity and 10-digit nonlegal statistical reporting categories. There is an HTS code number for every physical product traded from wheat to helicopter spare parts.

There are more HTS numbers than Schedule B export numbers. This reflects the greater amount of detail and scrutiny on products imported into the United States. Though matched at the 6-digit HS level, Schedule B and HTS codes for products may not be the same up to the 10-digit level. The government urges parties involved with filing import or export records to use the correct classification system, which can be easily found using online queries. U.S. HTS codes were revised in 2012. The next revision is scheduled for 2017.[9]

The codes are currently divided into 22 sections and 99 chapters. They begin with the least sophisticated trade goods such as animal and vegetable products. The codes reflect greater sophistication in the higher chapters covering such things as textiles, manufactured goods, computers, aircraft, and so on. A sample HTS code is reflected in Figure 9.2.

The gold scrap code is found in Section XIV of the HTS Code—Chapter 71: "Natural or Cultured Pearls, Precious or Semiprecious Stones, Precious Metals, Metals Clad With Precious Metal, and Articles Thereof; Imitation Jewelry; Coin."

Description: "Gold waste and scrap, including metal clad with gold but excluding sweepings containing other precious metals."

Note: In some instances, further specificity is detailed in the last four digits of the 10-digit code.

International Harmonized   U.S. Specific

71 12. 91. 00 .00

Chapter   Heading   Sub   Tariff   Statistical
                      Heading   Rate   Tracking

Figure 9.2 HTS sample code number for gold scrap

Table 9.1 Top Exports from the United States to Country X[10]

HTS	Commodity Description	Value
1001902055	Wheat and Meslin, except Seed	$237,275,300
8703230321	Passg Vehicle: Used; >1500<3000cc	$112,791,186
8803300050	Air, Helicopter parts	$106,681,778
1005902030	Yellow Dent Corn (Maize), U.S.	$83,389,530
8803300010	Air, Helicopter parts, other; civil	$76,273,523
1006309020	Rice, oth med gr sem/whol milld	$69,942,544
8802300070	Milt Aircrft>2000<1500 kg	$66,238,000
4703210040	Coniferous bleached woodpulp	$47.439,503
1001100090	Wheat/meslin-durum wheat other	$42,752,470
1551521000	Corn (Maize)	$42,543,754
8703240075	Pas Vehc: New>3000cc, eng>6cyl	$34,194,965
8525203055	Radio transceivers	$29,778,553
2403100060	Smoking tobacco	$23,093,527

Using HTS data, it is fairly easy to monitor trade. For example, Table 9.1 tracks the top exports from the United States to Country X over a given period of time. The descriptions and terminology are taken directly from a computerized printout. The items are classified by HTS number, description, and value. While this type of macro data might be interesting if a specific type of import does not make market or economic sense, real analysis involves drilling down into the product categories to identify the parties involved and specific transactions. In this way, anomalies or suspicious transactions can often be identified and further action taken.

WHAT ABOUT WEIGHT ANALYSIS?

Although most analysis of TBML focuses on price, unit analysis of weight can sometimes provide some interesting insights. For example, Dr. John Zdanowicz, an early pioneer in examining TBML, has studied the interquartile or the midrange statistical dispersion of weight characteristics of thousands of U.S. trade transactions. Table 9.2 lists a

Table 9.2 Abnormal U.S. Import Weights[11]

Country	Product	Weight
Egypt	Razors	15 kg/unit
Indonesia	Coffee	1.26 kg/kg
Germany	Sweaters	57 kg/dozen
Malaysia	Briefcases	98 kg/unit
Pakistan	Fabric	2 kg/sq meter
Indonesia	Pillows	55 kg/unit
Pakistan	Dish towels	2 kg/unit

few examples of actual import weights. Dubious weight/unit anomalies are easily identified. Weight analysis can also be useful in determining possible threats.

Of course, similar to unit/price analysis, the possibility always exists that individual data were erroneous, inputted incorrectly, or reflected statistical outliers or deviations. With TBML, generally analysis is possible because data exists. If an anomaly or suspicion is discovered, it should be treated as a starting point or an indicator. Good decision making is about understanding the data; there is no substitute for investigation. And particularly with abnormal weights for shipments transiting sea, land, or airports, abnormal weights could well have smuggling or national security implications.

A striking example of how suspect weight can trigger an investigation occurred in Canada. A criminal organization prepared a relatively small shipment of scrap metal, but indicated that it weighed several hundred tons. As discussed in this book, fraudulent invoices, bills of lading, and other documents were prepared supporting the shipment. However, when the cargo was loaded onto the ship, an alert Canadian customs officer noticed that the hull of the ship was riding well above the water line. If the ship was actually carrying the weight indicated, the ship would have been low in the water. As a result of the observation, the cargo was examined and an investigation pursued. It was assumed that the inflated value of the invoice as supported by the fraudulent weight of the shipment would have been used to transfer illicit funds to Canada.[12]

The HS has revolutionized the tracking of trade. Unfortunately, many (primarily underdeveloped countries) customs services have lacked the wherewithal and expertise to take advantage of the data generated. The Automated System for Customs Data (ASYCUDA) is a computerized system designed by the United Nations Conference on Trade and Development (UNCTAD) to administer a country's customs. Today, ASYCUDA is used in over 90 countries and territories.[13] The goal was to construct an analytic system to assist customs authorities all over the world to automate and control their core processes and obtain timely, accurate, and valuable information. The software does not have a robust analytic component and is largely focused on automating basic transaction-processing systems involved with the day-to-day clearing of cargo. When applied to customs enforcement, it focuses largely on day-to-day interdiction—not the long-term patterns and trends generally associated with TBML.

PIONEERING ANALYSIS IN TBML

In the early to mid-1990s, Senior Special Agent Lou Bock of the U.S. Customs Service became the "godfather" of TBML via his pioneering efforts to systematize the analysis of trade data to spot trade fraud, money laundering, and other financial crimes.

Lou was a former DEA inspector who had transferred to Customs. He had a rare combination of gifts that were enhanced by street-level investigative experience, coupled with his self-taught knowledge of computer programing. Lou was an incredibly bright, talented, and motivated agent. Despite a minuscule budget, working from Customs headquarters, Lou and a few colleagues tried to systematically examine trade data—specifically concentrating on spotting anomalies in trade transactions primarily using the HS and other data described above.[14]

With the help of Mark Laxer, a talented computer programmer, Lou was the driving force behind the creation of an innovative analytics program called the Numerically Integrated Profiling System (NIPS). Lou realized that most of his colleagues would accept only straightforward and user-friendly analysis—in other words, NIPS had to be "agent proof." So he provided technically challenged analysts and investigators (like myself) a new type of tool that would process large amounts of data, analyze it, and point to promising targets of investigation. The end result was in a user-friendly format that included graphics and visuals.

NIPS revolutionized trade analysis for criminal investigators. It let Customs do in a matter of keystrokes what it used to take countless days of legwork and the manual review of paperwork to do—analyze massive amounts of data to look for patterns or anomalies. For the first time, NIPS routinely enabled 100-gigabyte searches of trade data—or the equivalent of manually scouring through roughly 30 million full, single-spaced pages![15]

The data NIPS analyzed originated primarily from U.S. trade and financial data. At the time, much of the export data consisted of information compiled from outbound manifests that originated from commercial sources. Import data came primarily from Customs' Automated Commercial System (ACS) and import summary forms. On occasion, Lou was given access to limited foreign trade data from partner countries concerned about specific trade fraud allegations involving the United States.

NIPS used a *drill-down* method of analysis; the user would start with a general query such as "gold imports from the Dominican Republic." The user would then follow up with a continuing series of narrowing queries until a likely target of investigation was reached. Using analytical parameters, later versions of NIPS could automatically spot trade anomalies and discrepancies in trade transactions such as overvaluation or undervaluation, suspicious quantities, and suspicious countries of origin. The queries also overlapped with other databases that tracked the movement of money and people into and out of the United States.

Lou built into NIPS questions that every analyst and investigator should ask: *who, what, when, where?* However, then as now, even if an anomaly or likely target is identified, it is still up to the street investigator to find the answers to the two other important questions: *how* and *why?*

Lou's pioneering work was buttressed by simultaneous work conducted by two academics from Florida International University. They entered U.S. Department of Commerce international trade statistics into a computer program in an attempt to find interesting international trade patterns, but in the process found glaring inconsistencies in the pricing of some of the trade transactions. Similar to Lou's analysis, the professors concluded that money launderers were hiding illicit proceeds and transferring illicit value in the enormous world of international trade.[16]

TRADE TRANSPARENCY UNITS (TTUS)

While Lou was busy in Customs headquarters developing NIPS, at the same time I was assigned overseas to the American Embassy in Rome helping our Italian counterparts battle organized crime (the Mafia) by examining the flow of dirty money moving between Italy and the United States. Since our Customs Attaché office in Rome had regional responsibilities, I frequently traveled to numerous countries in the Middle East, sub-Sahara Africa, and parts of Europe pursuing a wide variety of customs investigations.

Through investigations into international criminal conspiracies and the development of excellent reporting sources, I gained a unique overseas perspective. And wherever my travels and investigations took me, I always seemed to bump into the misuse of international trade. I became increasingly concerned with trade fraud's overlap with international money laundering and underground financial systems.

In documenting my source debriefs and observations about the overlap between trade and money laundering in reports and memoranda to headquarters, I began using the term *trade-based money laundering*, or TBML. I believe that was the first use of the term. I did not realize I was coining a now well-known description. I simply felt a new classification of money laundering was needed. At the time—prior to September 11—both the FATF and U.S. policymakers concentrated their efforts on money laundering primarily associated with the "War on Drugs" where large amounts of dirty money sloshed around through Western financial institutions. Value transfer via trade was almost completely off their radar screens.[17] Because of my customs background and overseas vantage point, I felt strongly that we also needed to focus on a separate international money-laundering threat based on trade.

Lou's pioneering analytical work soon came to my attention. I became an early fan and supporter. Unfortunately, Lou's important work was handicapped by insufficient funding and the ebb and flow of high-level managerial support. In 1996, I departed Rome and transferred to FinCEN as the U.S. Customs liaison. I'm grateful for my experience at FinCEN because it allowed me to pursue my interest in international money laundering. I also gained additional exposure to the craft of analysis. Moreover, at the time, FinCEN management encouraged me to follow my interest in TBML, the misuse of the international gold trade, and study of underground financial systems. I took an active part in U.S. delegations to the FATF and I assisted in the growth of the Egmont Group of Financial Intelligence Units (FIUs), or foreign FinCENs.

During the period surrounding September 11, FinCEN management changed. The new management team insisted that similar to the dirty money battlefields in our War on Drugs, the new financial front-lines in the War on Terror Finance would evolve around the same kind of financial intelligence primarily produced by Western financial institutions. I doubted the efficacy of this approach. Moreover, I had severe philosophical and stylistic differences with the new FinCEN management team. I obtained a transfer to the Money Laundering Section of the Department of State's Bureau of International Narcotics and Law Enforcement Affairs (INL).

Shortly thereafter, I had the conversation with the Pakistani businessman I described in the Preface. His admonition that our enemies were laughing at us as they were transferring money and value right under our noses infuriated me. I subsequently discussed the issue with the head of the Indian customs service assigned to the Indian embassy in Washington D.C. We were mutually concerned about trade's link to underground finance and underground finance's link to terror. That evening, on a metro ride back home, I developed the concept and coined the term Trade Transparency Units, or TTUs.

It's a simple idea. Borrowing from the financial intelligence unit (FIU) model that examines suspicious financial transactions and other data, I suggested that the U.S. government examine the feasibility of establishing a prototype unit that collects and analyzes suspect trade data and then disseminates findings for appropriate enforcement action.

The objective was to establish a new investigative tool for customs and law enforcement that would facilitate trade transparency in order to attack entrenched forms of TBML, value transfer, customs fraud, and tax evasion. I hoped that it could also be a sorely needed "back door" into underground financial systems such as the BMPE and hawala that are being exploited by criminal organizations and terrorist adversaries. Coming from FinCEN, I hoped that one day there would be a worldwide TTU network that would be somewhat analogous to the Egmont Group of FIUs. (I also thought it important that we learn the lessons of the administrative and managerial mistakes of FinCEN and Egmont. The TTU network has to be enforcement oriented and directed.)

The wonderful thing about TTUs is that the data already exist. There is no need for vast new expenditures or to jump through labyrinths of bureaucratic hoops and approvals. As the reader has seen, every country already collects import and export data and often associated information. By comparing targeted trade transactions, it is a fairly straightforward analytical process to spot suspect trade anomalies. I knew the United States could simply build on Lou Bock's pioneering work. And I was confident that the concept would be attractive to other countries as well. Even for those that only paid lip service to fighting TBML and underground finance's link to terror, all governments are interested in combatting customs fraud and illicit value transfer because it robs them of needed revenue.

The State Department's Bureau of International Narcotics and Law Enforcement Affairs wholeheartedly endorsed the TTU initiative (and later provided funds to jumpstart the program in countries of concern). Likewise, the Department of Treasury provided crucial bureaucratic support. But the TTU initiative almost by definition dealt with trade and so had to be adopted and implemented by Customs. My former Customs colleagues, including Bock, fully supported and further developed the idea. I formally proposed the initiative in May 2003. (A copy of the original TTU proposal is included in Appendix B.) However, the suggestion overlapped with the creation of the new Department of Homeland Security and the dismemberment of Treasury Enforcement. It took a painfully long time for the government's stars to align and for sufficient resources to be devoted to finally initiate the TTU program.

The world's first TTU was established within ICE's headquarters. The NIPS program evolved into a specialized ICE computer system called the Data Analysis & Research for Trade Transparency System

(DARTT). Containing both domestic and limited foreign trade data, the computer system allows users to see both sides of a trade transaction, achieving trade transparency. Other investigative and financial databases were added, giving the analyst and investigator a more complete picture of a possible criminal conspiracy. In short order, the TTU concept proved itself. Countries collaborated and made a number of successful cases.

By 2007, the U.S. government made trade transparency and TTU development part of its National Anti-Money Laundering Strategy Report. Signed by the Secretaries of Treasury and Homeland Security, and the Attorney General, the strategy committed the United States to "attack TBML at home and abroad." Further, it promised, "Law enforcement will use all available means to identify and dismantle trade-based money laundering schemes. This strategy includes infiltrating criminal organizations to expose complex schemes from the inside, and deploying ICE-led Trade Transparency Units that facilitate the exchange and analysis of trade data among trading partners."[18]

Over the last few years, the TTU has evolved into an ongoing national investigative program for HSI. The program is embedded within the National Targeting Center—Investigations. According to Hector X. Colon, the director of the TTU, "Co-locating the TTU with Customs and Border Protection's targeting teams has better equipped HSI and CBP to successfully target, investigate, and dismantle transnational criminal organizations involved in TBML."[19]

The core component of the TTU initiative is the exchange of targeted trade data with foreign counterparts, which is generally facilitated by existing Customs Mutual Assistance Agreements or other similar information-sharing agreements. HSI/ICE is the only U.S. law enforcement agency capable of exchanging trade data with foreign governments to investigate international trade fraud and associated crimes.

By 2015, the HSI/TTU developed information-sharing partnerships with 11 foreign countries: Argentina, Australia, Brazil, Colombia, Dominican Republic, Ecuador, Guatemala, Mexico, Panama, Paraguay, and the Philippines.[20] Many other countries have shown interest in participating. They recognize the value of sharing trade data with the United States and possibly other TTU partners and gaining the analytical tools and expertise to more effectively examine their own data. By combining international efforts, the analysts and investigators can effectively follow the money and value trails.

 Since the creation of the domestic and international TTU initiative, more than $1 billion has been seized.[21]

In any government program dealing with data and analytics, there are justified concerns about privacy and international information sharing. So it is important to understand that foreign government partners that have established TTUs enter into a negotiated Customs Mutual Assistance Agreement or other similar information sharing agreement with the United States. They are granted access to specific trade datasets to investigate trade transactions, conduct analysis, and generate reports in the HSI TTU trade data subsystem.

HSI has two versions of their analytic program FALCON-DARTTS: one for HSI's foreign partners with access only to trade data shared pursuant to international information sharing agreements, and another for HSI users, which contains appropriate data from TTU partners as well as financial data and other law enforcement data. Foreign users do not have access to the HSI TTU financial and law enforcement datasets. Foreign users can only access trade data related to their country and the related U.S. trade transactions, unless access to other partner countries' data is authorized via information sharing agreements. Moreover, depending on the agreement and specific investigation, the data are aggregated and specific identifiers removed.[22]

According to Colon, "Most countries do not have access to foreign trade data to compare imports and exports and many countries' Financial Intelligence Units (FIUs) lack access to trade data or the expertise in identifying anomalies in trade transactions. The analysis of the trade data exchanged with foreign partners is facilitated by FALCON-DARTTS, an investigative tool that allows investigators and analysts to generate leads and support investigations related to TBML, smuggling, commercial fraud, and other crimes within the jurisdiction of HSI and foreign customs organizations. FALCON-DARTTS analyzes trade and financial data to identify statistically anomalous transactions that may warrant investigation.[23]

THE APPLICATION OF BIG DATA AND ANALYTICS

Over the last 10 years, there has been an explosion of "big data" and analytics. Nobody knows how much data and information are out there, but former Google CEO Eric Schmidt has claimed that we now create an entire human history's worth of data every two days![24]

Data alone are not that interesting. We need the knowledge that can be derived from the data. So we are fortunate that concurrent with the boom in data, both government and industry have pioneered exciting new analytic tools to systematically collect, harvest, mine, and examine data to uncover hidden insights, patterns, correlations, trends, and "intelligence." Much of the exciting new technology and analysis can be employed to tackle trade transparency.

For example, data warehousing and retrieval are enhanced by cutting-edge technologies that search, mine, analyze, link, and detect anomalies, suspicious behaviors, and related or interconnected activities and people. Unstructured data sources can be automated, scanned, and aggregated. Fraud frameworks can be deployed to help concerned government and commercial entities detect suspicious activity and anomalies using scoring engines that can rate, with high degrees of statistical accuracy, behaviors that warrant further investigation while generating alerts when something of importance changes. Text analytics can work with both structured and free-form text and identify numbers, words, and specific form fields. Predictive analytics use elements involved in a successful case or investigation and overlay these elements on other datasets to detect previously unknown behaviors or activities, enhancing and expanding an investigator's knowledge, efforts, and productivity while more effectively deploying resources. Social network analytics help analysts and investigators detect and prevent suspect activity by going beyond individual transactions to analyze all related activities in various media and networks, uncovering previously unknown relationships. Visual analytics is a high-performance, in-memory solution for exploring massive amounts of data very quickly. It enables users to spot patterns, identify opportunities for further analysis, and convey visual results via online reports or the iPad.[25]

We have already seen that classifying and monitoring trade and associated international travel, finance, shipping, logistics, insurance data, and more generates tremendous information that can be applied to promote trade transparency. For example, web analytics and web crawling alone can search shipping companies and customs websites to review shipment details and compare them against their corresponding documentation. Advanced analytics can also be deployed to develop unit price analysis, unit weight analysis, shipment and route analysis, international trade and country profile analysis, and relationship analysis of trade partners and ports.[26]

Of course, there has also been a proliferation of classified data that could be better exploited to examine certain questionable aspects of trade.

I am technology challenged, but it appears to me that we have barely scratched the surface in applying analytics to the data that are currently available and could be made available. Discounting the unattainable, by using modern analytic tools to exploit a variety of relevant big data sets, I believe international trade transparency is theoretically achievable or certainly possible at a factor many times over what we have today.

CASE EXAMPLE: OPERATION DELUGE

In 2006, the U.S. and Brazilian TTUs collaborated in Operation Deluge. The TTUs jointly targeted a scheme that had undervalued U.S. exports to Brazil to evade more than $200 million in Brazilian customs duties between 2001 and 2006.[27] In a huge bust, 950 Brazilian federal police officers and 350 customs agents executed search warrants at 238 locations in various Brazilian states.[28] They also executed 128 arrest warrants that netted both government officials and the directors and owners of several large Brazilian companies. Nine of the detainees were employees of Brazil's Internal Revenue Service.[29] During the joint operation, U.S. ICE agents in Miami seized approximately $500,000 in goods slated for export to Brazil.[30]

The United States and Brazil accused the defendants of tax evasion, document fraud, public corruption, and the undervaluation of exports. The commodities included an assortment of goods including electronics and telecommunications equipment, orthopedic equipment, surgical gloves, fruits, plastic bottles, garments and textiles, batteries, vehicles, dietary supplements, and perfumes.[31]

According to Brazilian authorities, the leader of the ring was Marco Antonio Mansur. Mansur was arrested with his son—a co-conspirator—in their apartment in an upscale neighborhood of Sao Paulo. Mansur was a wealthy businessman who once lived in Paraguay.[32] Police accused him of creating dozens of front companies to carry out his undervaluation scheme; the companies were registered in Uruguay, Panama, the British Virgin Islands, and Delaware.[33]

NOTES

1. For an excellent overview of trade-finance, see the 2014 US FFIEC Bank Secrecy Act/Money Laundering Examination Manual, p. 267, available online: https://www.ffiec.gov/bsa_aml_infobase/pages_manual/manual_print.htm.

2. "Advisory to Financial Institutions on Filing Suspicious Activity Reports regarding Trade-Based Money Laundering," FinCEN (February 18, 2010), available online: http://www.fincen.gov/statutes_regs/guidance/html/fin-2010-a001.html.

3. Ibid.

4. Ibid.

5. U.S. Trade Online: https://usatrade.census.gov/usatrade.nsf.

6. "Tariff Schedules," Office of the United States Trade Representative, available online: http://www.ustr.gov/trade-topics/industry-manufacturing/industrial-tariffs/tariff-schedules.

7. Ibid.

8. Ibid.

9. Export.gov website, available online: http://www.export.gov/faq/eg_main_017509.asp.

10. Disguised data given to the author by U.S. Customs.

11. John S. Zdanowicz, Florida State University, "Trade Based Money Laundering and Terrorist Financing," *Review of Law and Economics*, 5 (2) (2009), p. 868.

12. "Trade Based Money Laundering," Financial ActionTask Force (June 23, 2006), see case example 2, available online: http://www.fatf-gafi.org/media/fatf/documents/reports/Trade%20Based%20Money%20Laundering.pdf.

13. See the ASYCUDA website for additional information; http://www.asycuda.org/.

14. The information in this section comes from personal knowledge and from: John Cassara, *Hide & Seek: Intelligence Law Enforcement and the Stalled War on Terrorist Finance* (Washington, DC: Potomac Books, 2006), pp. 151–153.

15. Sharon Theimer, "U.S. Customs Database Used to Track Terrorist Financing," *DSstarr*, available online: http://www.tgc.com/dsstar/01/1211/103779.html.

16. Kenneth Rijock, "An Emerging Money Laundering Threat Facing Compliance Officers," Financial Services Technology (Sept. 3, 2008), available online: http://www.world-check.com/media/d/content_pressarticle_reference/Rijock_FST_0908.pdf.

17. The author develops this argument in detail in his book, *Hide & Seek: Intelligence, Law Enforcement, and the Stalled War on Terrorist Finance.*

18. *2007 National Anti-Money Laundering Strategy,"* p. 7, available online: http://www .treasury.gov/resource-center/terrorist-illicit-finance/Documents/nmls.pdf.

19. March 26, 2015, e-mail exchange between the author and Hector X. Colon, the unit chief/director of the TTU.

20. "Written testimony of ICE Homeland Security Investigations, National Intellectual Property Rights Coordination Center Director Lev Kubiak for a Senate Committee on Appropriations, Subcommittee on Homeland Security hearing titled "Strengthening Trade Enforcement to Protect American Enterprise and Grow American Jobs," July 16, 2014, available online: http://www.dhs.gov/news/2014/ 07/16/written-testimony-ice-senate-committee-appropriations-subcommittee-homeland-security, and updated in a March 26, 2015, e-mail exchange between the author and Hector X. Colon, the unit chief/director of the TTU.

21. March 26, 2015, e-mail exchange between the author and Hector X. Colon, the unit chief/director of the TTU.

22. "Privacy Impact Assessment for the FALCON Data Analysis & Research for Trade Transparency System," January 16, 2014, available online: http://www.dhs.gov/ sites/default/files/publications/privacy_pia_ice_falcondartts_january2014_0.pdf.

23. March 26, 2015, e-mail exchange between the author and Hector X. Colon, the unit chief/director of the TTU.

24. Jeff Vance, "Big Data Analytics Overview," *Datamation* (June 25, 2013), available online: http://www.datamation.com/applications/big-data-analytics-overview .html.

25. The author has proposed data and analytic solutions in many forums including prepared testimony before the House Homeland Subcommittee on Counterterrorism and Intelligence, May 18, 2012, "Terrorist Financing since 9/11: Assessing the Evolution of al Qaeda and State Sponsors of Terror," available online: http://homeland .house.gov/sites/homeland.house.gov/files/Testimony%20-%20Cassara.pdf.

26. "Goods Gone Bad: Addressing Money Laundering Risk in the Trade Finance System," PWC, January 2015, available online: http://www.pwc.com/us/en/risk-assurance-services/publications/trade-finance-money-laundering.jhtml.

27. Stephanie Ayres, "Investigation by New Trade Transparency Unit Leads to Hundreds of Raids in Brazil," *Financial Crimes News* (January 8, 2007).

28. Kenneth Rijock, "Operation Deluge, Brazilian-American Joint Operation Shuts Down $234m Trade Fraud Scheme," *World-Check* (August 21, 2006).

29. "79 Arrested in Brazil's Biggest Foreign Trade Fraud," *People's Daily Online* (August 17, 2006), available online: http://en.people.cn/200608/17/eng20060817_294109 .html.

30. "ICE Assists Brazilian Officials in Dismantling $200 Million Trade Fraud Scheme," ICE News Release (August 18, 2006).

31. Ibid.

32. Francisco Neves, "Brazilian Police Have No Rest: They Bust International Importing Gang," *Brazil Magazine* (August 16, 2006).

33. "ICE Assists Brazilian Officials."

CHAPTER **10**

Red-Flag
Indicators

BML can be complex, confusing, and often hiding in plain sight. For bank compliance officers, the situation is made more difficult due to one of the basic tenets of trade finance: "Banks deal with documents and not with goods, services or performance to which the documents relate."[1]

According to the Wolfsberg Group, an association of global banks that promote AML/CFT standards, banks do not get involved with the physical goods, nor do they have the capability to do so. These limitations define the degree of scrutiny and understanding a financial institution can bring to the identification of suspicious activity.[2] Yet despite these self-imposed parameters, compliance officers might well have occasion to suspect unusual or suspicious activity. I also believe that financial institutions involved with financing transactions will face increasing pressure to assume a more proactive role in scrutinizing trade.

Hector X. Colon, the head of the U.S. TTU, acknowledges the debate and the difficulty and appeals for help: "TBML presents probably one of the most complex and dynamic forms of illicit money movement which undermines legitimate business and commerce. It is important that compliance officers report suspicious activity that could help law enforcement identify and investigate TBML."[3]

Fortunately, a number of concerned organizations have issued *red-flag indicators* or warning signs that could be indicative of TBML. Some of the best originate from the 2006 FATF Typology Report on Trade Based Money Laundering,[4] the 2012 Asia Pacific Group Typology Report on Trade Based Money Laundering,[5] the 2014 Federal Financial Institutions Examination Council's Bank Secrecy Act/Anti–Money Laundering Examination Manual,[6] and a 2010 FinCEN Advisory to Financial Institutions on Filing Suspicious Activity Reports Regarding Trade Based Money Laundering.[7]

Many of the indicators identified in the above-referenced sources are duplicative and/or overlap. Some also focus on different subsets of TBML that have been discussed in this book, including underground financial systems, FTZs, and others. Many of the red flags deal with trade finance. This chapter includes many indicators from the above-cited references. I also add a few of my own. The red flags listed in this chapter are not in any particular order, category, or priority.

By combining them in a single list, I believe the student of TBML will see the broader context and also be able to pick and choose the indicators that are of most interest.

Trust your instincts. If something doesn't make market or economic sense, take a closer look. In other words, be guided by the law enforcement principle of JDLR—it "just doesn't look right."

Of course, red flags by themselves are not proof of illegal activity. They are simply indicators that the transaction *may deserve closer scrutiny.* The concerned compliance officer, analyst, or investigator must take into consideration other factors, including the normal transaction/business activity of the subject/s, the particulars of the trade item and the transaction, its recognized value (which can sometimes be subjective), financing, the geographic locations involved with the transaction, any previous history of trade fraud or criminal associations, the presence of financial intelligence on any of the parties involved, and other factors included in Chapter 9's discussion of monitoring trade.

POSSIBLE RED-FLAG INDICATORS OF TBML

- Significant discrepancies exist between the description, quality, and quantity of the commodity on the bill of lading, invoice, and actual goods shipped.
- Significant deviation between the value of the commodity as reported on the invoice and a normal "arm's-length" fair-market price.
- The weight of the shipment does not match the listed contents.
- The shipment is inconsistent with the exporter's normal business (e.g., an exporter of consumer electronics shipping paper supplies).
- The size of the shipment appears inconsistent with the exporter's normal business activity.

- Invoices or bills of lading include inaccurate information about the product being shipped or information that is not commonly accepted (e.g., an invoice listing the square feet of granite tile being imported when the accepted norm is pricing by the ton).

- Invoices contain inaccurate or incomplete product descriptions; for example, an invoice for 1,000 kilograms of frozen shrimp is not sufficient to analyze its market value because there are multiple U.S. harmonized codes for frozen shrimp reflecting imports of different sizes.

- The commodity is being shipped to/from or through areas of "high risk" for money laundering.

- Companies are operating out of foreign countries where it is very difficult to determine the true ownership or controlling persons of the company or where the type of business is not fully apparent.

- A party is unable or unwilling to produce appropriate documentation upon request.

- Documentation appears fraudulent.

- The routing of the shipment is circuitous, not direct, is illogical, or is being transshipped through a questionable area for no apparent economic reason.

- A shipment of goods destined for an end-user has no need for the product (e.g., electronics manufacturing equipment sent to a destination that does not have an electronics industry).

- Shipments involve suspect free trade zones or special economic zones.

- The method of payment is inconsistent with the normal business practice of the parties involved, inconsistent with the characteristics of the transaction, or using advance payment for a shipment from a new supplier in a high-risk country.

- The transaction involves the receipt of cash.

- International wire transfers are received as payment for goods into bank accounts where the exporter is not located.

- The transaction involves a third party that has no apparent connection to the buyer or seller.

- Payment is made from multiple sources and/or multiple accounts.

- The transaction involves the use of front or shell companies.

- The parties involved are not transparent and use "Delaware"-like shell corporations with lack of beneficial ownership information.

- Numerous sole-proprietorship businesses or private limited companies are involved in the transaction or established by proxies or where false addresses are involved.

- The transaction and payment appear to have unnecessary and complex layers involving multiple accounts and multiple jurisdictions that combine to obscure the true nature of the transaction.

- Money services businesses or money exchange bureaus located in third countries are used as intermediaries for the transfer of goods or money.

- The transaction involves a frequently amended letter of credit.

- Shipment locations or description of goods are not consistent with the letter of credit.

- Transactions that involve payments for goods through checks, drafts, or money orders are not drawn on the account of the entity that purchased the items.

- Unusual deposits of cash, cash deposits in round numbers, or structured cash deposits under the reporting threshold into a bank account are used to fund the trade transaction.

- Sequentially numbered checks drawn on domestic bank accounts are negotiated through foreign money services businesses.

- The contract is other than an arm's-length transaction (see abusive transfer pricing).

▦ Related-party transactions are involved (e.g., familial relationships).

▦ Goods that are commonly associated with TBML schemes are involved (e.g., scrap gold, precious metals and stones, trade in tobacco, consumer electronics, automobiles, etc.).

▦ Goods present valuation difficulties (precious stones, artwork, scrap gold, etc.).

▦ A freight-forwarding firm is listed as the commodity's final destination.

▦ Goods involved are frequently used in bartering schemes (e.g., gasoline and tires).

▦ A shipment does not make economic sense (e.g., the use of a 40-foot shipping container to transport a relatively small volume of goods).

▦ Carousel transactions are involved—the repeated or circular importation and exportation of the same high-value commodity.

▦ Packaging is inconsistent with the commodity or shipping method involved.

▦ Upon inspection or verification, the manufacturing entity has no physical address, no or limited production capability, limited or no inventory at its business premises, and so on.

▦ Phantom shipment—no goods are actually shipped but payment is made. Confirmation of shipment and delivery should be requested in a suspect case of TBML.

▦ There are multiple invoices for suspect goods. A frequently repeated suspect pattern of numerous invoices involves the same or similar items and where the actual physical shipment is never physically verified.

▦ The exporter requests payment of proceeds to an unrelated third party.

▦ The quantity or quality of the goods is padded, or inflated.

■ Counterfeit invoices are used. If an invoice looks suspicious, try to compare it with a known genuine invoice. Note any differences in the quality of the printing, company letterhead, design or other visuals, different contact numbers, e-mail addresses, or other items recorded in previous correspondence.

PRUDENT STEPS

In addition to being familiar with TBML methodologies and the above red-flag indicators, a prudent compliance officer should consider the following steps:

■ All documentation should be examined. If specific data or documents are not made available, ask for them! Depending on the financial institution and their internal policies, much of the information will be required in order to arrange financing. Legitimate clients should have no compunction about turning over requested documents for review.

■ In dealing with suspect TBML activity, follow standard due diligence and KYC policies. Know your customer and know your customer's customer. The recipients or customers of the client should also be the subject of due diligence inquiries, particularly if the client is located in a suspect location.

■ If possible (and appropriate), conduct unannounced visits to the company involved. Does the company actually exist? Is the company really engaged in manufacturing the subject trade goods or does it have a need for the imported product?

■ Adhering to internal policies, file a suspicious activity report. Provide as much detail and explanation as possible for your suspicions and clearly indicate why you believe the transaction is representative of TBML, the BMPE, hawala, etc.

■ Contact law enforcement. If a proposed trade-based transaction has obvious law enforcement or national security considerations, reach out directly to the applicable federal, state, or local government agency or department. Realistically, you might not get the feedback you desire but in many cases law enforcement authorities will use the tip and either intercept or monitor the shipment or transaction. (They might also use an undercover approach.)

GUIDANCE

The United Kingdom's Financial Conduct Authority (FCA) has warned banks about TBML and urged them to improve their monitoring efforts. According to a recent study, many banks "had no clear policy or procedures document for dealing with trade-based money laundering risks … were unable to demonstrate that money laundering risk had been taken into account when processing particular transactions … [and] made inadequate use of customer due diligence information gathered by relationship managers or trade sales teams."[8] I imagine the above shortcomings hold true for most countries around the world.

I'm convinced that TBML is the next frontier in international money laundering enforcement. There will undoubtedly be increasing regulatory pressure applied to financial institutions involved with trade-finance. I urge prudent trade organizations and financial institutions to become familiar with TBML methodologies, establish best practices regarding risk in the trade finance system, and develop analytics-focused AML/CFT monitoring capabilities to identify suspicious TBML transactions.

NOTES

1. The Wolfsberg Group, *Wolfsberg Trade Finance Principles* (2011), p. 3; available online: http: http://www.wolfsberg-principles.com/pdf/standards/Wolfsberg_Trade_Principles_Paper_II_(2011).pdf.

2. Ibid.

3. March 26, 2015, e-mail exchange between the author and Hector X. Colon, Unit Chief/Director of the HSI TTU.

4. 2006 FATF Typology Report on Trade Based Money Laundering, available online: http://www.fatf-gafi.org/media/fatf/documents/reports/Trade%20Based%20Money%20Laundering.pdf.

5. 2012 Asia Pacific Group Typology Report on Trade Based Money Laundering, available online: http://www.fatf-gafi.org/media/fatf/documents/reports/Trade_Based_ML_APGReport.pdf.

6. 2014 Federal Financial Institutions Examination Council's Bank Secrecy Act/Anti-Money Laundering Examination Manual, available online: https://www.ffiec.gov/bsa_aml_infobase/documents/BSA_AML_Man_2014.pdf.

7. 2010 FinCEN Advisory to Financial Institutions on Filing Suspicious Activity Reports regarding TBML, available online: http://www.fincen.gov/statutes_regs/guidance/pdf/fin-2010-a001.pdf.

8. "Banks Control of Financial Crime Risks in Trade Finance," Financial Control Authority (July 2013), available online: http://www.fca.org.uk/static/documents/thematic-reviews/tr-13-03.pdf.

CHAPTER 11

Conclusions and Recommendations

GET SERIOUS ABOUT TBML

In 2005, I wrote my first book, *Hide & Seek: Intelligence, Law Enforcement and the Stalled War on Terror Finance*. The final chapter of the book contained a number of "steps forward." The first recommendation was, "Get Serious about TBML." It should come as no surprise that, years later, I have exactly the same conclusion and priority recommendation!

I would like to quote from the earlier recommendation in *Hide & Seek*: "The misuse of trade should be the next frontier in anti-money-laundering programs. Just as a generation ago the United States promoted financial transparency, today it is time to promote trade transparency. International trade is a back door for money laundering, illegal value transfer, customs fraud, tax cheating, and various alternative remittance systems."[1] That earlier prescription is in fact the theme of this book.

Nothing has changed my mind in the intervening years: trade transparency should be the new priority in AML/CFT enforcement. In Chapter 1, we discussed the magnitude of international money laundering. Worldwide estimates are in the trillions of dollars. As demonstrated, if we honestly examine the sheer volume of illicit proceeds laundered and the increasing recognition that tax evasion is another form of money laundering, our success rate as measured by the one meaningful bottom-line metric—convictions—is pitiful.

So it is time to question the effectiveness of our current counter-measures. The status quo isn't working. At the same time, we have essentially ignored one of the chief components of international money laundering—trade. While time, attention, and resources are devoted to new-age "sexy" money-laundering topics such as cyber-currency, the overwhelming majority of dirty money being laundered today takes place via old-fashioned methods that we have not yet been able to control. In point of fact, trade-based value transfer is arguably the oldest money-laundering system in the world.

The international community must now focus on this essential missing link. We should follow hidden value transfer trails by looking comprehensively across countries *and* commodities.

As I wrote in *Hide & Seek*, "For a variety of reasons, [bureaucracies] have been reluctant to focus on this issue [TBML]. The competing interests of commerce and enforcement and between liberties and the government's need to know will undoubtedly influence any future debate on how to combat the misuse of trade. Yet just like in the area of traditional money laundering through financial institutions, compromises can be found, necessary safeguards implemented, and a balance achieved."[2] I'm convinced we can do this.

So what are some new steps forward?

DEFINE THE MAGNITUDE OF THE PROBLEM

In Chapter 1, I wrote, *"Including all its varied forms,* the argument can be made that TBML is perhaps the largest and most pervasive money-laundering methodology in the world." Estimating the overall magnitude of global money laundering has proved difficult.[3] The scope of TBML has never been systematically examined. But I believe it is possible for economists, statisticians, and analysts to come up with a fairly accurate estimate of the overall magnitude of global TBML and value transfer. Narrowing it down to specific problematic countries is easier still. The primary reason this is doable is that data are available for most of the trade-based methodologies discussed in this book. That is not necessarily true for money laundering in general.

Academics and nonprofits such as Global Financial Integrity have done tremendous work in developing models that measure aspects of TBML. Using these pioneering insights, I believe the World Bank or the IMF should study the global magnitude of the problem and develop an overall estimate. If those international organizations are unwilling to undertake the task, I urge the Department of Treasury's Office of Intelligence and Analysis (OIA) to at least examine U.S.-related data and come up with an official estimate for the amount of TBML that impacts the United States.

A generally accepted estimate of the magnitude of TBML in all its varied forms is important for a number of reasons: (1) it will provide clarity; (2) it will focus attention on the issue; (3) from an enforcement perspective, the supporting analysis should provide both excellent insight into specific areas where criminals are vulnerable and promising opportunities for targeting; and (4) systematically cracking down on TBML and customs fraud will translate into enormous revenue gain for the governments involved.

I also believe an approximate ratio of the estimated amount of TBML to the amount a government should recover by enforcement is possible to determine. The carrot of enticement will prove important. From experience, I have found that for most countries it is not political will that finally drives effective action to combat TBML and value transfer. Rather, it is revenue enhancement for income-starved governments that is the catalyst for action. Whatever the motivation, it is time to get started.

FOCUS FROM THE TOP

As we have seen, TBML impacts a variety of issues of growing international concern, including transnational crime, terrorism, tax evasion, customs fraud, abusive transfer pricing, sanctions busting, capital flight, trade diversion, underground finance, informal remittances, and others. These are all incredibly important issues that impact both the developed and developing worlds. The promotion of trade transparency requires global visibility. Effective countermeasures necessitate a comprehensive and worldwide approach. Thus, in my opinion, trade transparency should be an agenda item for the G-20, the Organization of Economic Development (OECD), the World Customs Organization (WCO), and the Financial Action Task Force (FATF).

Trade fraud also impacts societal and cultural issues such as corruption, the transfer of national wealth, environmental degradation, the exploitation of national resources, endangered wildlife, illegally logged timber, conflict gold and diamonds, and other worrisome challenges. I would like to see nonprofit organizations involved in these issues, such as Global Witness, promote trade transparency for both industry and government.

A FATF RECOMMENDATION

In the world of AML/CFT, the FATF makes things happen. The FATF recognizes TBML is a huge concern and calls it "one of the three largest" money-laundering methodologies in the world. There is a special FATF typology report on TBML. Unfortunately, when the current FATF Recommendations were reviewed and promulgated in 2012, TBML was not specifically addressed.

In years past, I was active in the discussions about making TBML a "special" FATF recommendation. However, it should not come as a surprise that not all countries want trade transparency. Some benefit from the status quo. Moreover, expanding FATF's mandate into international trade matters would be a huge leap outside of its traditional domain of focusing on banks, money services businesses, and designated nonfinancial businesses and professions (DNFBPs). But I believe it is now only a matter of time before the FATF expands its self-imposed constraints. The FATF must be flexible and confront varied identified threats to the increasingly interconnected global financial order. If it does not move to systematically address one of its self-identified top-three global money-laundering methodologies, the organization will lose credibility. Accordingly, I believe the FATF and its sister FATF-style regional bodies should work toward developing a consensus that TBML should be subject to its own recommendations.

This consensus will undoubtedly take time. In order to be effective, any new recommendation on TBML must encompass not only financial institutions but also designated sectors involved in international trade. This will include firms transporting or arranging the transport of goods such as brokers, freight forwarders, and carriers. In addition, any new mandate on trade transparency should include manufacturers and companies involved in global trade. This will necessitate a huge expansion of the current AML/CFT umbrella. Entirely new categories of nonfinancial companies that are currently not the least bit knowledgeable or concerned about AML/CFT safeguards must be included. This admittedly controversial and costly proposed expansion would inevitably involve new industries in AML/CFT customer due diligence, record keeping, and the filing of financial intelligence reports such as CTRs, 8300s, and SARs.[4]

There are some signs that Treasury is moving in this direction. For example, in April 2015, FinCEN issued a temporary geographic targeting order (GTO) directed against 700 exporters of consumer electronics and cellular phones in the city of Doral in Miami–Dade County. The GTO requires the businesses to report all cash transactions involving $3,000 or more instead of the normal $10,000. Over the last few years, there has been increasing intelligence that electronics exporters in Doral, which operate in a free trade zone near Miami International Airport, were "vulnerable to abuse," particularly being used as witting or unwitting accomplices in facilitating TBML and BMPE schemes. John Tobon, the ICE Assistant Special Agent in Charge of HSI investigations in Miami, said that he hopes the electronics exporters will support their role in combating international money laundering via trade. According to Tobon, "We're trying to start creating that culture of compliance" (in industries outside of financial services).[5]

These and similar measures will undoubtedly generate pushback because of cost, burdensome record keeping, and the prevalent attitude among most businesses that they do not have a role to play as policemen. So realistically, a FATF Recommendation on TBML is not a near-term countermeasure. But building awareness and consensus and implementing targeted enforcement operations is a good place to start.

CURTAIL THE COMMERCIAL MISUSE OF TRADE

As noted in Chapter 7, both the criminal and commercial misuse of trade works hand-in-hand. I agree wholeheartedly with Raymond Baker of Global Financial Integrity that "we cannot succeed in stopping the criminals while at the same time telling multinational corporations that they can continue to misinvoice as they choose."[6] Abusive and fraudulent pricing techniques are used every day by thousands of multinational corporations around the world to move money and transfer value across borders. Current AML/CFT countermeasures turn a blind eye to legitimate actors' use of shadow financial systems, questionable financial flows, offshore havens, and assorted gray techniques used for the purposes of tax evasion, wealth preservation, and increasing profits. Yet at the same time, authorities will aggressively pursue criminal organizations' use of the same techniques to move tainted money across borders. This type of intellectual and political disingenuousness and hypocrisy contributes to our underwhelming success in effectively combating money laundering and other types of financial crimes.

Global corporations must embrace legitimate trade. Legitimate actors should demand trade transparency. This means respecting customs duties, VAT assessments, currency exchange regulations, AML/CFT regulations, and more. The FATF and other concerned international bodies should work to define illicit financial flows that are facilitated via trade and then create effective and enforceable measures to curtail trade misinvoicing. The human costs of commercial trade-based money and value transfer are the strongest arguments for international trade transparency and why this issue must be the next frontier in financial crimes enforcement.

ENHANCE WIRE TRANSFER REPORTING

In 2010, FinCEN issued a notice of proposed rulemaking that would lower the reporting threshold on cross-border electronic fund (wire) transfers from $10,000. (There was discussion regarding the amount of the new limits for both inbound and outbound wires.) The rule was authorized by the Intelligence Reform and Terrorism Prevention Act of 2004. The proposed rule would require banks directly transacting with foreign financial institutions to report all cross-border wire transfers to FinCEN. Currently, financial institutions are subject only to reporting suspicious wire transfers. FinCEN estimated that the proposed rule would annually create 500 million to 700 million new reports.[7] Currently, financial institutions and MSBs file approximately 17 million financial intelligence reports with FinCEN every year.

FinCEN believes that the proposed cross-border wire transfer requirements would close certain loopholes that are exploited for money laundering, terrorist financing, and tax evasion. For a number of reasons, the proposed rule was subsequently withdrawn.

The focus of the rule was not TBML. However, such a rule if implemented would greatly enhance trade transparency. According to HSI investigator John Tobon, "We have full visibility of the trade data and if we could get full visibility on the financial picture attached to the trade data, it would be like getting lasik surgery and being able to throw away your glasses."[8]

I endorse augmented cross-border wire reporting because the new intelligence will assist criminal investigators in combatting not only TBML but many other financial crimes. Candidly, my principal concern is that FinCEN has proven itself incapable of fully exploiting the financial intelligence it currently receives.[9] The proposed wire data would be a 40 times increase of current annual BSA data filed. So this recommendation is conditional upon long-overdue effective congressional and Treasury oversight of FinCEN.

TBML ANALYTICS

Most large financial institutions and many money services businesses have automated AML/CFT programs. Some of these programs are commercially available and others are developed in-house. Depending on their level of sophistication, they use some of the above-described techniques to monitor transactions, adhere to anti—money laundering compliance programs, and follow internal policies and guidelines.

Over the last few years, there has been increasing emphasis within AML/CFT compliance to be much more proactive in analysis. For example, by "spinning the dials" of monitoring systems, obligated entities sometimes search for telltale indicators of human trafficking. The point is that alerts are not generated unless programmed to do so.

Unfortunately, up to now, little has been done to include and detect TBML. There hasn't been any "dial spinning." Thus, I suggest AML/CFT compliance analytic programs be expanded to cover suspect trade and value transfer. For financial institutions, as discussed in Chapters 9 and 10, most scrutiny will likely be focused on trade finance. However, today it is also possible to code or engineer TBML red-flag indicators into traditional AML/CFT software. The technology and expertise exists so that analytics can provide alerts when there is a likelihood of specific TBML methodologies such as hawala, trade pricing anomalies, the likelihood of trade fraud, and so on. I would like to see associations involved with banking, fraud, trade, financial crimes, and anti—money laundering press for the incorporation of TBML analytic programs. Financial intelligence units around the world, including Treasury's FinCEN, should enthusiastically champion this countermeasure. I'm confident the data and analytics industry are ready to assist.

EXPAND THE INTERNATIONAL TTU NETWORK

Trade Transparency Units (TTUs) have proved to be an increasingly important means to link international customs and law enforcement agencies. In the few years of their existence, TTUs' analytic, investigative, and enforcement efforts have identified and disrupted the activities of transnational criminal organizations involved in fraudulent trade schemes. There are enough data and "success stories" to make an informed judgment that the concept has proved effective.

In addition to being an innovative countermeasure to TBML and value transfer, as we have seen, systematically cracking down on trade-fraud is a revenue enhancer for participating governments. Frankly, it is for this reason that many countries have expressed interest in the concept. In essence, these governments understand that they are not collecting the appropriate amount of taxes and duties due to rampant customs fraud. Finding new revenue is increasingly an imperative for governments around the world. And establishing a TTU is a rare example of a government program that returns far more revenue than it consumes!

I asked Hector X. Colon, director of the U.S. TTU for his vision for the TTU concept. According to Colon:

> I would like to see the TTU program grow within the U.S. and internationally. Domestically, the TTU can be capable of supporting not only HSI, but other law enforcement partners that have cases with a nexus to trade. In order to do so, it will require additional manpower and funding. Over the past few years, the TTU has been reduced in manpower and budget despite a significant increase in the number of investigations and foreign TTUs it supports. Internationally, the WCO appears interested in adopting the TTU program. A partnership with the WCO could expand the TTU program beyond HSI's current TTU international footprint. Additional WCO members that embrace the TTU methodology of developing cooperative relationships with foreign counterparts to enhance information sharing will build the framework for HSI to successfully conduct international trade and money laundering investigations, capable of prosecuting and dismantling the transnational criminal networks engaged in TBML and other illicit customs crimes.[10]

I fully support Colon's vision and wholeheartedly endorse the U.S. TTU model and its nascent international network. I am a proponent of eventually having a standard and globally recognized TTU partnership along the lines of the Egmont Group of Financial Intelligence Units (FIUs). Yet any country or jurisdiction can also create its own internal and independent TTU outside of the U.S.-sponsored initiative. An independent or nontraditional TTU could even be integrated into a current FIU or customs service. A compelling argument could also be made for the establishment of regional TTUs to examine distinct area-wide TBML and value transfer issues. Once again, such TTUs do not have to be affiliated with the U.S. DHS/HSI TTU program.

For example, Lou Bock and Mark Laxer (introduced in Chapter 9 as pioneers in TBML analysis and enforcement) recognize the power of traditional TTUs but are frustrated with their limitations as they serve only a small number of countries and generally focus on rather narrow aspects of crime such as terror finance and drug-related money laundering.[11] Another problem is that trade fraud controls are fragmented and reflect a division of labor among specialized agencies that only act when misconduct falls within their jurisdiction and mandate. For most jurisdictions, there is currently no holistic, systematic collaborative effort to bring data together, conduct analysis, investigate, and prosecute. A lack of expertise is another roadblock.

I have called corruption the "great-facilitator" in TBML. Bock and Laxer agree. In their experience, targeting takes place deep within the framework of government bureaucracies where there is too often a negative incentive to root out massive fraud. Not only does fraud embarrass and sometimes point to powerful entities, aggressive investigation takes political courage and resources and can shake up the comfortable status quo at that very institution.

So Bock and Laxer are now promoting nontraditional TTUs. They have identified innovative ways in which TTU functionality can be scaled for the diverse needs of countries. Nontraditional TTUs can target many different types of criminal behavior such as illicit trade flows and environmental crime. The duo have also developed a system by which the data and analysis reside outside member governments as a way to bypass corruption and inefficiencies often found in large bureaucracies. Nontraditional TTUs could also help lift the veil on the commercial misuse of trade. And they have worked to incorporate a variety of open source, publicly available data in their analysis.

So with the above in mind, I suggest the international expansion of the TTU initiative—with or without affiliation with the U.S.-led network. In addition, countries around the world should significantly bolster their customs services and provide training for how to better recognize and detect various forms of TBML and value transfer.

REEMPOWER TREASURY ENFORCEMENT

It has been well chronicled that both the CIA and the FBI failed in their missions—both foreign and domestic—to protect the homeland against the September 11 terrorist attacks. Other agencies also failed in aspects of their particular duties, such as the then Immigration and Naturalization Service, the Federal Aviation Authority, and Treasury's FinCEN. Yet in the rush to react to the events surrounding September 11, politicians from both parties hurried to reward the CIA and FBI with increased budget, mission, and manpower. And the Department of Treasury's enforcement arm that had virtually nothing to do with missing the signs of the impending terrorist attacks was punished.

With the resulting creation of the Department of Homeland Security (DHS), proud legacy Treasury law enforcement agencies such as the Secret Service and the U.S. Customs were jettisoned and shifted to the new DHS. The Bureau of Alcohol, Tobacco, and Firearms (ATF) was transferred to the Department of Justice. The move was aided and abetted by a Treasury secretary who had no interest in the proud legacy and tradition of Treasury law enforcement.[12]

The resulting dysfunction within the DHS has been well documented. In my opinion, the primary reason that DHS doesn't work as designed is that it is simply too large. It was created in 2002 by incorporating entities from 22 agencies and departments. Today, it has over 200,000 employees and a FY 2015 gross discretionary budget of approximately $45 billion![13] In my opinion, one unfortunate result of this colossus of an organization is that our AML/CFT efforts are stalled.[14]

In the Department of Justice, TBML and value transfer are subsets of other underlying crimes or specified unlawful activities. For example, the DEA focuses on money laundering only as it relates to the predicate offense of narcotics trafficking. The FBI does wonderful work reacting to bank robberies and white-collar criminals but knows very little about trade fraud and underground value transfer. Treasury, on the other hand, has a more holistic and systematic approach to money laundering in all of its forms. Moreover, the domestic financial industry sees Treasury as its natural government interlocutor—not the Departments of Justice or Homeland Security.

In the post–September 11 Treasury Department, the Office of Terrorism and Financial Intelligence (TFI) is primarily relegated to making AML/CFT policy and recommendations. It's a fact of bureaucratic life that outside recommendations are often ignored. And because its enforcement arm was crippled when DHS was created, Treasury no longer has the buttons to push and levers to pull to make things happen and implement those same policies. Some observers will argue that Treasury's use of sanctions and designations is an effective tool. Personally, I agree with the sage observation of retired U.S. diplomat Douglas Paal: "Sanctions always accomplish their principal objective, which is to make those who impose them feel good."[15] Besides, Treasury needs additional means to implement its enforcement mission.

So in conjunction with a long-overdue congressional review of the efficacy of the DHS, I suggest that thought be given to reestablishing the Department of Treasury's ability to conduct some types of financial crimes investigations.[16] (I am not including Treasury's Internal Revenue Service Criminal Investigations in this discussion because its primary focus revolves around taxes.) The easiest way of doing this would be returning the United States Secret Service and the United States Customs Service to a reconstituted Treasury Office of Enforcement. (Full disclosure: I proudly served in both the Secret Service and the legacy Customs Service before their unwarranted departure to DHS.)

The Secret Service was founded in 1865 and was in the Department of Treasury until the creation of DHS. Its recent well-chronicled administrative and operational breakdowns are in part due to larger unresolved issues within DHS. The dual missions of the Secret Service—protection and financial crimes investigations—are actually complementary. Agents assigned to protection details learn a variety of skills working financial crimes investigations on the street. We would benefit by having an elite Secret Service skilled in twenty-first-century financial crimes enforcement back in its historical parent—the Department of Treasury.

Congress created Customs in 1789 and placed it within the new Department of Treasury. At the time, its primary mission was the collection of customs-related revenue. Over the centuries, its enforcement mission expanded. By the time I joined Customs in the mid-1980s, its Office of Enforcement was charged with enforcing over 400 laws, more than the FBI handled! With the exception of immigration, its authority had to do with the border of the United States. Since it was part of the Department of Treasury, its investigative special agents had expertise in financial crimes investigations related to the cross-border movement of illicit money, value, and trade. Many customs investigators had unique insight into underground financial systems that are in large part based on trade.

But Customs no longer exists. It is now part of Immigration and Customs Enforcement (ICE) within the DHS. The forced merger with the former Immigration and Naturalization Service and expansion of its mission into immigration enforcement has not been successful. Its expertise, skillsets, budget, and staffing were diluted. It is time to return the oldest federal law enforcement agency back to the place of its birth. A reconstituted Treasury-based U.S. Customs Service would then be able to devote more focused attention to TBML and value transfer enforcement and our overall AML/CFT countermeasures.

THE MISUSE OF TRADE IS A LAW ENFORCEMENT ISSUE—NOT JUST A CUSTOMS ISSUE

When I retired from the U.S. government, I was honored to join the State and Local Anti-Terrorism Training (SLATT) program. It is funded by the U.S. Department of Justice, Bureau of Justice Assistance (BJA). The SLATT program is dedicated to providing specialized multiagency anti-terrorism detection, investigation, and interdiction training and related services at no cost to our nation's law enforcement officers, who face the challenges presented by the terrorist and violent criminal extremist threat.[17]

I assist the SLATT program by periodically traveling around the country and speaking with federal, state, and local law enforcement groups about terror finance and international money laundering. During my presentations, I am often stunned with the lack of knowledge regarding the importance of following the money and our financial countermeasures. I have also been amazed with the almost total unfamiliarity with TBML and value transfer. Even though I can demonstrate how TBML affects state and local law enforcement, most often the consensus is, "Trade is a customs issue. It doesn't concern me or my department."

Yet it is precisely because law enforcement officers are on the front lines in their communities and know their operating environment well that they should notice if a local business or commercial activity does not make market or economic sense. For example, a normal business should not remain in operation for long with sporadic commercial activity or when consistently selling products at a loss. Numerous businesses in the United States and elsewhere are involved at the local level in TBML schemes and deal with goods that are frequently manipulated to transfer value. Businesses involved with the BMPE—large and small—are found throughout the United States. And, of course, as we have seen, local underground financial networks such as hawala and fei-chien often depend on trade and local business networks. Numerous examples of local businesses' involvement in trade-based value transfer are found throughout this book.

Accordingly, I urge my state and local law enforcement colleagues to become more familiar with issues surrounding TBML schemes and how they affect the local community. Where appropriate, trade fraud and associated crimes should be part of their financial investigations education. With an expanded TTU, there should be more sharing of targeted trade data with local law enforcement. And state and local law enforcement should play an increased role in appropriate federal task forces that deal with the threats of money laundering, financial crimes, and terror finance.

We have plenty of laws, rules, and regulations on the books that enable law enforcement to combat financial crimes, including TBML. What we need is a renewed emphasis on enforcement.

NATIONAL TASK FORCES ON UNDERGROUND FINANCE

Although most underground financial transactions are benign, unfortunately criminals and terrorists are attracted to them. During our discussion, we have seen that they are nontransparent. Alternative remittance and value transfer systems are ethnic based and generally hidden to outsiders. Unfortunately, law enforcement at all levels does not have adequate representation from ethnic groups that often use underground financial systems. So the level of expertise is low.

I have made the argument that trade transparency could be the back door into some of the underground networks. Trade is generally used as a method of countervaluation or a means of balancing the books between brokers. I believe law enforcement and customs personnel should be more aware of these systems and how to better follow the value trail. But we also need more robust countermeasures.

Australia has a huge problem with ethnic organized crime groups that use underground financial systems to launder illicit proceeds and repatriate funds back to their home countries. Sometimes these underground financial systems are used for terror finance. In 2012, Australian law enforcement officials developed an effective enforcement tool to reduce money-laundering risks inherent in the money remittance sector and informal value transfer systems. It is called the Eligo National Task Force (ENTF). The ENTF initiative involves the Australian Crime Commission, the Australian financial intelligence unit (FIU)—AUSTRAC, the Australian Federal Police, Australian Customs and Border Protection Service, and local law enforcement. The ENTF also works collaboratively with representatives from the U.S. FBI and the DEA. Each member of the task force brings his or her particular areas of expertise and sources of information.

A wide range of ENTF countermeasures resulted in disruptions to criminal entities and identified hundreds of criminal targets previously unknown to law enforcement. The ENTF has uncovered dozens of separate money-laundering schemes in Australia, including some that are cleaning the proceeds of drug sales and filtering the money to exchange houses in the Middle East, which are then sending the money back to drug traffickers in South America.[18] Eligo-initiated investigations have resulted in seizures of hundreds of millions of Australian dollars' worth of cash and drugs. Perhaps most importantly, the ENTF is fostering professionalism within the remittance sector. The Eligo National Task Force conducts outreach and even releases fact sheets for the remittance sector that give guidance on detecting and deterring money-laundering activity. This makes it more resistant to organized crime.[19]

I propose that the ENTF model be copied. Task forces should be established in the United States and other concerned countries. The argument could be made that the United States already has task forces aplenty: Joint Terrorism Task Forces (JTTFs), High Intensity Financial Crimes Areas (HIFCAs), High Intensity Drug Trafficking Areas (HIDTAs), SAR Review Teams, and others. But none of these task forces specifically concentrate on remittance and value transfer networks. Some observers will point out that remittance companies must register with FinCEN and be licensed in most of the states. They feel that is sufficient. The problem is that most problematical underground transfer agents do not follow the rules. By their very nature, they are "underground." The same thing applies in other countries where underground financial systems are rife such as Pakistan, Afghanistan, India, and the UAE. All of these countries call for the registration and licensing of remittance dealers. They are also (*chuckle, chuckle*) supposed to file suspicious transaction reports with their country's FIU! In short, our current countermeasures for underground finance may look good on paper but they have proved ineffectual.

Specialized law enforcement task forces are effective. The concept has been proven around the world. A coordinated crackdown on remittance networks will give us insight into organized crime and terror finance and drive clients toward regulated and transparent money transfer companies that are not based on hidden trade-based countervaluation schemes.

 Outside of crimes of passion, criminals and criminal organizations are motivated by greed. And it is laundered money—in all its varied forms—that enables transnational criminal organizations to run their operations.

I opened this book with a sobering taunt from our adversaries. Because of our inability to see and understand TBML and value transfer techniques that are hidden in plain sight, criminals and terrorists are laughing at us.

Yet I see promising signs that TBML in all it varied forms is finally being recognized as one of the primary methodologies criminals and their facilitators use to launder staggering amounts of money around the world. There is also increasing acknowledgment that curtailing the criminal use of TBML cannot succeed unless we also curb the commercial misuse of trade, such as trade misinvoicing and abusive transfer pricing. I am also hopeful because over the last few years, there have been incredible advances in analyzing the kind of big data that international trade generates. Increasing globalization and trade interdependency necessitate steps toward transparency and accountability.

While it is not realistic to eradicate TBML, it is entirely within our power to promote and implement trade transparency and associated countermeasures. There are tremendous benefits in doing so. I remain optimistic that we can meet the challenge presented in this next frontier.

NOTES

1. John Cassara, *Hide & Seek: Intelligence, Law Enforcement, and the Stalled War on Terror Finance* (Washington, D.C.: Potomac Books, 2006), p. 231.

2. Ibid.

3. For example, when I was assigned at FinCEN in the late 1990s FinCEN hired an economist and assigned her with the task of estimating the magnitude of global money laundering. After a few years of futile attempts at research, she simply gave up. Similar studies elsewhere have also been frustrated. That is why I use the generally accepted IMF estimate quoted in Chapter 1 of approximately 2–5 percent of the world's GDP.

4. This proposal has been advanced by many other observers. For example, see Ross Delston, "The 41st FATF Recommendation: Why Preventive Measures Targeting Trade-Based Money Laundering Should Reach Beyond Banks," *Money Laundering Bulletin* (March 15, 2002), available online: http://www.jdsupra.com/legalnews/the-41st-fatf-recommendation-why-preven-24691/.

5. Brett Wolf, "Banks Should Track Miami Electronics Exporters Following Crackdown, U.S. Official Says," Thomson Reuters (April 27, 2015).

6. Raymond Baker in June 1, 2015, e-mail to the author.

7. "Proposed Rule Targets Cross-Border Wire Transfers," Federal Reserve Bank of Atlanta (November 8, 2010), available online: http://portalsandrails.frbatlanta.org/cross-border-wires/.

8. Wolf.

9. See my discussion of FinCEN in *Hide & Seek*, chapters 6 and 7. Years after my observations and despite new directors, staffing, and substantial budget increases, FinCEN has still not realized its "promise and potential."

10. Hector X. Colon, unit chief/director of the U.S. TTU, in March 25, 2015, e-mail exchange with the author.

11. Mark Laxer in May 26 and June 29, 2015, e-mails to the author.

12. See my discussion in *Hide & Seek* regarding the dissolution of Treasury enforcement. See also Juan C. Zarate, *Treasury's War* (New York: Public Affairs Books, 2013).

13. Dan Verton, "DHS Tech Spending, Where the Money and Challenges Will Be in 2015," *FedScoop* (January 26, 2015), available online: http://fedscoop.com/dhs-tech-spending-where-the-money-and-the-challenges-will-be-in-2015.

14. This is in part the theme of my first book, *Hide & Seek*

15. David Ignatius, "A Sober Approach to Sanctioning Iran," *Washington Post* (March 7, 2010), available online: http://www.washingtonpost.com/wp-dyn/content/article/2010/03/05/AR2010030502970.html.

16. This proposal was originally made in *Hide & Seek*, p. 242.

17. The Institute for Intergovernmental Research (IIR) serves as the technical service provider for ongoing training, research, and analysis services to the SLATT Program through the support of grant awards received from the Bureau of Justice Assistance. IIR supports the SLATT Program by providing project coordination activities, training assessment, and meeting coordination. See the IIR/SLATT website for additional information: https://www.iir.com/WhatWeDo/Criminal_Justice_Training/SLATT/.

18. "Hezbollah Funding Scheme Loops Cash from Crime to Terrorism," *Financial Crime Asia* (January 23, 2014), available online: http://financialcrimeasia.org/2014/01/23/hezbollah-funding-scheme-loops-cash-from-crime-to-terrorism/.

19. For more information about the Eligo Task Force see the Australian Crime Commission website, available online: https://www.crimecommission.gov.au/organised-crime/joint-task-forces-and-initiatives/eligo-national-task-force.

APPENDIX **A**

Money-Laundering Primer

utside of crime of passion (e.g., murder committed in a jealous rage), criminals and criminal organizations commit crime because they are motivated by *greed*. Greed is a vice as old as humanity and is considered in Christian ethics to be one of the "seven deadly sins." And once greedy criminals start accumulating large sums of illicit money, they have to try to hide its origins.

 Money laundering is the disguising or concealing of *any* criminally derived income to make it appear legitimate.[1]

Nobody knows the origin of the term *money laundering*, but in the United States it is thought to have originated in the 1920s or 1930s during the era of Al Capone, Meyer Lansky, and other infamous gangsters. They took illicit cash that originated from a variety of criminal enterprises such as gambling and Prohibition-era alcohol sales, and mixed it with clean money in cash-intensive businesses such as laundromats and restaurants. In other words, they tried to wash their dirty money and make it appear clean and legitimate.

The term gained use in the early 1960s with the proliferation of the sale of illegal narcotics. It became more widely known during the Watergate investigation of the 1970s, in which suitcases of cash played a role in the eventual resignation of President Richard Nixon. The pithy and memorable term "follow the money" was reportedly coined by the "Deep Throat" informant who helped unravel that same scandal.

Ironically, it was also President Nixon who declared the "War on Drugs." In order to give criminal investigators tools so they could follow the narcotic money trails, in 1970 Congress started passing a series of laws later augmented by rules and regulations that collectively are known as the Bank Secrecy Act (BSA).

 Bank secrecy is a misnomer. It really equates to financial transparency.

Although money laundering had been around for a long time, the BSA was the first legislation that systematically tried to control the growing problem. The BSA mandated a series of reporting and record keeping requirements. The data are now commonly called "financial intelligence," "financial transparency reporting requirements," or simply "BSA data." Today, Treasury's Financial Crimes Enforcement Network (FinCEN) acts as the designated administrator of the BSA.

FINANCIAL INTELLIGENCE

There are various types of financial intelligence. The original BSA required the first three record-keeping requirements listed below. Over the years, additional types of financial intelligence have been created. A few of the most important reports follow.

Currency Transaction Reports

Banks and other financial institutions are required to report currency transactions (deposits or withdrawals) of $10,000 or more by or on behalf of the same person on the same business day. The form used is popularly called the Currency Transaction Report (CTR). There are exceptions to the filing requirements for these large transactions if they are between domestic banks and for transactions conducted with certain retail cash-intensive businesses and government agencies.

Unlike the Suspicious Activity Reports described in this appendix, generally a client is informed about the obligation to file a CTR. Sometimes money launderers try to *structure* transactions to avoid the reporting requirement by depositing smaller sums of money under the threshold. Runners, sometimes known as *smurfs,* are also recruited by professional money launderers to deposit small sums of illicit money in multiple financial institutions.

 FINCEN FORM 104

Today, the official form for a CTR is the FinCEN Form 104. Approximately 150 data fields are included in the form. The information (name, address, other identifiers, account data, etc.) represents a wealth of information for law enforcement professionals tracking financial crime. The CTR represents the largest volume of BSA data filed; approximately 14 million CTRs are filed with Treasury's FinCEN every year. A sample of FinCEN Form 104 and other financial intelligence forms can be found on the FinCEN website (www.fincen.gov).

Currency and Monetary Instrument Report

A customs report must be filed by individuals or entities that transport $10,000 or more in cash (including in foreign currencies) or negotiable monetary instruments into or out of the United States. These entities include banks and armored car companies.

For example, if the reader flies into or out of the United States from Washington Dulles Airport, he or she must be notified or given forms inquiring whether the passenger is transporting $10,000 or more. The same holds true for those crossing a land border by foot or vehicle or those entering or departing the United States by sea. Of course, it is not illegal to transport money in large amounts across the border. In fact, the government encourages foreigners to bring money to spend! The only obligation is that a form must be filed.

 FINCEN FORM 105

At the time of the BSA, the original cross-border currency declaration form was known as a "Report of International Transaction of Currency or Monetary Instruments," commonly known as a CMIR. Today, the official designation for a CMIR is the FinCEN Form 105. Hundreds of thousands of these forms are filed every year. Each form has approximately 70 data fields containing useful identifying information and financial intelligence.

Report of Foreign Bank and Financial Accounts (FBAR)

Citizens and resident aliens of the United States are required to file a report with the IRS if they maintain a financial interest or a signature authority over a foreign bank account, brokerage account, or other type of foreign account that exceeds certain thresholds. Originally, the report was filed on IRS Form 90–22–1 and was known as a "Foreign Bank Account Report" (FBAR). It is known today as the FinCEN Form 114.

Form 8300 (Cash over $10,000 Received in Trade or Business)

This is an IRS form and is required for cash transactions over $10,000 by businesses not otherwise covered by BSA reporting such as real estate agencies, car dealerships, and jewelers and dealers in precious metals and stones. The form must be filed when a covered business receives more than $10,000 in cash in one transaction or in two or more related transactions.

Similar to other types of financial intelligence, Form 8300 has detailed identifying information, including the customer's name, address, the amount of cash received, and the date and nature of the transaction. Generally, the customer is not notified when the form is filed. In addition to submitting the forms to the Department of Treasury, businesses must maintain associated records for at least five years.

Form 8300 was originally used primarily for tax purposes. Similar to other tax reports, the release of the data to law enforcement outside of IRS was restricted. Over the past few years, 8300 data have become more available.

Suspicious Activity Reports

Suspicious Activity Reports (SARs) were initiated in the United States in 1996. They were modeled in part after the Suspicious Transaction Report (STR) disclosure system that was already in existence in Europe.

Financial institutions and money services businesses (MSBs) should file an SAR if a transaction is inconsistent with normal account activity or otherwise appears suspicious. Banks are obligated to "know your customer" and practice due diligence. As a result, banks and increasingly nonbank financial institutions have compliance programs that help spot suspicious transactions. Although the numbers vary, over one million SARs are filed annually in the United States. The total fillings are very roughly divided between SARs filed by banks and those filed by MSBs such as currency exchangers, gold and jewelry dealers, and money remitters.[2]

The information on SAR filings has proven very helpful for law enforcement. In addition to the identifying data, SARs also provide a narrative field for the filers to include their observations and reasons why they feel the transaction is suspicious in nature. Some of the narratives are short, perhaps only a few sentences. Others are quite lengthy and provide detailed information and an explanation as to why the transaction is suspicious. Banks and other institutions that file SARs are also required to maintain supporting documentation for the reports and make it available upon request.

The SAR form also contains a field in which the filing institutions can indicate the type of suspicious activity encountered. Categories include money laundering (structuring), counterfeit financial instruments, false statements, mortgage loan fraud, identity theft, check fraud, counterfeit currency, terrorism financing, and others. Investigators can tailor their data queries by specifying the type of SARs they are interested in by date, geographic location, and categories of suspicious transactions.

HOW IS FINANCIAL INTELLIGENCE USED?

The tens of millions of financial intelligence reports that are produced in the United States and other countries (see discussion of the Egmont Group) every year have proven to be a tremendous resource to help criminal investigators follow the money trails. The financial data are valuable not only in money-laundering investigations but also in providing some financial transparency in other types of criminal activity as well. Querying a subject's name in the financial databases may disclose further identifying information, including an address, telephone number, or business association that might be keys to the investigation. The intelligence might also provide some insight or at least a snapshot of the suspect's financial transaction, which could be very valuable to investigators. However, financial intelligence alone rarely makes a case. Generally, law enforcement will have to combine the financial intelligence with information from other databases (for example: criminal databases, immigration databases, customs databases, commercially available information about businesses, social network sites, etc.). By connecting the dots between individuals, companies, bank accounts, and so on, a picture of financial relationships and money flows begins to develop.

Most often, financial data are used *reactively* by law enforcement. In a reactive case, a crime has occurred and a criminal investigator is assigned to solve the crime through a variety of investigative techniques, including interviews, developing informants, performing surveillance, and conducting an undercover investigation. Financial intelligence can help in developing identifying data, establishing networks, and constructing a paper trail.

Financial crimes investigations can also be *proactive* in nature. In these situations, a criminal violation has not yet occurred. Instead, law enforcement examines financial intelligence (CTRs, CMIRs, SARs, etc.) and tries to identify anomalies, suspect patterns, and trends. The information is then used to intercept criminal activity in progress and take appropriate countermeasures.

AVAILABILITY OF FINANCIAL INTELLIGENCE

Treasury's FinCEN is responsible for the collection, warehousing, analysis, and dissemination of financial information in the United States. It is the country's Financial Intelligence Unit (FIU). In theory, official consumers of financial intelligence at the federal, state, and local levels can contact FinCEN and ask for appropriate queries to be made of the financial databases. There are various programs and platforms for these official inquiries. Queries should be as specific as possible and include known identifying information. Of course, FinCEN only has access to financial intelligence that has a nexus or link to the United States. FinCEN also grants certain law enforcement entities such as the FBI direct bulk downloads of financial information.

Official consumers can also request financial intelligence from an appropriate interagency/departmental task force. A representative from the Department of Treasury (FinCEN or the IRS) or the Department of Homeland Security (Immigration and Customs Enforcement) should have direct access to most of the same financial databases. Generally, non-Treasury and DHS enforcement agencies are limited in their abilities to make direct queries.

Law enforcement can also gain access to financial intelligence through regional federal, state, and local task forces; these include Joint Terrorism Task Forces (JTTFs), High Intensity Financial Crime Areas (HIFCAs), and U.S. Attorney SAR Review Teams.

In 1996, FinCEN was a founding member of the Egmont Group of Financial Intelligence Units. The idea behind Egmont was for member countries around the world to obtain, analyze, and disclose financial intelligence. The FIU's focus is to support host-country law enforcement and other officials, but Egmont Group members also support official requests for information from other Egmont Group members. In effect, a FIU is a foreign FinCEN. Today, there are approximately 150 FIUs officially accredited to the Egmont Group. Although there are different FIU models (some are investigatory in nature and some are administrative), and different countries have various types of financial intelligence and reporting thresholds, all have the equivalent of SARs—known frequently overseas as Suspicious Transaction Reports (STRs).

LEGISLATION

In 1986, the United States became the first country in the world to make money laundering a crime and enacted a law that is still one of the most powerful in the world (Title 18, U.S. Code Section 1956, also known as the Money Laundering Control Act). It provided federal agents and prosecutors the necessary tools to fight money laundering and made several significant amendments to the BSA, including criminalizing structuring to evade BSA reporting requirements and increasing civil and criminal penalties for money laundering. An amendment to the Right to Financial Privacy Act made it easier for banks to furnish suspicious transaction data to federal enforcement agencies without the risk of being sued by clients.[3]

The law also has an extraterritorial reach if at least part of the offense takes place in the United States or even if money is only transferred through the United States. As a result, the United States can insert itself into dollar-based transactions or U.S. dollar transfers that are settled through correspondent bank accounts in the United States.

The Money Laundering Control Act was followed by other legislation over the years that strengthened the U.S. AML/CFT regime. Noteworthy laws include the Anti-Drug Abuse Act of 1988, the Annunzio-Wylie Anti-Money Laundering Act of 1992, the Money Laundering Suppression Act of 1994, the Money Laundering and Financial Crimes Strategy Act of 1998, and the USA PATRIOT Act of 2001.[4]

INVESTIGATING MONEY LAUNDERING

The U.S. intelligence and law enforcement communities agree that dirty money is laundered in three recognizable stages, as discussed in Chapter 2: *placement, layering,* and *integration.*

In the placement stage, illicit cash must somehow be deposited into financial institutions. Criminal organizations attempt to put their money in banks for the simple reasons that they want to be able to spend it and protect it. Because large amounts of cash are involved, law enforcement feels that criminals are at their most vulnerable when they try to deposit or place illegally obtained funds directly into a bank account. For example, in the United States, if one uses the estimate that $100 billion is laundered every year from the street sales of narcotics, that translates into approximately 20 million pounds of currency![5] It poses a tremendous logistical challenge for criminal organizations to place that much cash into banks in ways that do not raise suspicions. The most common way this is done is by smuggling the dirty money out of the country to destinations where the cash will be readily accepted. For example, tens of billions of dollars of bulk cash representing the proceeds of narcotics sales are smuggled across the southern U.S. border into Mexico every year. Another common placement technique used by money launderers is to use runners, couriers, or *smurfs* that deposit small amounts of money in financial institutions in ways that do not trigger mandatory currency reporting requirements imposed by the BSA.

During the layering stage, criminals and criminal organizations attempt to separate the source of the funds by way of complex transactions such as wiring funds to multiple accounts in multiple jurisdictions. Criminals do this in order to make it difficult for law enforcement to follow the money trail.

Finally, in the integration stage, criminals and criminal organizations try to create the appearance of legitimacy by, for example, investing the placed and layered funds in tangible goods such as property, businesses, or even investing in the stock market.

Traditionally, money laundering has been equated with the proceeds of the sale of narcotics. While narcotics trafficking still represent a hefty percentage of dirty money in the world, the United States recognizes approximately 300 "predicate offenses" or "specified unlawful activities" for charging a defendant with money laundering. Predicate offenses include fraud, smuggling, weapons trafficking, and terrorist finance. The international standard as championed by the FATF is "all serious crimes." And as we have seen, there is increasing discussion about recognizing tax evasion as a predicate offense for money laundering. The primary predicate offense for TBML is customs fraud.

DIFFERENCES BETWEEN MONEY LAUNDERING AND TERROR FINANCE

Although money launderers and terrorist financiers use many of the same techniques and methodologies, there are three primary differences in their use of tainted money:

1. Money launderers are motivated by greed. Terrorists are generally motivated by ideology or religion. However, there are signs that terrorists are increasingly driven by the quest for money, power, and control.
2. In money laundering, generally large amounts of illicit funds are involved. In comparison, the cost of terrorist attacks is quite small.
3. By definition, money launderers seek to disguise the proceeds of illegal activity. In terror finance, funding may be from both legal and illegal sources.

MONEY-LAUNDERING METHODOLOGIES

Per our discussion in Chapter 1, in 1989 the G-7 created the FATF. The international anti–money-laundering policymaking body championed 40 recommendations for countries and jurisdictions around the world aimed at the establishment of AML and after September 11 CFT countermeasures. These included the passage of AML/CFT laws, the creation of financial intelligence, know your customer (KYC) compliance programs for financial institutions and money services businesses, the creation of Financial Intelligence Units (FIUs), and other safeguards. Over the years, FATF-style regional bodies (FSRBs) have spread around the world. The FATF and FSRBs conduct mutual evaluations, support member countries in formulating AML/CFT regimes, and periodically conduct studies on money-laundering threats and methodologies.

According to the FATF, there are three primary methods of laundering money:

1. Via financial institutions and nonbank financial institutions. This includes the placement and structuring of deposits of tainted money into banks, wiring or layering the dirty money to multiple accounts in multiple banks in multiple jurisdictions to confuse the paper trail, and then using the laundered money by integrating it into the economy by way of purchasing high-value properties and goods.

2. Bulk cash smuggling is the physical smuggling of illicit cash from one jurisdiction to another where it will be more readily accepted for deposit.

3. Trade-based money laundering. This also includes underground financial systems, because historically and culturally most are settled on the misuse of international trade, including customs fraud.

Although not currently included in the FATF top-three methodologies, the FATF and concerned international observers are calling attention to *new payment methods* (NPMs). They are also sometimes called *e-money* or *digital cash*. Examples include Internet payment services, cyber-currency, stored-value cards, prepaid calling and credit cards, digital precious metals, mobile payments (m-payments), or the use of cell phones to send/receive/transfer money and digital value.

The use of *shell corporations* that lack transparent beneficial ownership information is not necessarily considered a top money-laundering methodology. However, the use of such phantom companies is extensive in various money-laundering schemes.

Criminals often mix or use many of the above methodologies and techniques in combination, thereby increasing the difficulty of following the money, digital-cyber, or value trails. And criminal and terrorist organizations are adept at exploiting vulnerabilities in our global AML/CFT countermeasures and the challenges posed by differing venues, jurisdiction, and lack of expertise. They are also attracted to countries that have weak enforcement or lack the political will to enforce their laws. And, as we have seen, corruption is the great facilitator.

NOTES

1. Most of the material in this appendix comes from the author's knowledge. Background texts that were helpful include:

    John Cassara and Avi Jorisch, *On the Trail of Terror Finance: What Law Enforcement and Intelligence Officers Need to Know* (Washington, DC: Red Cell Publishing, 2010). See Chapter 2 on Sources of Financial Information.

    John Cassara, *Strategic Financial Intelligence: A Primer on Middle Eastern and South Asian Value Transfer Techniques* (Washington, DC Lockheed, 2008). See Chapter 1, "An Overview of Financial Intelligence."

    Robert E. Powis, *The Money Launderers* (Chicago: Probus Publishing, 1992). See Prologue.

2. See FinCEN "SAR Stats," formerly FinCEN "SARs by the Numbers," available online: http://www.fincen.gov/news_room/rp/sar_by_number.html.

3. Powis, p. xii.

4. For a brief history and description of U.S. AML/CFT legislation, see: http://www.fincen.gov/news_room/aml_history.html.

5. John A. Cassara, *Hide & Seek: Intelligence, Law Enforcement and the Stalled War on Terrorist Finance* (Washington D.C: Potomac Books, 2006), p. 131.

APPENDIX **B**

Original Trade
Transparency Unit
(TTU) Proposal

The author wrote the following proposal for the creation of TTUs in May 2003. At the time, he was detailed from Treasury's FinCEN to the Department of State's Bureau of International Narcotics and Law Enforcement Affairs (INL). However, the proposal was more of an individual initiative. It was eventually routed through the interagency process and approved (see Chapter 9).

MAY 2003 PROPOSAL: TRADE TRANSPARENCY UNITS

By SSA John Cassara

Summary Proposal

Establish and possibly link an international network of country Trade Transparency Units (TTUs), loosely analogous in concept to the Egmont Group of Financial Intelligence Units. The purpose of the TTUs is to identify anomalies in international trade transactions from customs data. These identified anomalies could be an indicator of trade-based money laundering, financial crimes and/or terrorist financing. An international system of trade transparency, working in conjunction with current financial transparency reporting requirements, could alleviate many other previously intractable trade related problems. An international system of trade transparency could also potentially provide revenue to governments around the world. This initiative, builds upon, but does not duplicate previous U.S. initiatives.

Defining the Problem

Over the last generation, the United States has championed the concept of financial transparency for the formal financial sector including banks, conventional wire remitters, casinos and other formal financial sectors. Working primarily with the Financial Action Task Force (FATF) and its regional bodies, the Egmont Group of Financial Intelligence Units, and exerting bilateral and regional leadership around the world, the United States has helped create anti–money laundering programs and policies that have been implemented around the world.

The events surrounding September 11, however, demonstrate anew the threats posed by financial flows outside the formal sectors, including trade-based money laundering and alternative remittance systems. Trade-based money laundering and terrorist financing systems can bypass, in whole or part, the Bank Secrecy Act and other anti–money laundering and financial crimes regulations. Trade-based systems act as a kind of a parallel method of transferring money and value around the world. Systems such as hawala, the black market peso exchange, and the use of commodities such as gold and diamonds that are not captured by current financial reporting pose tremendous challenges for law enforcement using current financial reporting requirements. Moreover, many of these alternative remittance systems are ethnic-based, making them even more difficult for U.S. investigators to understand and target. As the United States and other countries around the world tighten the noose of financial regulation and reporting for the formal and even informal financial sectors, the use of trade-based money laundering and alternative remittance systems will assuredly grow. It is essential, therefore, that we work to put into place an international mechanism capable of detecting trading anomalies that could point to money laundering, terrorist financing, and other financial crimes.

Investigating Trade-Based Money Laundering

Experience has shown the best way to analyze and investigate suspect trade-based activity is to have systems in place that can monitor specific imports and exports from/to given countries. In fact, U.S. Customs pioneered this approach through its creation of the Numerically Integrated Profiling System (NIPS), a computer system that uses U.S. trade data, examines suspect anomalies, and identifies likely targets of investigation. Unfortunately, the opportunities presented by NIPS have never been fully exploited. NIPS, using U.S. data alone, also has limitations, the most important of which is that, to be most effective, NIPS analysts need to compare trade data from other countries. Moreover, it is difficult to follow the trade flow when goods are transshipped from country X to Y via Z. An additional challenge occurs when the U.S.

wishes to monitor suspect trade that does not enter into the commerce of United States, for example, following suspect trade related to terrorist financing that may move goods from Karachi to Dar Es Salaam via Dubai.

If country X exports goods to country Y, in theory country X's export records regarding price, quantity, and general description should match (with some recognized variables) the corresponding import records of country Y. Unfortunately, there is a growing worldwide trend towards trade fraud. For example, concern over the sale of conflict diamonds from the Gambia to Belgium resulted in a comparison of trade data that showed the Gambia exported $100 million worth of diamonds to Belgium between 1996 and 1999, even though the Gambia has no diamond production. U.S. Customs has used this same technique of examining trade anomalies to combat the Colombia black market peso exchange, to examine suspect gold shipments from Guyana, and examine transshipped textiles from the Middle East. In these instances, Customs was able to match U.S. trade data with cooperating countries' trade data and look for suspicious indicators.

The desired trade data are already collected in every country around the world. All countries have customs services and all countries impose tariffs and duties for revenue purposes. In fact, lesser-developed countries are dependent on customs duties to generate revenue. Although there are some differences in the way trade data are gathered and warehoused, the U.N. and the IMF are promoting uniform standards such as ASYCUDA that collect and manage customs data in approximately 80 (primarily lesser developed) countries. ASYCUDA is a computerized customs management system which covers most foreign trade procedures including manifests, customs declarations, transit procedures, etc. (NIPS is fully compatible with ASYCUDA). In addition, acting on a U.S. initiative, the G-7 proposed the adoption and implementation by customs services worldwide of a standard data and reporting format. The World Customs Organization (WCO) developed the WCO Data Model with a Global Standard Format. The EU subsequently made a political commitment to adopt the WCO Data Model, which is also supported by the Asia Pacific Economic Cooperation (APEC). The U.S. has also committed to making its Automated Commercial Environment (ACE) system compatible with world norms. Thus over the last few years a foundation has already been established governing customs compatibility. The below proposals do not deviate from U.S. policy and initiatives, but rather seek to use the above foundation as a point of departure that will give law enforcement enhanced tools concerning the misuse of global trade.

Proposal 1: The U.S. should actively promote in appropriate forums the concept of "trade transparency" whereby countries agree to collect, automate, and disseminate under appropriate restrictions and guidelines customs trade data in order to combat trade-related crime. The data would capture specific declared shipments, inbound and outbound. Countries' trade data systems should be made compatible with an international norm.

Proposal 2: Borrowing from the successful Financial Intelligence Unit (FIU) model, the U.S. would build upon the NIPS program to establish the world's first Trade Transparency Unit (TTU) that will collect, analyze, and disseminate suspect trade data. The U.S. should work towards the establishment of a worldwide TTU network (Proposal 3 below).

A U.S. TTU would be charged with looking for trade anomalies that could be indicative of a wide variety of predicate offenses, including trade-based money laundering, customs fraud, alternative remittance systems, and even terrorist financing. The TTU would act in a similar manner to an FIU; its primary purpose would be to support law enforcement by responding to requests to further investigations and by looking proactively for anomalies that would indicate likely targets of investigation. (The value of the TTU analytical product would undoubtedly be enhanced if the information was cross-checked with an FIU.)

A TTU would be able to obtain trade data of interest directly from another TTU or "pull-down" the data of interest from an administrative gatekeeper. (See Proposal 3 below governing TTU Group administrative functions.) For example, if the U.S. TTU was interested in examining suspect trade anomalies between India and the United States, the U.S. TTU could contact the Indian TTU and arrange for the exchange of the data. By comparing declared imports and exports from both sides, it is a relatively simple process to determine indications of possible overinvoicing, underinvoicing, fictitious invoicing, export incentive fraud, etc. Over- and underinvoicing, for example, are often used in money laundering and alternative remittance systems such as hawala. In another example, if the U.S. TTU was concerned with the possibility of terrorist financing via trade that does not enter into the commerce of the U.S., the same TTU system would have access to the needed trade data, either directly from the concerned countries or through the administrative gatekeeper.

The Egmont Group of Financial Intelligence Units (FIUs) was created in 1995 as a kind of "club" where likeminded FIUs could gather periodically to discuss common concerns about the collection, analysis, and dissemination of financial intelligence. When Egmont was formed, there were only 12 FIUs. By mid-2003, there will be over 80 members in the Egmont Group. Egmont does not have a permanent secretariat. There are no dues. Egmont is totally separate from the FATF and other money laundering organizations. Membership in the Egmont Group is completely voluntary.

Proposal 3: Following the Egmont model, a completely voluntary TTU network could associate themselves into a Group that would share specific trade data with Group members upon request. The Trade Transparency Group would develop procedures for admitting new members, protocols for exchanging trade data, secure methods for transmitting the data, etc. As with Egmont, there is no need for a permanent secretariat or affiliation with an international organization. However, as was true during the first years in the development of Egmont, the U.S. TTU may have to play a key role in the administration of the Trade Transparency Group.

Customs has already pioneered the technique of customs data exchange with other countries based on the NIPS platform. For example, Customs currently shares some trade data with [countries redacted]. [Other countries redacted] already engage in a two-way exchange of customs data with the U.S. The exchange of data has resulted in major cases and the collection of millions in revenue. However, the exchange of customs data is not adequately coordinated nor part of comprehensive U.S. policy. The exchange of customs trade data has also not been systematically examined for indications of terrorist financing. (Customs Container Security Initiative —CSI—is addressing some of these issues, and protocols have been established under the CSI program that may prove valuable with trade transparency.) Yet countries are enthusiastic about the trade transparency concept, and if a Trade Transparency Group were developed, there are indications that countries would line-up to join.

The costs involved with developing a TTU in the United States would be minimal. Customs already has most of the reporting and analytical systems in-place. In the post–September 11 environment, TTU location, agency protocols, organization, staffing and budget will hopefully not become major obstacles. Developing TTUs in other countries will be dependent on many variables. However, the technology exists to engineer trade transparency compatibility and any costs incurred in other countries will be more than compensated for by immediate returns. In lesser-developed countries, particularly those judged to be at risk for terrorist financing, the U.S. could offer technical assistance in automating their trade data and making it available for TTU interface.

If we adopt a system of international trade transparency modeled on the above, many benefits could result:

- It would be an excellent tool to help monitor and combat trade-based money laundering. There is currently very little available data on money laundering systems that involve trade nor effective countermeasures.

- It would help more fully identify and disrupt the Colombian black market peso exchange (BMPE), the largest narcotics-related money laundering methodology in the Western Hemisphere. An international trade transparency network would be particularly helpful in combating BMPE networks where there are transshipments through multiple countries, for example, goods exported from Italy to Colombia via Panama.

- Since traditional hawala is trade based (commodities are used to provide countervaluation) it could have a dramatic impact on some forms of hawala transactions.

- It could help reduce the misuse of the international gold trade, an embedded money laundering methodology that has stymied criminal investigators around the world.

- Customs fraud would be reduced.

▨ Many countries would be better able to combat export incentive fraud.

▨ Tax and tariff revenue would increase.

▨ It would be an effective analytical tool for monitoring trade quotas.

▨ An international system of transparent trade would help monitor the trade in conflict diamonds, conflict timber, etc.

▨ There would be a reduction in many forms of smuggling, including narcotics.

▨ We could better control trade diversion schemes.

▨ It would give law enforcement agencies better tools to combat the worldwide trade in counterfeit goods.

▨ It would help detect trade-related capital flight.

▨ Transparency in trade would help reduce multilayered corruption.

▨ Trade transparency could help give trade sanctions teeth, by making trade flows easier to monitor. This could help give policy makers additional options in international conflicts.

Although there will undoubtedly be skeptics, trade transparency will be attractive to governments around the world because it will protect the integrity of their markets and provide tax and tariff revenue. Many times countries do not take action to combat money laundering or terrorist financing, but when it is demonstrated that action on transparency enhances revenue, those same countries become very interested. Moreover, a system of trade transparency could provide infusions of tax and duty dollars for the USG. Academic studies show that the U.S. Treasury is routinely shortchanged billions of dollars every year via methods to circumvent required trade reporting.

In the dissemination of financial intelligence, there is always a balance struck between enforcement and privacy concerns. Although there is not as great an expectation of privacy with trade, it is crucial to the success of these proposals that we build in appropriate steps to safeguard sensitive data. For example, the data will be used only by government agencies. Private industry will not have access to the information. In the United States, business already gives much the same information to government agencies including Customs, the I.R.S. and sometimes Commerce. Moreover, if a particular industry or company feels that the inadvertent release of transactional data could jeopardize business, software rules could be written whereby sensitive or identifying information in the data fields would not have to be included. In addition, the dissemination of trade data does not mean the blanket release of information for "fishing expeditions." Rather, as with FIU analysis, specific queries would be formulated either in response to a request from law enforcement or perhaps a category or field would be analyzed proactively searching for anomalies that might warrant subsequent investigation. The above should actually be attractive to most international U.S. business interests. Transparency will help foster fair competition, and U.S. business excels on a level playing field in the international arena.

Conclusion

So long as there are profits to be made, or zealotry to be pursued, systemic money laundering, financial crime and terrorist financing will continue. To the extent that we deny these criminals the front door of the domestic and international formal financial systems, they will utilize informal and trade-based systems. In order to identify and attack these non-formal systemic abuses, we must create mechanisms, akin to the Bank Secrecy Act, the USA Patriot Act and other anti–money laundering regulations and reporting, that will capture the possible use of trade to finance crimes. We must advocate and press for an international mechanism to attain international trade transparency as a complement to that of financial transparency.

As described above, the basic idea of trade transparency is simple and straightforward. For a variety of enforcement and revenue enhancing reasons, trade transparency is already attractive to many governments around the world. The costs involved establishing a transparency network would be minimal. The information already exists. The potential returns are enormous.

The war on terrorist financing is stalled. The USG emphasis thus far has been to concentrate on money moving through traditional financial institutions. The results have been mixed at best. It is time we systematically addressed trade-based crime. The trade transparency proposals outlined above do not duplicate existing programs but rather use the infrastructure already in place as a point of departure. The April 2003 edition of the *Homeland Security Journal* states, "The ideal would be actions to encourage other nations to share information with the United States so that it can be evaluated using NIPS, with the eventual goal of trade transparency. This is an efficient means of expediting a counter-terrorist action to understand the scope of the problem faced by the United States and the world."

If adopted, the proposals outlined above will launch us toward this "ideal."

Glossary

Arbitrage The nearly simultaneous purchase and sale of an asset in order to profit from a difference in the price. It exploits price differences of identical goods in different market locations.

Arm's-length transaction If two unrelated companies trade with each other across international boundaries, there is generally negotiation on price, resulting in a fair or market-driven charge, which is acceptable for tax purposes.

ARS—Alternative Remittance System See *IVTS*.

AML/CFT—Anti–Money Laundering/Combating the Financing of Terrorism Collective term generally used to describe the legal and regulatory framework and other obligations countries must implement. See also *FATF 40*.

APG—Asia Pacific Group A FATF-style regional body, the APG wrote a comprehensive 2012 TBML typologies report.

ASYCUDA—Automated System for Customs Data A computerized system designed by the United Nations Conference on Trade and Development (UNCTAD) to administer a country's customs.

ATT—Afghan Transit Trade A regional agreement between landlocked Afghanistan and its neighbors that allows goods to be imported into the country with preferential duties. The trade has resulted in massive smuggling and trade fraud, and it continues to facilitate the laundering of narcotics proceeds and contributes to the financing of terrorist groups operating in South Asia.

BMPE—Black Market Peso Exchange One of the most pernicious money laundering schemes in the Western Hemisphere. It is also one of the largest, processing billions of dollars a year from Colombia alone via TBML and other schemes.

BSA—Bank Secrecy Act Officially known as the "Currency and Foreign Transactions Reporting Act," it requires financial institutions to help various government agencies detect and prevent money laundering. Specifically, the BSA requires banks and other financial institutions to file reports of currency transactions exceeding $10,000, to keep records of cash purchases of negotiable instruments, and to report suspicious activity.

Bulk cash smuggling (BCS) The physical transportation or smuggling of bulk cash currency in order to place it in a jurisdiction with less stringent financial transparency reporting requirements.

Capital flight Wealth, capital, and assets are moved from a country when there is a loss of confidence. Generally this is due to an event or policies that have economic consequence such as political instability, monetary uncertainties, increase in taxes, or currency depreciation.

Carousel fraud The practice of importing goods from a country where they are not subject to Value Added Tax (see *VAT*), selling them with VAT added, then deliberately not paying the VAT to the government. The fraudster charges VAT on the sale of the goods and instead of paying it to the government simply absconds—taking the VAT with him. It is a form of "carousel" or "merry-go-round" fraud when sometimes goods are cycled between companies and jurisdictions collecting ever more fraudulent VAT revenues. Sometimes in TBML, carousel fraud also refers to the process of cycling trade goods (genuine or fictitious) in and out of non-VAT markets in order to justify payment abroad.

CBP—Customs and Border Protection See *ICE*.

CDD/KYC—Customer Due Diligence/Know Your Customer The first step financial institutions must take to detect, deter, and prevent money laundering and terrorist financing; i.e., maintain adequate knowledge about their customers and their financial activities.

CMIR—Report of International Transportation of Currency or Monetary Instruments The United States has established a declaration system that applies to all incoming and outgoing physical transportation of cash and other monetary instruments. It is illegal to transport more than $10,000 (or its foreign equivalent) in cash or other monetary instruments into or out of the country without filing a CMIR, also known as FinCEN Form 105.

Countervaluation Often employed in settling debts between traders and those involved with underground finance. For example, a party in a transaction may over- or undervalue a commodity or trade item such as gold, thereby transferring value to another party and/or offsetting debt owed.

CTR—Currency Transaction Report Financial institutions are required to file a CTR with FinCEN whenever they process a currency transaction exceeding $10,000. These reports include useful identifying information about the transaction. Once FinCEN receives them, they are input into a BSA reporting database that is available to federal banking regulators and—with restrictions—the law enforcement community.

Delaware corporation See *shell corporation.*

DARTT—Data Analysis and Research for Trade Transparency A computer system designed to analyze anomalies in import and export data. Anomalies are often indicators of illicit activity such as money laundering, smuggling, and trade fraud.

Egmont Group The international standard-setter for financial intelligence units. An organization created with the explicit purpose of serving as a center to overcome the obstacles preventing the sharing of financial intelligence and other information between member FIUs.

Export incentives Tax, legal, and/or regulatory payments or allowances that encourage domestic companies to export goods or services.

FATF—Financial Action Task Force Also known by the French name *Groupe d'action financiére sur le blanchiment de capitaux* (GAFI), FATF was created by the G-7 leaders in 1989 in order to address increased concerns about money laundering's threat to the international financial system. This intergovernmental policymaking task force was given the mandate of examining money-laundering techniques and trends, reviewing domestic and international actions, and setting the international standard for combating money laundering and terrorism financing. FATF-style regional bodies associated with FATF are found throughout the world.

FATF 40 The FATF-issued international standards for preventing, detecting, and suppressing both money laundering and terrorist financing. Although they are technically just "recommendations," they carry the force of "mandates for action" throughout much of the international community and financial sector.

Fei-chien A very old Chinese underground financial system originally designed to pay taxes. Over the centuries it evolved as an underground money and value transfer system. Today, fei-chien, sometimes also known as "flying money," and other similar indigenous Chinese parallel financial systems are used to fill the needs of both Chinese entrepreneurs and migrants around the world. Skirting official financial restrictions and regulations that impede commercial efficiency, fei-chien facilitates capital flight, tax evasion, the repatriation of profits, and the remittance of wages.

FinCEN—Financial Crimes Enforcement Network A bureau with the U.S. Department of Treasury, FinCEN is the U.S. financial intelligence unit.

FIU—financial intelligence unit In many countries, a central national agency responsible for receiving, requesting, analyzing, and/or disseminating disclosures of financial information to the competent authorities, primarily concerning suspected proceeds of crime and the potential financing of terrorism. An FIU's mandate is backed up by national legislation or regulation.

Flying money Also known as *fei-chien, hui kuan,* and *chiao hui,* flying money is an ancient Chinese underground financial and alternative remittance system. See *IVTS* and *fei-chien.*

FTZ—free trade zone Designated geographic areas outside of normal customs areas and procedures. FTZs and similar districts such as special economic zones, enterprise zones, free ports, and export processing zones generally offer duty- and tax-free access and sometimes incorporate a number of other incentives for businesses. They provide a preferential environment for goods and services usually associated with exports.

FSRB—FATF Style Regional Body These bodies—which are modeled on FATF and are granted certain rights by that organization—serve as regional centers for matters relating to AML/CFT. Their primary purpose is to promote a country's implementation of comprehensive AML/CFT regimes and implement the FATF 40 recommendations.

HS—Harmonized Tariff Schedule Developed by the World Customs Organization, the HS comprises about 5,000 commodity groups, each identified by a common six-digit code. The HS is supported by well-defined rules to achieve uniform classification. The system is used by more than 200 countries as a basis for their customs tariffs.

Hawala A centuries-old broker system based on trust, found throughout South Asia, the Middle East Africa, and the Americas. It allows customers and brokers (*hawaladars*) to transfer money or value without physically moving it, often in areas of the world where banks and other financial institutions have little or no presence. Historically and culturally, trade is often used to settle accounts between hawaladars. Hawala-like systems are used by many different cultures but under different names.

Hawaladar   A broker in a hawala or hawala-type network.

Hundi   In Pakistan and Bangladesh, hundi is the term used to describe hawala.

HSI—Homeland Security Investigations   An investigative arm of the Department of Homeland Security active in combating criminal organizations illegally exploiting America's travel, trade, financial, and immigration systems. HSI is a part of ICE that employs special agents to do investigations. ICE has other divisions.

ICE—Immigration and Customs Enforcement   Part of the Department of Homeland Security, ICE executes its mission through the enforcement of more than 400 federal statutes, and focuses on immigration enforcement, preventing terrorism and combating the illegal movement of people and trade.

INCSR—International Narcotics Control Strategy Report   A congressionally mandated report released annually in March by the U.S. State Department Bureau of International Narcotics and Law Enforcement Affairs. Volume I describes international narcotics production, and Volume II describes money laundering and related financial crimes in countries around the world.

IVTS—informal value transfer systems   Sometimes known as *parallel banking, underground banking*, or *alternative remittance systems*, IVTS refers to any system, mechanism, or network that transfers money for the purpose of making an equivalent amount of funds payable to a third party in another geographic location, whether or not in the same form. The transfers often take place outside of conventional banking systems and often use trade-based value transfer systems to settle accounts between brokers.

Integration   This is the last stage of the money-laundering process. The laundered money is introduced into the economy so that it appears to be normal business earnings, making it very difficult for law enforcement to detect. Some methods of integration include real estate purchases, buying luxury vehicles, investing in the stock market, and investment in trade goods. See also *placement* and *layering*.

IRS/CI—Internal Revenue Service/Criminal Investigations   This U.S. law enforcement agency investigates potential criminal violations of the Internal Revenue Code, Bank Secrecy Act, and related financial crimes.

KYC—know your customer KYC is the process of a bank or business knowing the true identity and activity of a client or customer. See *CDD*.

Layering This is the second stage of the money laundering process. The purpose of this stage is to make it more difficult for law enforcement to detect or follow the trail of illegal proceeds. Methods include converting cash into monetary instruments and moving money between bank accounts. See also *integration* and *placement*.

MSB—money services business Any individual or business that engages in accepting and transmitting funds by any means through a financial agency or institution. All informal financial operators in the United States, including hawaladars, are legally categorized as MSBs. Examples include currency dealers, check cashers, and issuers of travelers' checks, money orders, or stored value.

Overinvoicing When money launderers and those involved with value transfer, trade fraud, and illicit finance misrepresent goods or services on an invoice by indicating that they cost more than what they are actually worth. This allows one party in the illicit transaction to transfer money to the other under the guise of legitimate trade.

Parallel banking See *IVTS*.

Placement This is the first stage of the money-laundering process. Illicit money is disguised or misrepresented, then placed into circulation through financial institutions, casinos, shops, and other businesses, both local and abroad. A variety of methods can be used for this purpose including currency smuggling, bank complicity, currency exchanges, securities brokers, blending of funds, asset purchase, and so forth. See also *integration* and *layering*.

Remittance code In underground money and value transfers such as hawala and fei-chien, brokers sometimes provide the customer with a code when they receive the money to be remitted. The customer in turn communicates this code to the intended recipient of the money. When the money is actually delivered, the recipient presents the code to the courier or partner hawaladar to complete the transaction.

SAR/STR—Suspicious Activity Report/Suspicious Transaction Report If a financial institution suspects or has reasonable grounds to suspect that the funds involved in a given transaction derive from criminal or terrorist activity, it is obligated to file a report with its national FIU containing key information about the transaction. In the United States,

SAR is the most common term for such a report, though STR is used in many other jurisdictions.

Service-based laundering Instead of laundering money or transferring value through trade goods, services are used. Similar to TBML, service-based laundering revolves around invoice fraud and manipulation.

Shell company An incorporated company with no significant operations, established with the sole purpose of holding or transferring funds, often for money-laundering purposes. As the name implies, shell companies have only a name, address, and bank accounts; clever money launderers often attempt to make them look more like real businesses by maintaining fake financial records and other elements. Generally, there is a lack of beneficial ownership information.

Smurfing/structuring A money-laundering technique that involves splitting a large bank deposit into smaller deposits to evade the U.S. government's CTR and SAR requirements for financial institutions.

Task force In the United States, a task force is a collaborative effort between federal, state, and local law enforcement designed to target a particular criminal activity, and often in a particular geographical area. Resources, expertise, and jurisdictions are combined. The task force has proven to be an effective way to combat crime. There have also been international law enforcement task forces. The FATF is an international policymaking task force. See *FATF*.

TBML—trade-based money laundering The process of disguising the proceeds of crime and moving value via trade transactions in an attempt to legitimize their illicit origin.

Trade diversion In an international trade situation, a business or broker that offers a lower-cost product for importation into a particular country tends to create a trade diversion away from another importer or local producers whose prices are higher for a similar product.

Transfer pricing In the context of TBML, transfer pricing is what subsidiaries of the same multinational charge each other for goods and services. It is generally done to shift tax liability to a tax-free or low-tax haven.

Tri-Border Area The frontier junction of Paraguay, Argentina, and Brazil. This area is known for its illicit activity, including TBML, terrorism financing, customs fraud, drug smuggling, intellectual property rights violations, and tax evasion. The geography of the region makes it very difficult to monitor, facilitating and promoting organized crime and related activities.

TTU—Trade Transparency Unit   TTUs examine trade between countries by comparing, for example, the export records from Country A and the corresponding import records from Country B. Allowing for some recognized variables, the data should match. Any wide discrepancies could be indicative of trade fraud (including TBML). Anomalies could also be the back door to underground remittance and informal value transfer systems that are based on trade such as hawala. The first TTU was established in the United States and is currently directed by Homeland Security Investigations. TTUs have since been established around the world.

Underground banking   See *IVTS*.

Underinvoicing   When money launderers and those involved with value transfer, trade fraud, and illicit finance misrepresent goods or services on an invoice by indicating that they cost less than what they are actually worth. This allows the traders to settle debts between each other in the form of goods or services.

VAT—value added tax   A type of consumption tax by which the value of an article is increased at each stage of its production or distribution.

WCO or World Customs Organization   Esablished in 1952 as the Customs Co-operation Council (CCC), the WCO is an independent intergovernmental body whose mission is to enhance the effectiveness and efficiency of 180 Customs administrations across the globe that collectively process approximately 98 percent of world trade.

Index

Printed and bound by CPI Group (UK) Ltd, Croydon, CR0 4YY

16/04/2025

14658455-0002